Advance Praise for

Reading Youth Writing

"I keep wondering why someone hasn't already written a book like *Reading Youth Writing!* Youth writing/youth production is such an important component of youth culture, and issues of voice in particular are critical. But I am delighted that it is Michael Hoechsmann and Bronwen E. Low who have finally taken on this project. Here they bring together their individual and collective experiences as community activists and media specialists. But they are also academics who are committed to a pedagogy of change. *Reading Youth Writing* tells a story that will change the landscape of how those who work with and for young people in such areas as communication, cultural studies, education and youth studies think about youth as producers."

Claudia Mitchell, James McGill Professor, McGill University

Reading Youth Writing

new
literacies
¶

AND DIGITAL EPISTEMOLOGIES

Colin Lankshear, Michele Knobel,
and Michael Peters
General Editors

Vol. 26

PETER LANG
New York • Washington, D.C./Baltimore • Bern
Frankfurt am Main • Berlin • Brussels • Vienna • Oxford

MICHAEL HOECHSMANN
& BRONWEN E. LOW

Reading Youth Writing

"New" Literacies, Cultural Studies & Education

PETER LANG
New York • Washington, D.C./Baltimore • Bern
Frankfurt am Main • Berlin • Brussels • Vienna • Oxford

Library of Congress Cataloging-in-Publication Data

Hoechsmann, Michael.
Reading youth writing: "new" literacies, cultural studies, and education /
Michael Hoechsmann, Bronwen E. Low.
p. cm. — (New literacies and digital epistemologies; vol. 26)
Includes bibliographical references and index.
1. Youth—United States—Social conditions. 2. Teenagers' writings, American.
3. Mass media and teenagers—United States. 4. Literacy—Social aspects—United States.
5. Urban youth—Education—United States. I. Low, Bronwen E. II. Title.
HQ796.H624   305.2350973'090511—dc22   2007003555
ISBN 978-1-4331-0177-9
ISSN 1523-9543

Bibliographic information published by **Die Deutsche Bibliothek**.
Die Deutsche Bibliothek lists this publication in the "Deutsche
Nationalbibliografie"; detailed bibliographic data is available
on the Internet at http://dnb.ddb.de/.

Cover illustrations by Bruce Cobanli

© 2008 Peter Lang Publishing, Inc., New York
29 Broadway, 18th floor, New York, NY 10006
www.peterlang.com

Table of Contents

Acknowledgments

Writing a book is a journey. And we would like to thank the fellow travelers who helped us along our trek. We would like to acknowledge Colin Lankshear and Michele Knobel who encouraged us to undertake this work, and Chris Myers and Sophie Appel at Peter Lang who supported us along the way. Miranda Campbell and Jonathan Langdon, two graduate research assistants at McGill, played key roles. Miranda, in particular, helped guide us in the most difficult moments, steering us through the lexical, syntactical and typographical quagmires with her meticulous editorial work. Bruce Cobanli shone the light of his artistic talents on the cover art, and the design staff at Peter Lang helped to focus that light. Staff and participants at Young People's Press, and the teachers and students Bronwen worked with, inspired this work and gave us food for thought, as did documentary filmmakers Katie McKenna, Josh Dorsey, and Alyssa Kuzmarov. We each drew scholastic sustenance from great colleagues on our travels, far too many to list. Those that played key roles on the development of this work, however, include Suzanne de Castell, Shirley Steinberg, Tom Painting, Reenah Golden, Warren Crichlow, and Joanne Larson. Several chapters of this book build on earlier work published elsewhere. Thanks are due here to the *Journal of Curriculum Theorizing*, *Taboo*, *English Quarterly*, and *The Review of Education, Pedagogy, and Cultural Studies*. Finally, we would like to acknowledge our families who welcomed us home from this journey and were there for us all the while. This book is dedicated, in no particular order, to Marnie, Max, Lucas, David, Arwen and Beatriz.

CHAPTER ONE

Reading Youth Writing:
Who's Paying Attention?

There's a myth surrounding my generation—a sad and terribly far-fetched belief that paints us as arrogant and selfish people...It is not difficult for teenagers to portray the image that many see and expect from them: self-centered, reckless, rebellious, ignorant of the needs of others, on a selfish destructive course to seek our own gratification. That image is the best and often the only way to hide our hurt and our confusion.

—Barathy N., Young People's Press

We have heard it all before. Youth in trouble, without moral compasses, either out of control or not worth talking about. Stories about young people are most often not written by youth and are usually tempered by moral opprobrium and generational bewilderment. The mass media bear the burden of responsibility for the widespread discourses of youth deviance or disaffection, given that their reports are often sensationalist and bear only exaggerated relation to actual conditions. In the media or around the water cooler, we tend to hear about youth committing outrageous acts of violence or minor incidents of foolhardiness. We pay attention when they upset our expectations, or hurt themselves or others. We zero in on spectacular transgressions and analyze them in every way imaginable, asking not what went wrong with this one individual in a given circumstance, but rather what is wrong with youth today. How have they gone astray, once again? Take, for instance, the finding that as the national homicide rate for youth and adults in the United States fell by 20% between 1992 and 1996, the coverage of youth homicide increased by 721% on the three major television networks (Center on Media and Public Affairs, cited in Goodman, 2003). A 2007 study conducted in the UK found that fewer than 1 in 4 stories in the nation's media are positive and that 87% of stories on youth in the broadcast media are unfavorable. The study, conducted by TNS Media Intelligence for *Young People Now* magazine, also found that when interview subjects are sought, young people are quoted in only 11% of stories while adults are quoted in 38% of them (Ahmed, 2007). In general, we want exceptions to help explain the rule, for instance, that young people lack common sense, and that parents, teachers, the media, computer games, or their trouble-making friends let them run astray. For the most part, adults pay little attention to youth when they are behaving, when they are helping themselves or others, or when they are quietly writing about their lives.

With this book we wish to carve out a space for reading youth writing. At this historical juncture when the places and cases of youth writing, both print and multimodal, have opened up exponentially, it is opportune to consider the conditions and contexts of youth writing and cultural production more generally. While we explore changing literacy contexts, forms, and practices, we focus on both emergent and residual forms of literacy—not just new literacies, but also old literacies in new times. Our particular interest is in charting the "situated literacies" (Barton, Hamilton, & Ivanic, 2000) of youth, and our approach foregrounds youths' communicative intentions and raises questions about the contexts of production and reception, of authorial intention and audience negotiation. In order to do this, we turn to some of the analytic methods and theoretical frameworks of cultural studies: we make a case for the importance of cultural studies in the theorizing of new literacies. Cultural studies offers an explicitly interdisciplinary lens attuned to popular meaning-making practices; in this book, we demonstrate what cultural studies can offer the reading of youth writing and the more general project of better understanding contemporary communicative conditions and relations. We contend that a cultural-studies approach opens up key questions that help us straddle the old and the new, pay attention to situated and contextualized forms of production, consider both authors and audiences, and seek meaning in the words young people use. It asks us to carefully consider the significance and interplay of both the forms and content of expression. And it demands that we recognize the urgency and poignancy of youth voice and embrace what is said, both the serious and the frivolous manifestations, as situated utterances, modes of expression that stem from specific cultural conditions that may be reflective of lived realities, or may not. Even if not, they can offer insight into young people's imaginations and visions of how things could be otherwise.

Youth writing might be read as one of the arts of getting by, of forging forward through indifference, misunderstanding, and high expectations. Or it might give us a better understanding of contemporary forms of leisure, of goofing around, being cool, having fun, or making one's friends laugh. Young people, growing up in an era of cultural, economic and technological flux, have a lot to contribute to our shared understanding of ourselves. Ultimately, studying youth and their cultural practices is not only about coming to grips with the realities of young people. Because youth culture both drives and reflects changes in culture more generally, youth can teach us about changing communicative practices in a world in which the rapid pace of change makes anticipating what literacy and life skills are needed now, let alone in the near future, very challenging. Youth are both inheritors of previous ways of doing things and trailblazers of the new. They can also be the canaries in the coal mine of cultural change.

We open the discussion with the very scenario we hope to critique, a moral panic centered around the scribblings of a deeply troubled young man, a spectacular incident of reading youth writing. We do so in order to unpack some of the relations between adult readers and youth writers, to situate ourselves within the context we seek to rework. We have both witnessed youth trying to explain their inherited realities to adult audiences, and the frustrations this often occasions.

Panicky Readings

Life is like a video game, you gotta die sometime.

—Kimveer Gill (Gerard-Cosh, 2006)

When you find a young person with a gun in their hand, you're more likely to listen to them than when they have a pencil or are sitting at a computer terminal.

—Michael Hoechsmann (Doskoch, 2006)

Maybe I should stop writing this useless stuff?

—Kimveer Gill ("11 Hours Before Murder," 2006)

On September 13, 2006, a young man armed with a semi-automatic rifle walked into Dawson College in Montreal and began shooting. A blogger and an avid player of video games such as *Postal 2* and *Super Columbine Massacre RPG*, Kimveer Gill acted out a simulated fantasy, a first-person shooter walking through a crowd of young people, killing anyone who came into his range of fire. One of his last acts before going on his murderous spree was to log on to the blog he maintained at Vampirefreaks.com and leave these final notes: "Whiskey in the morning, mmmmmm, mmmmmmmmm, good!" and "I call white people niggahs too, it's just fun." Gill had stayed up late writing the night before, posting comments to his blog about Artie Lange, kittens, freezies, and German heavy metal. At 3:33 a.m., presumably before going to sleep one last time, Gill wrote "Maybe I should stop writing this useless stuff?" ("11 Hours Before Murder," 2006). In the days and months leading up to the whiskey-fueled moment he climbed into his car with a loaded rifle on board, Gill had scripted his whole day and the terrible tragedy it would occasion.

Whether his writing was useless or not is a question of conjecture. Its publication certainly didn't cause any alarm bells to sound. But when the dust had settled and the media discovered his Web archive of hate, despair, and nihilism, his writing was widely circulated and carefully dissected.

His postings reflect a troubled soul and read retroactively, premeditate his eventual crime down to such details as a description once posted about drizzling rain (the weather which prevailed on the day of the shootings): "It will be a quiet and peaceful morning. A light drizzle will be starting up. The clouds will be grey, so grey. Just the way I like" (Montgomery & Heinrich, 2006). Along with a perhaps predictable range of rants against society, the police, principals, jocks, bullies, and the unfair nature of life, Gill posted up a series of photos showing him posing with a variety of weapons and an image of his own tombstone which read "Kimveer/Lived fast died young/Left a mangled corpse" (Heinrich, Cherry, Larouche-Smart & Bruemmer, 2006). When he wrote his morning entry on the fatal day, he was listening to a bilingual song by the heavy metal band Megadeth called "A Tout le Monde": "A Tout Le Monde (to everyone), a tout mes amis (to all my friends), je vous aime (I love you), je dois partir (I must leave), these are the last words I'll ever speak, and they'll set me free" ("Sample of Song Lyrics," 2006). Gill, it appears, had not been misread. He had simply not been read at all, at least by anyone who might have been able to make a difference in his life. This example of their voices being ignored is typical of the circumstances for youth. As Dick Hebdige (1988) says,

> youth is present only when its presence is a problem, or regarded as a problem. More precisely, the category of "youth" gets mobilised in official documentary discourse, in concerned or outraged editorials and features, or in the supposedly disinterested tracts emanating from the social sciences at those times when young people make their presence felt by going "out of bounds"... (p. 17–18)

Like Gill's, the writings of the Columbine shooters, Dylan Klebold and Eric Harris, were similarly studied after they killed 13 people and themselves. Again, youth voice was dissected in the homicide lab after the fact. The Sheriff's Office of Jefferson County, Colorado, seized over 900 documents from their homes including school assignments and chat-room manuscripts. Once released from the scrutiny of law enforcement, a selection of these writings, now seen presumably as insights into the minds of mad young people, was published by Harper's Magazine ("First-Person Shooters," 2006). According to Hebdige (1988), young people who go out of bounds "get defended by social workers and other concerned philantropists [and] explained by sociologists, social psychologists, by pundits of every political complexion. In other words, there is a logic to transgression" (p. 18). Of course, Hebdige was not talking about mass murder, but rather more modest forms of transgression such as "resisting through rituals, dressing strangely, striking bizarre attitudes, breaking rules, breaking bottles, windows, heads, issuing rhetorical challenges to the law" (p. 18). Dressing strangely and issuing rhetorical challenges to the law did nothing to draw any attention to Klebold, Harris and Gill. But picking up guns certainly did. A few days after Gill's rampage, a 15-year-old in the Montreal vicinity was arrested for posting a similar online threat: "This will happen at Hudson High School Senior, and when it does, I can't wait to die, or help in the process" (Harrold, 2006). The fact that this young person's message surfaced and was read literally demonstrates that the community was in what Stanley Cohen (1980) calls a period of "moral panic" when "a condition, episode, person or group of persons emerges to become defined as a threat to societal values and interests" (p. 9). Cohen points out that one of "the most recurrent types of moral panics...has been associated with the emergence of various forms of youth culture...whose behaviour is deviant or delinquent" (p. 9). Our point here is not to minimize the consequences of the actions of Gill. The moral panic that blew over Montreal and Canada in the wake of the Gill shooting is born from a truly tragic and senseless event. Our point, however, is that it took such a tragedy to shine the spotlight back onto alienated youth and youth transgression and violence. And shining that spotlight in this era of hyper-literacy involves scrutinizing what youth are saying in and across multiple contexts of cultural production.

After the Gill shooting, Michael was tossed into the media frenzy in the role of pundit reading youth. On the evening news that night and the morning after on several live newscasts, Michael argued that Gill's case was anomalous, that he does not represent the condition of youth in general, but that we are not making enough effort to listen to them or to read their writing. Goth youth had been thrust into the spotlight because Gill claimed to belong to this subculture. These youth, whose theatrical displays of darkness were apparently abnormal enough to appear deviant, were vulnerable to generalizing misreadings just as they had been seven years earlier. When the Columbine shootings took place, Michael had been working with Young People's Press (YPP). Just like the Dawson incident, Columbine thrust the Goth subculture into an unfortunate light, so YPP sent youth journalists out into the community to write a feature story on these socially maligned young people, later published in the *Toronto Star*. In an interview with Canadian Press, Michael drew from his previous analysis of Goth youth to make the claim that the very fact that many Goth teens have Web sites and blogs and write poetry makes them a real literary group. He extolled the virtues of blogging in Goth life and in youth culture in general, saying that young people are exhibiting a "literary sensibility of using language in playful and provocative ways. It's extraordinary what's going on right now. There's a wildfire out there on the

Internet of young people's cultural production and we are hardly paying any attention to it. Someone has to pick up a gun before we'll listen to it" (in Anthony, 2006).

Tracking the Wildfire

That wildfire of youth cultural production is what interests us in this book. We want to move outside of the discourses of moral panic and read the youth writing, which is omnipresent and everyday. Central to the wildfire's spread are the affordances of new media. For instance, youth "voice" or writing is increasingly finding a vehicle and a home in online contexts. The e-mail, IM, and chat worlds are the typical vehicles, and the blogosphere and Web 2.0 sites are the venues. While Web 2.0 sites are typically home to multimodal writing, blogs are home to a type of literary discourse inherited from the private side of the letter form and the public dimension of Op/Ed journalism. The explosive growth of the blogosphere has enabled the spread of youth writing in the public sphere, bringing out of the closet the energy channelled all these years into personal diaries, journals, and creative writing. Literacy events that were once primarily private are increasingly taking place in the public sphere of the Internet, often demonstrating the ambivalence of cultural production in a period of transformative technological change. Particularly popular among youth are MySpace and YouTube. MySpace is a social networking Web site which dramatically simplified the process of setting up a personal Web site and made it free. Rather than having to rent server space and learn to use webpage markup language or even an off-the-shelf Web design application, any would-be user is given a webpage at no cost (other than consuming the ads on the site). MySpace is currently the world's sixth most popular English-language Web site (Alexa, 2007) with a reported 630,000 new registrations every day (Sellers, 2006). Kissing cousin to the blog is the videoblog or "vlog." Since the origins of digital video, the medium has been embraced by media activists and educators as cheap and user friendly, especially in relation to film (a topic we explore further in chapter 3). Home-use and "prosumer" digital video cameras and editing software have flooded the market and brought the possibilities of filmmaking into homes, schools, and community centres. And when video meets the blog, the vlog is born. Through advancements in video streaming software and the advent of free video-sharing sites, the home video now has jaw-droppingly huge audiences. The most popular video sharing site is YouTube, the world's fourth most popular site (Alexa, 2007). YouTube was founded in February 2005 on the same principles as MySpace as a site where users (many of whom are teenagers) can upload, share, and view videoclips for free. Much of its early popularity was due to the links to the site that MySpace users would embed in their pages. In keeping with YouTube's corporate slogan "Broadcast Yourself," original first-person video diary vlogs are a tremendously popular genre on the site, especially among youth.

A discussion of the explosion of contemporary youth writing would be incomplete without considering Hip-Hop culture, arguably the most resonant vehicle today for contemporary cultural production by black and Hispanic youth in North America and an important influence on youth culture internationally. Born out of African-American and Caribbean oral and musical traditions, Hip-Hop emerged in the 1970s in the streets and party halls of the Bronx. It has from the beginning been a space of self-expression and social critique for blacks and other minorities on the margins of mainstream North American society and is now, more and more, an international language of youth resistance (Mitchell, 2001; Sarkar, Low & Winer, 2007). Hip-Hop culture is made up of four central art forms: rapping (reciting lyrics to a beat or music), deejaying, breakdancing, and graffiti. It also includes ways of speaking, dressing, dancing, and moving, making up a whole culture of style, as in rapper KRS-One's (2000) mantra "rap is something you do, Hip-Hop is something you live." Hip-Hop culture is attractive to a small but growing number of literacy educators because rap music celebrates the power of language, poetry, and writing, with rappers proudly proclaiming themselves as word warriors who draw upon the pen as sword. Hip-Hop has made being a poet cool even, and especially, for young black men. For instance, take the following description by the male members of a young Montreal rap crew, the Bartenders, about why they write rap lyrics:

Maxime: Like if you're mad, you're mad and you can say what you want, you're sick of politics, well you can speak out loud in the street but it won't make a difference, people will ignore you, but on your paper at least there is someone who, you know, your pencil—

Dace: That welcomes you, man, that extends you a hand.

Antoine: There are people who are ready to listen to what you have to say and I think that's also a reason to write, to pass on a message.

Kobir: It is people who connect, that's it, for connecting with the peeps.

(in Sarkar, Low, & Winer, 2007, translated from the French)

Not only does Hip-Hop culture offer a space of self-expression and communication but it also promotes ongoing lexical invention and is driven by a "theory of language" that advocates linguistic experiment and the use of language as a raw material for creative production and self-invention (Low, 2001). Hip-Hop's emphasis on creativity, innovation, and performance are part of what we think makes it such a vital and driving element of youth writing today. We explore in this book some of this commitment in relation to concepts of poetics, which foreground the importance of linguistic renewal through creative language use, and which argue that by acting on the language through which we are, in part, constructed, we open up the possibilities for the renovation of the self.

Reading Youth Writing examines and reflects upon some of the range of genres and spaces of contemporary youth writing and self-expression: Web 2.0 environments; Hip-Hop culture, including "spoken word" culture more generally; documentaries which give youth cameras in order to give youth "voice"; and more traditional youth media writing in the context of one organization, Young People's Press, which gave a national audience to the journalistic writing of young people typically confined to the school newspaper. Both of the authors of this book have experience working with youth and youth writing in this transitional era, including direct involvement in youth writing projects that would be considered traditional—or "residual," a concept from Raymond Williams that we examine in the next chapter—but which are prescient beacons of the new youth writing that is now flowing freely in new media contexts such as Web 2.0 habitats. Our experiences straddle schooled and non-schooled spaces. Bronwen helped develop and teach a spoken word poetry curriculum over several years in an urban school in a mid-sized U.S. city, and Michael was executive director of a non-profit, by and for youth national news agency in Canada. In relation to both experiences, we want to consider the conditions that enabled an outpouring of youth writing and to reflect upon what dominant topics, themes, and questions arose when young people were given the space to express what was on their mind. We are interested in moving beyond simply applauding the fact that youth still write, in this way resisting what Heath (2004) has referred to as the "romance of voice," by also reading critically, for this is an essential aspect of taking youth cultural production seriously and engaging youth on their terms. Finally, we read contemporary youth writing as blended, or liminal, or transitional genres, and study a diversity of forms—some of which seem to speak more directly to more traditional forms of literacy and others to the affordances of new media—and so also hope to complicate conversations about old and new literacies.

There are of course others paying close attention to youth writing. For instance, a great deal of work within language arts education puts forward teaching methods which might help youth write more and better (Atwell, 1987; Calkins, 1994; Gallagher, 2002). Our commitment to re-imagining literacy education in light of adolescent out-of-school literacies means that one of *Reading Youth Writing*'s aims is to contribute to this ongoing discussion about motivating and developing youth writers. As a result, two of the books' chapters share details of the different writing pedagogies which shaped the youth writing projects we were involved with. However, we are as interested in what youth writing can tell us about youth—their opinions, perspectives, dreams, and commitments—as in what it can tell us about teaching. We want to theorise the implications of what youth write for understanding adolescent identities in real social and cultural contexts. We also work in the tradition of popular works that celebrate and demand an audience for youth writing and perspectives and voice (see for instance, Talarico's (1995) account of his poetry/basketball program in recreation centres in Rochester, N.Y., and Shandler's (2000) collection of essays, commentaries, and poems by adolescent girls on a range of issues). These popular works also include the many collections of adolescent writing which continue to be published in print (i.e., *Wordscapes: British Columbia Youth Writing Anthology*, 2007) and, increasingly, on the Internet (e.g., *Teen Voices Online*, "the original magazine written by, for, and about teenage and young adult women" and the print monthly magazine, *Teen Ink*, both found at www.speakuppress.org). Unlike these sorts of publications, we want to move beyond distributing youth-produced texts and celebrating the fact that youth do write to critically engaging with what they say in their writing and situating what they say in relation to theories of literacy and culture.

We come to this task with the presupposition that at one level writing is a form of recognizing and representing one's own location within a broad nexus of social relations, some oppressive and some empowering. While many critical ethnographers bring their drafts back to the subjects of their study to complete a feedback loop, to read youth writing for and in the public sphere is to engage with data that is emergent: neither qualified, nor quantified. This raw data is an always incomplete reading of everyday life, but one with a socio-historical urgency, fleetingly "authentic" in its moment of articulation, a palimpsest that speaks for, and of, other youth caught in the same nexus. Given, as new literacy theorists have been arguing, that literacy is a social practice, then it is necessarily tied to specific ways of being in the social, and to particular identities. Gee (2003) makes a relation between identity and "deep" or "active, critical" learning, arguing that a commitment to the latter requires seeing oneself "in terms of a new identity...as the *kind of person* who can learn, use, and value the new semiotic domain" (p. 59, emp. in the original) that this learning engages. In this book, we interrogate what youth writing can tell us about the kinds of persons—and the kinds of worlds—that young people imagine for themselves, and we consider what sorts of literacy practices are both enabled and restricted by these imagined and model identities.

Researching New Literacies

These are complicated times for literacy research. There is a shared sense in a number of research currents such as the new literacy studies and critical literacy that literacy as traditionally taught in schools is inadequate for multiple and different reasons. Widely held conceptions of what literacy is are out of date in a rapidly evolving present whose communicative needs are driven by new media technologies and the economic, political, and cultural conditions of globalization. They are also frequently disconnected from the literacy practices of everyday life outside of schools, in families, and communities, and from the meanings and modalities embedded in popular culture. Models of literacy are challenged to keep up with the shifting multiliteracies that are required and cultivated by new media and information technologies, expanding cultural horizons associated with new global multicultures, and the proliferation of representational forms of a media-saturated culture (Cope & Kalantzis, 2000; Lankshear & Knobel, 2006). Those currents of literacy research that are committed to better understanding the complexity of contemporary literacy practices tend to focus on the ways literacy gets lived—across and through different individuals, contexts, and media (Barton & Hamilton, 1998; Gee, 1996, 2004; Street, 1995, 2005). That said, such alternative perspectives often flow against the dominant stream of writing and thinking about the teaching of literacy in schools, much of which is dominated by "back to basics" educational policies in places like the United States, Australia, and parts of Canada. The rhetoric of a "literacy crisis" remains pervasive in many academic journals, government policy documents, and the media (Lewin, 2003). Graff (1987) dated the origins of the widespread concern about declines in literacy to the mid-70s, despite the near universality at the time of basic reading and writing skills in North America. Symptomatic of this concern are the complaints from parents and teachers that today's youth no longer read and that television shows, music videos, and films have supplanted literature as entertainment, while visual technologies like video games and windows-based computers have eroded adolescents' ability to read and write. Graff (1987) argued that these complaints and the "literacy myth" in general speak less to a decline in literacy skills than to the difficulty of recognizing evolving communicative practices, or new literacies, as well as to profound misconceptions about the nature and significance of reading and writing. And a good deal of research on literacy within the new media era shows unequivocally that, rather than reading and writing less, youth in digital spaces are reading and writing more than ever (Alvermann, 2002; Lankshear & Knobel, 2006). In this book, we take up some of the very targets of contemporary anxieties about youth literacy—youth popular cultures driven by the linguistic and cultural innovations of African-American and other minority youth, and the electronic media with its visual and oral modalities—as important sites for understanding these evolving spaces of communication and new literacies.

This book enters into conversation with new literacy research in both senses of the "new" as outlined by Lankshear & Knobel (2003): research in the "New Literacy Studies" (NLS) which is new as in theoretically and methodologically different from traditional literacy research and research into literacies—often multimodal—which are chronologically new. New Literacy Studies understands literacy as a social practice and models of literacy as ideological rather than autonomous. It argues that there is often a powerful, ideologically motivated disconnect between schooled forms of literacy and home/community literacies which can further the social marginalization of racial, ethnic, and language minority youth (Heath, 1983; Luke & Freebody, 1997). In order to better understand what and how literacy means in particular contexts, NLS often draws upon ethnography and discourse analysis as methods of inquiry. Of particular significance to our study of contemporary youth writing is New Literacy Studies research on youth literacy practices in out-of-school contexts, which has convincingly demonstrated the range and complexity of these forms (Hull & Shultz, 2002; Mahiri, 2004). Hull and Shultz (2001) ask "how might out-of-school identities, social practices, and the literacies that they recruit be leveraged in the classroom?" and "how might teachers incorporate students' out-of-school interests and predilections but also extend the range of the literacies with which they are conversant?" (p. 603). Bronwen's spoken word curriculum development was in part motivated by such questions, and the discussion here of its implementation explores the course as a response to them. We also take up such questions in our examinations of the writing pedagogies Michael helped to develop at Young People's Press.

Our interest in the multimodal meaning-making practices demanded by digital technologies and media culture also puts us into relation with research in the field of chronologically new literacies. Central to this field is the work of Lankshear & Knobel (2003, 2006) and many of the writers collected in *Adolescents and Literacies in a Digital World* (Alvermann, 2002). Given how generative digital and media spaces have been for youth writing, these studies also help inform ours, as we work to extend this literature through new engagements with what youth are trying to express in these digital spaces. We are as interested in what youth are saying in this writing as in the fact that they are writing. While the temptation in this transitional period is to focus on the medium, we don't want to sever form from content, the how from the what. We are as interested in the message the medium facilitates as the medium itself, and in the interplay between medium and message, and, in some cases, in the medium as message (although we also resist the technological determinism McLuhan's phrase implied). It can seem that the new forms are enabling not so much *new content* as *new contexts* for speech acts which have long histories. And in our study of new incarnations of old practices, we wonder about both continuities and changes. In relation to "new literacies," Hull (2003) notes that by "juxtaposing and joining a variety of semiotic systems and technologies," youth are "reinventing and invigorating what it means to communicate" (p. 230); in turn, we wonder what gets reinvented, what gets invigorated, and how we might tell the difference.

In order to better understand the overlay of the past and the present, and the complexities of how change happens, we move in the next chapter to the work of Raymond Williams (1977), and his model of the complexity and co-existence of cultural change in the form of dominant, residual, and emergent forms. We also find useful Marshall McLuhan's concept of the tetrad: whenever there is technological change, particularly in forms of communication, some things of the past are enhanced, some retrieved, some reversed and some obsolesced (McLuhan & McLuhan, 1988). Much of what is reversed or obsolesced is at the level of form: the personal letter cedes to the e-mail, which in turn cedes to the instant message; the essay cedes to the blog; graffiti and class notes cede to postings on Facebook; depth of thought cedes to breadth, to networked thought. Paul Levinson (1997) has utilized McLuhan's tetrad to demonstrate the ironies of technological change. He argues, for example, that Thomas Edison developed the phonograph as what would be today an answering machine. He created a tool that went on to be used for other reasons, primarily as a musical recording playback machine, and that also rescued radio at the time when competition from television made it difficult to sustain it as a live performance medium. The phonograph enabled radio to begin a Top-40 format of prerecorded music that lives on today. The same ironies emerge when we look at literacy through a rearview mirror. From the era of the Gutenberg parenthesis (Pettitt, 2007), when print literacy was hegemonic, emerge literacy practices that are both text-driven and share elements of a pre-print era. Ong (1982) described these forms in terms of a "secondary orality" that carries with it many of the traits of primary orality, including immediacy and the use of formulas, but which depends for its existence upon print literacy. As we'll discuss further in chapter 7, "Jamming the signal: Rap music and the poetics of technology," rap music is an interesting combination of traditional and contemporary literacy practices: it relies upon some of the most ancient forms of entertainment, including oral storytelling, performance, and the poetic principles of rhyme and rhythm, but its intense, multi-layered sound is the product of very sophisticated sound technologies, and in particular, of rap producers' and deejays' experiments with digital samplers, sound boards, synthesizers, and keyboards. We also read these experiments in terms of the concept of poetic innovation, and suggest that rap music offers a kind of anchor to other ways of languaging and communicating in an era of new literacies.

Some of the richest new literacy practices are those of the smart mobs, the collective intelligence of those engaged in the new collaborative and creative spaces of communication afforded by Web 2.0 and other domains. These new collaborative cultures, seen for instance at Wikipedia but coming to new domains of human inquiry as quickly as millions of people can get together about what matters to them, demonstrate the enhancement and retrieval of content that is now loosened, at some potential risk, from the realm of experts and made broadly open to input and innovation by individuals and groups worldwide. Content, too, continues to flow through the articulations of young people. The problem, however, underscored by Richard Lanham (2006), is that amidst the massive data flow, apparently 1.5 billion gigabytes per year (adding up to 2.5 million megabytes per person on earth), much of what is said goes unheard and so in effect the pursuit of attention is more significant than the pursuit of communication. Multiple cartographers of the new literacies notwithstanding, we are still in relatively uncharted waters. For this reason, we wish to eschew to some extent the allure of new platforms and new contexts of writing to look at how youth are articulating themselves in the liminal spaces between and around new forms. We feel that the great flood of text and texting provides a fruitful context for reading youth writing. Lanham's *Economics of Attention* (2006) also interests us because we feel that it is precisely a sense of deficit in the attention economy that fuels the imaginary of youth anomie and the generative, albeit fictional, space recorded in the Generation X literature at the end of the last century. Youth anomie as imaginary construct feeds both ways; it is at once proof of adult indifference and youth slackerdom. Outside of a real appreciation for reading youth writing, generations of adults misinterpret youth intentions and practices while youth sense indifference and inattention to their needs and desires. It is a vicious circle, as real as the set of symbolic exchanges that occur in the circuits of consumption. There, the opposite happens. Adults, or more specifically marketers, spend great resources and time trying to understand youth. While Lanham helps us to identify the new conditions of scarcity—not information but attention—it is precisely attention that youth have been clamouring for throughout the years, both at a biographical level as young people growing up and at a generational, sociological level as a social demographic.

We referred above to the role played by new media in helping to ignite the "wildfire" of youth writing and cultural production more generally. As we gradually inch away from the old monolithic one-way flow mass media to the new "interactive" environment of MySpace and YouTube, there has clearly been a shift in the conditions in which having a voice in the public sphere is even possible. While new digital divides are increasingly apparent, the middle-class kid with a modem has the capacity today to create sophisticated media and to podcast it. That is an extraordinary new development that cannot be minimized. Power is a scarce resource for young people, and if we consider its social, political, economic, and cultural arenas, then we should see at the least the potential advantage that many young people have over previous generations of a comparable demographic. While some corporations are making a fortune producing and selling the new relatively low-cost hardware and software for the new hypermedia generation, the reality is that the costs of production and distribution have dropped so low that millions of young people can join the new virtual studio, some becoming instant celebrities and some just having the feel-good moment of being a part of the hypermedia world. What we have both seen in our direct work with young people engaged in writing for a real audience is that when youth are given the opportunity to express themselves within contexts where they think adults will be listening or reading, they tend to raise the serious issues of the day. They seek our attention, as they always have. Youth media organizations such as Young People's Press, profiled later in this book, have been productive sites of youth voice, channelling rhetorical intentions into communicative moments. We also think that the innovative approaches of many youth media projects to using technology as tools for communicative praxis have something to teach schools about educating through and with technology. The draw to projects and organizations that offer a real chance of disseminating youth voice was always one of making a difference, speaking up against the tide of experts and authors, teachers and parents, who seemed to have the upper hand in defining the very conditions of youth. The same can be said, in a much different manner, about initiatives that enable young people to determine content in school settings. Programs such as the slam poetry initiative described later in this volume open spaces within the strict confines of epistemological control in schools to say the unsaid, to speak against the grain, to challenge inherited scholastic tradition with emergent forms congruent to youth conditions outside of school walls. That said, if youth can be savants, commentators of their cultural contexts, one would not always surmise this by examining youth taste cultures (Bourdieu, 1984). Much of what youth consume as media and text in general is centered around superficial pop culture tropes. The media production in youth-driven spaces produced largely for peer audiences is often very playful, media savvy, parodic, sarcastic, and sometimes silly: intended to impress or make peers laugh rather than principally committed to making people think. Youth communication is profoundly contradictory. Nonetheless, we have found that when given the opportunity to address hybrid or adult audiences, youth often draw on latent desires to have/find a voice in public debates. In our work with youth we have found that when youth think adults are listening, they often share aspects of their most thoughtful selves. This is one of the central arguments of this book.

The Challenges of Reading Youth Writing

That said, what does one need to know in order to listen and to listen well? The task for adults of reading youth writing is complicated by layers of difference which are always generational but also often based in other differences that importantly include culture. In order to read well, one needs to know the language; this means knowing the conventions of emergent genres as well as popular idiom. The near impossibility of keeping up has meant that many parents and teachers can't make sense of and so stop listening to or watching youth popular culture. And many teachers avoid integrating popular culture into curriculum for fear that being "hip" to rapidly changing youth culture is impossible (Alvermann, Moon & Hagood, 1999). Youth culture can make a teacher feel vulnerable, in that students' insider knowledge can shift the balance of authority and expertise (Callahan & Low, 2004; Mahiri, 1996). As well, not only is youth writing contradictory, but so is popular culture: the controversial language and content—including representations of violence, women, sexuality, and materialism—of a good deal of popular music, film, and television, can lead to significant tensions between schools and popular youth culture. Such concerns are especially strong in response to rap music; a discourse of "moral panic" surrounds Hip-Hop culture, as Koza (1999) makes clear in a study of media representations and public debates "that have constructed rap, rappers, and rap fans as the deviant, lacking, undesirable, or evil other" (p. 91). These sorts of anxieties around rap are not confined to the U.S.; in the political and social fall out following the 2005 Paris suburb riots, approximately 200 French deputies and senators demanded an inquiry into the role five French rap groups might have played in inciting the rioters (even though three of the five had been disbanded for years) (Rioux, 2005). As Ross (1994) reminds, rap has broken new grounds of expression as "arguably [the] first black musical form in which *anything could be said*, and for which testing the limits of free speech in a recognizably racist society had become a matter of conscious habit, if not necessity" (p. 2). Such testing has taken the form of critical politically conscious rap (which can include black nationalist political rhetoric—see Public Enemy, Dead Prez), the nihilism of some gangsta rap (e.g., NWA), and the hypermaterialism and sexism of some "Mack" rap (e.g., Ice-T, Too $hort). Distinctions between positive and harmful rap expression are also complicated by the presence of language and themes easily characterized as misogynist, violent, materialistic, and homophobic across the genres. Despite such controversial representations, those interested in youth still need to engage with rap music because youth do. We cannot ignore youth culture, hoping it will go away. In the terms of socio-cultural learning theory, culture doesn't just provide a context for individual learning (Rogoff, 2003). Instead, the individual is embedded within culture, actively producing culture and being produced by it: popular youth culture is always already present in classrooms and other spaces in which adults and youth come together. And importantly, Hip-Hop's contradictions reflect those found in the larger cultures it is embedded in and therefore need to be grappled with. Finally, given Hip-Hop's appeal and the critical consciousness embedded in a good deal of rap music, much of it "underground," the cultural movement has tremendous potential for the education and political mobilization of youth (Kitwana, 2002). The challenge for literacy researchers and educators is how to engage, understand, and respond to this culture in meaningful ways.

We close this introduction with an anecdote about the difficulty of reading youth well, which serves as an example of the kinds of stories we are using this book to tell. It helps us unpack some of the layers of difference which shape communicative and interpretive relationships between adults and youth across cultures. The performance poetry curriculum, which Bronwen helped to develop, worked to capitalise on poetry's newfound cachet among youth by drawing on rap music as a prompt for discussions about art and politics, poetic principles, and meaning. In the first year the course was offered, rap also was at the centre of a school controversy. Gerard, an African-American student in the performance poetry course, told the class the following tale about a recent school event. It was the school talent night. Gerard and another high school senior were rapping to the backbeat of an instrumental track entitled "Special Delivery." After a few minutes, they asked the audience how many wanted to join them and dance the Harlem Shake on stage. The rappers were then to announce that they had a special delivery, and two male students would be wheeled out on a cart, dancing, up onto the stage. After this brief skit, the rappers would resume. However, Gerard and his friend never made it past the initial shout-out to the audience: their microphone was accidentally unplugged, and the principal stepped in and cut the act. He first explained, as paraphrased by the student (and filtered through his memory and perspective), "that it was old people in the crowd and he didn't want things to get out of hand and get chaotic," but then said, "I don't want to hear any cursing or sexual obscenities in your raps...I don't want to hear it." This event prompted a series of conversations between Gerard, his poetry teacher Tim, the teacher-organizers of the event, and the principal (all of whom, except for Gerard, are white). Tim had recently learned from his students the distinction between freestyle (improvised) and written raps; he explained it to the principal who then decided Gerard must have been freestyling at the talent night. Neither the principal nor Tim knew the student had had his lyrics approved by the teacher-organizers. And neither of them knew that the invitation onto the stage was not real but instead part of a rap "skit," a common convention of the genre. Finally, the teacher-organizers could not tell if Gerard had stuck to the text because they couldn't understand him in performance. The miscommunications emerged as increasingly complex as the story unfolded: Gerard had been asked to provide the teacher-organizers with some translations of the AAVE and Hip-Hop terms in the lyrics and in his glossary he purposefully mistranslated terms he thought they might find fault with.

There are a number of implications of this story for the reading of youth writing by adults. It is an example of how official school discourse can ignore, deny, or close down youth voice by censoring and censuring its expressions, which don't fit neatly into school ways of doing literacy. It is also an example of the difficulty of interpreting across differences. Tim, in conversation with Bronwen, concludes that the principal's confusion about whether the rap was a freestyle or written down "points to the fact that we as adults have to know the language" before making any judgments about it. At the same time, the story speaks to the importance of working towards cross-generational and cultural communication, because without it Gerard was not given informed guidance about the choices he made in terms of his identity construction, writing, and performance by the very people who were employed to help him grow. As we mentioned above, we have seen some of the most powerful youth expression in contexts facilitated and supported by adults.

In our school- and community-based projects with young people and in this book we work towards meaningful engagements with, understandings of, and responses to youth writing and cultural expression. In chapter 2, we argue for the value of cultural studies as an analytic method and theoretical framework for reading youth writing. We introduce Richard Johnson's (1996) heuristic for cultural studies, an approach to cultural analysis that links questions of production, text, audience, and lived culture in a dynamic tension. We also put forward Raymond Williams' (1977) framework for thinking about processes of cultural change, in which residual, dominant, and emergent forms coexist in a given cultural practice or historical moment, and argue for its value in examining contemporary literacy practices. Additionally, we offer an overview of scholarship on youth, youth cultures, and youth conditions that grounds subsequent chapters in a social, cultural, and economic analysis of growing up in a post-Fordist era of fast capitalism and a postmodern era of mobile subjectivities and identities. Chapter 3 further explores the question of what it means to read youth writing well and interrogates the concept of youth "voice" by examining a series of documentary films which equip youth with video cameras to enable them to tell their stories. Here we consider some of the impediments to "giving voice"—technological, aesthetic, ethical, philosophical, economic, and political. In the subsequent chapters we move through some of the different spaces of contemporary youth self-expression, starting with those which are explicitly emergent through some shaped more obviously by residual forms. Despite these distinctions we consider them all in relation to Lankshear & Knobel's (2006) notions of new stuff, technologies, and mindsets and wonder about the possibilities they open up for youth literacies. Chapter 4 explores some paradigmatically "new" digital spaces of expression, and considers the non-formal learning and amateur production taking place primarily in Web 2.0 domains. Here we consider how audience conditions what is communicated by youth. We explore this context of peer-to-peer learning and communication, recognizing some of its potentials and pitfalls.

In the fifth chapter, we turn to print journalism and look in depth at the pedagogies and outcomes of a non-profit youth media organization, with an orientation to what youth are saying when given a voice in the mainstream media. It includes a content analysis of just under 300 articles published in newspapers and online. This chapter also considers the conditions of production of youth writing, including how the institutional formation shapes to some extent what is expressed by youth. Chapter 6 turns to Hip-Hop and spoken word culture and examines slam poetry in the context of a performance poetry course offered to senior English students in an urban U.S. high school. By drawing on two years of classroom data and four years of performance data, examined through the lens of theories of poetics, we pay close attention to what these students say, when given the opportunity, to audiences of their teachers, community members, and peers. We also explore the implications of youths' growing interest in performance poetry for understanding adolescent literacies and identities, and popular culture more generally. Chapter 6 explores a dimension of rap music that has been less studied than its lyrics, particularly in relation to literacy: we examine rap's complex soundscapes, produced in part through the deliberate misuse of contemporary technologies of sound production, and explore what they might tell us about the popular, out-of-school ways youth are thinking about and working with technology. We start building a theory of technological literacy which brings to the fore creativity and innovation. In chapter 8, we consider some of the implications of the social, cultural, and semiotic readings young people make of popular cultural texts and turn to the question of media education in and for new times. We argue that much of what is articulated in the media derives from careful studies of youth worldviews conducted by media professionals, and articulate a broad and comprehensive agenda for media education. This chapter does not resolve the problems raised in this book—it is not the pedagogical cure for all that ails us—but rather suggests a necessary corollary for reading youth writing in a media education that situates the consumption and production of media texts within a meaningful engagement in the lives of young people. The conclusion to *Reading Youth Writing* draws upon the analyses and arguments from the various chapters in order to build a theory of education and of literacy in transition situated in a period of cultural and economic change. Here we set an educational agenda for new literacies and old, and a pedagogy of possibility that speaks to work futures and life pathways and the role of literacy within it.

CHAPTER 2

Growing Up Young:
Cultural Studies and New Literacies

One thing is certain: By not standing up to be counted, you could be part of that volatile concoction that begins to destroy those around you. And when the flames begin to lick at your own feet, there might not be anybody left to lift you out of the fire.

—Sarah T., Young People's Press

Reading youth writing. Unpack this phrase and you end up with several important questions worthy of further analysis. Reading *youth* means interpreting youth behaviour, hypothesizing youth values and worldviews, and analyzing the trends and transformations of youth cultures. Reading *youth writing* means recognizing young people as social actors and cultural producers and as innovators of (sometimes large scale) cultural change. And reading youth *writing* means taking a long and critical look at what young people are saying, writing and producing, the amalgam of so-called youth voice. To undertake such a task, we need a powerful tool or lens, interdisciplinary in nature and focused on the world(s) around us when engaging a scholarly question. This chapter makes a case for *reading youth writing* through the lens of cultural studies. We argue that cultural studies offers a theory and method of inquiry which is flexible and dynamic enough to help make sense of the complex and contradictory spaces of contemporary youth cultures and cultural production. We first give an overview of the history of cultural studies, mapping the trajectory of its central concerns and debates and describing the particular cultural studies heuristic that structures the book as a whole. We next explore cultural studies' relationship to education and to studies of literacy in particular. We draw on Richard Johnson's heuristic for cultural studies to make sense of youth writing and media in a complex interaction of writing, text, reception, and cultural context. We then explore the question of "newness" so central to popular writing about contemporary adolescent literacy practices, in relation to Raymond Williams' model of uneven and contingent cultural change. We close the chapter with an overview of scholarship on youth, youth cultures, and youth conditions, which grounds subsequent chapters in a social, cultural, and economic analysis of growing up in a post-Fordist era of fast capitalism and a postmodern era of mobile subjectivities and identities.

What Do We Mean By Cultural Studies?

On the surface, the task of mapping out the field of cultural studies appears a daunting one, given that so much energy is spent by scholars debating "what is cultural studies?" (cf. Storey, 1996). Ultimately, we feel that this centrifugal impulse of cultural studies to avoid a common definition is counterproductive. Cultural studies is an interdisciplinary approach to reading the artifacts and practices of the present as an historian would read those of the past. One takes an element of the synchronic moment, and brings the most critical theoretical concepts and methods from a range of academic fields to the table to analyze it. The origins of British cultural studies are in post war adult education (Williams, 1989). Alongside other instructors toiling in adult education, founding figures of cultural studies such as Raymond Williams and Richard Hoggart came to recognize the disconnect between the lives of their mostly working-class students and the traditional subject matter of education. They realized that their learned perspectives on culture were ignorant of the lives and conditions of the students with whom they wished to communicate and that to teach they must be willing to learn. And so they shifted the curriculum's focus away from official histories and knowledge grounded in the Leavisite tradition of static and elitist notions of culture as something inherently edifying. Instead they envisioned culture as something lived. In classes and in research, they began investigating working-class and popular culture, resulting in texts such as Raymond Williams' *Culture and Society* (1958) and Richard Hoggart's *The Uses of Literacy* (1957), the latter establishing an early precedent for cultural studies of literacy. Rejecting the cultural elitism that disregarded popular art as unworthy of study, Hoggart deployed the tools of literary analysis to make sense of popular literature such as "penny dreadfuls." Drawing on his own working-class background, he looked at how people used the texts in their everyday lives and analyzed how the texts construct and position particular kinds of readers and communities of readers. Hoggart juxtaposes what he sees as the banal, cynically commercial, and sentimental nature of a good deal of popular literature with more authentic working-class culture; the text is both a celebration of the traditional values and cultural practices of the working classes and a rejection of the so-called popular culture he felt was eroding them. As these teachers and researchers turned to the popular as subject of inquiry, they dismantled fixed oppositions between high and low culture and raised the central cultural studies question of how people make meaning.

With the founding of the Birmingham Centre for Contemporary Cultural Studies (CCCS) in 1964, a generation of cultural studies scholars began to emerge who focused on the study of contemporary culture, and frequently, on those most involved in changing it: young people. Undoubtedly the most influential theorist of cultural studies has been Stuart Hall who has remained at the forefront of this socially engaged area of inquiry over the past four decades. Accepting an honorary degree at the University of Massachusetts-Amherst in 1989, Hall summed up the project of cultural studies as "thrusting onto the attention of scholarly reflection and critical analysis the hurly burly of a rapidly changing, discordant and disorderly world" while "testing the fine line between intellectual rigour and social relevance" (1989). Central to the British cultural studies commitment to social relevance has been the foregrounding of questions of power. In order to raise and understand such questions, cultural studies has drawn upon Marxist theories of historical materialism, cognizant of the importance of economic analysis to understanding social conditions and development. Studies of the workings of class and critiques of capitalism have been mainstays of British cultural studies. That said, the tradition has also posed an ongoing challenge to orthodox Marxism's economic determinism. The innovation which early cultural studies texts like Raymond Williams' *Culture and Society* (1958) signalled was an increased sensibility to cultural manifestations of social concerns. More specifically, and in relation to E. P. Thompson's *Making of the English Working Class* (1963) in particular, Stuart Hall (1980) states that this involved the "foregrounding of the questions of culture, consciousness and experience, and an accent on agency," while breaking with "technological evolutionism," "reductive economism" and "organizational determinism" (p. 58). Thus, structures and technologies were not to be given more than their due as causal conditions for the real conditions people experienced in their everyday lives.

Stuart Hall (1980) distinguishes between two major paradigms in the first decades of British Studies: the "culturalist" tradition initiated by Williams, Hoggart, and Thompson, and the later interventions of French "structuralisms." Hall describes the culturalist paradigm as "opposed to the base-superstructure way of formulating the relationship between ideal and material forces" while conceptualizing culture as "interwoven with all social practices; and those practices, in turn, as a common form of human activity: sensuous human praxis, the activity through which men and women make history" (p. 63). This conception views culture as "whole ways of life"

(Williams, 1961, p. 46) rooted in the livid experiences of communities and individual people. Despite its formalism, the work of French Structuralists, most notably Claude Levi-Strauss, Roland Barthes and Louis Althusser, also had an enormous impact on British cultural studies. The translation of Ronald Barthes' *Mythologies* in 1972 and of Louis Althusser's essay on "Ideology and Ideological State Apparatuses" (1971) helped to turn the debates in the early 1970s towards the issue of symbolic and institutional forms of domination. The primary innovation of the structuralist intervention was an emphasis on ideological structures. The corresponding buzzword was "determination," as the emphasis strayed from the "make their own history" to the "on the basis of conditions which are not of their choosing" side of Marx's famous formulation. With the belated discovery of the texts of Antonio Gramsci, the debate on signification, ideology, and popular struggle in cultural studies wandered back to the "make their own history" side of the coin with the recognition that common sense articulations of culture are actively made, not passively inherited.

The emergence of cultural studies on the American continent offered a conjuncture for a reflection on and a revision of the project of cultural studies originally articulated in the British context. At best, the newly emergent U.S. cultural studies flattened out the vertical axis of British cultural studies' class centeredness. Perhaps this levelling comes with the territory, a culture described by Andrew Ross (1989) where "popular culture has been socially and institutionally central" (p. 7) and where the "popular sovereign goes forth in a more modest, republican garb, and drinks a less expensive, carbonated version of the water of life" (p. 13). More significantly, however, the movement of cultural studies in the U.S. towards a more horizontal, if unevenly developed, axis of analysis signals the "articulation" of critical theory with the (post Marxist) social movements of the past thirty years: civil rights, feminism, black/Chicano/First Nations consciousness, and gay and lesbian rights. The result of this shift for cultural studies, according to Ross (1990) is to move "its traditional focus away from the conflict between dominant and popular cultures, conceived as unified blocs, [to] turn its attention to the axis between central and marginal cultures, conceived as pluralities" (p. 28). This shift allows, or requires, that social change be seen as an uneven, often contradictory, process. At worst, however, cultural studies in the US emerged as a type of "reader response" theory of the media, overlaid by a sometimes impenetrable dose of high theory.

Stuart Hall responded to this trend in the U.S. at the "Cultural Studies: Now and in the Future" conference in 1990 at the University of Illinois at Urbana-Champaign, a major international gathering of top cultural studies scholars, which occasioned another round of interrogation of what it meant to do cultural studies. Hall remarked that though he did not want to close or to police the field, he was nonetheless concerned about "the overwhelming textualization" (1992, p. 286) of theories of power, politics, race/class/gender, exclusion, marginality, etc. Hall expressed "nagging doubts" about "the ways of constituting power as an easy floating signifier which just leaves the crude exercise and connections of power and culture altogether emptied of any signification" (p. 286). Vital for Hall was the notion that theoretical and socio-political questions are kept in constant tension, but that theory also be recognized "as a practice which always thinks about its intervention in the world in which it would make some difference, in which it would have some effect" (p. 286). This ultimately requires not confusing academic and intellectual work, but striving "to produce some kind of organic intellectual political work" (p. 286).

In *Reading Youth Writing* we try to respect Hall's warnings, forging a conception of popular politics, which retains the political edge of a Marxian analysis of production, but which takes up the challenge of the postmodern market of meanings: a conception which works from, and takes seriously, a multiplicity of subject positions. Such an integrative concept of cultural studies was articulated by Hall and other presenters at the Urbana-Champaign conference. The editors of *Cultural Studies* (1992), which is a volume of the conference proceedings, state that cultural studies is a transdisciplinary field, "committed to the study of the entire range of a society's arts, beliefs, institutions, and communicative practices" (Grossberg, Nelson & Treichler, 1992, p. 4). It undertakes to study culture "*both* as a way of life—encompassing ideas, attitudes, languages, practices, institutions, and structures of power—and a whole range of cultural practices: artistic forms, texts, canons, architecture, mass-produced commodities, and so forth" (p. 5). Given the range of objects and domains of study, cultural studies is necessarily and unapologetically eclectic in its theories, approaches, and methods. Cultural studies theorizing often draws upon approaches from anthropology, sociology, philosophy, feminist theory, postcolonial and anti-racist theory, literary studies, film criticism, and media studies. As a research method, cultural studies mobilizes close reading strategies from literary studies, linguistics, and semiotics as well as ethnographic modes of inquiry. For these reasons, cultural studies is typically described as a "movement" or "network," rather than a field. It resists the reifications of disciplinarity through its theoretical openness and versatility, its self-reflexivity, and its critical stance towards other traditions, which are "approached both for what they yield and for what they inhibit. Critique involves stealing away the more useful elements and rejecting the rest" (Johnson, 1996, p. 75). One would be forgiven to conclude that cultural studies is a network of theory poachers, but there is a practice and praxis of social and political change that fuels the best of cultural studies work.

A cultural studies heuristic we have found particularly useful as a starting place for thinking about the study of cultural processes and phenomena comes from Richard Johnson. His model is illustrated as a circle, or circuit, with four topoi (places of analysis), resembling the east, north, west, and south points of a compass. Johnson takes the traditional author-text-reader triad of literary studies, opens up the terms, and then adds a fourth: The four points of the circuit, each interconnected with the other, are (1) production, (2) textual or material form, (3) reception, and (4) influence on lived culture. As Johnson describes it, each box represents a moment in the circuit, each moment depends on the others but is also distinct, and each is indispensable to the study of the cultural form as a whole. The model demands a holistic mode of inquiry which takes into consideration all four elements. An example of this model in use is Michael's analysis of Air Jordan shoes (Hoechsmann, 2001). Drawing on Johnson's model, Michael explores the political economy of production associated with the Nike corporation, the semiotics and symbolism of Michael Jordan and Air Jordan shoes, empirical studies of youth in America, and the culture of race, urban America, and basketball behind the whole phenomenon. While Johnson's model is useful for the study of mainstream media texts and cultural artifacts, we draw on it in this book to analyze the more informal contexts of youth writing and cultural production.

We have been thinking about *Reading Youth Writing* as enacting as a whole this process of inquiry into contemporary cultural production by youth. Under production, we consider a widened sense of authorship to encompass collaborative or singular productions as well as the particular conditions and contexts of production. We wonder, who writes? When and where? For what reasons? The latter section of this chapter helps us to establish some of the larger social, political and economic contexts of contemporary youth cultural production. As well, many of these issues related to authorship more particularly are raised in our chapter on Young People's Press, "From the classroom to the newsroom," and in our chapter on a performance poetry curriculum, "Slammin' School." Next, the study of textual forms and literacy practices is at the heart of our analysis, including questions about what genres, forms, modalities, tropes, etc. get deployed and to what purpose. "Slammin' School" contains close readings of the texts produced by youth, as does the chapter on rap music, "Jamming the Signal: Rap Music and the Poetics of Technology," the chapter on video and youth self-representation, "Says Who?," and the chapter on Web 2.0 writing, "I'm Speaking to You!" The notion of "readings," or how people make sense of the texts, is central to "I'm Speaking to You!" and "Says Who?," as we explore questions such as, what is the nature of the audience? What does the audience bring to the moment of reading? What are the limits of understanding? This question is taken up in some detail in the "Slammin' School" chapter which draws upon ethnographic experiences working with youth. Like Johnson (1996), our understanding of some of the conditions which shape readings include "asymmetries of resources and power, material and cultural" (p. 83). What do we need to know in order to read youth writing well? This sparks a discussion on media education and social change in the penultimate chapter, "Educating Bono."

The final stage in Johnson's framework considers how cultural forms affect everyday cultural life, and how cultural change feeds back on the moment of production. This might be the conundrum at the heart of all of our work, but it grounds the body of research and observation that make up the various chapters of this book, and is ultimately the key aspect of our cultural studies approach to the new literacies. All of the chapters inquire into the embedded nature of these processes in forms of cultural life, shaped by particular social relations. The important caveat here is that the conceptual framework Johnson lays out does not presume a narrow casting of 'effects,' but rather issues the "so what?" challenge. Why do we do what we do? How are our writings and readings made significant? In other words, we cannot simply interpret conditions of production, textual forms and practices, and audience readings as resonant sites of meaning without some consideration of the interplay between them and the broader social and cultural contexts in which they are made meaningful. What we need are more broadly integrative models. This problem and these questions are what we grapple with throughout this book.

Writing and researching about youth cultural production brings us into classrooms, but it also takes us to community centres, libraries, non-profit projects, Internet cafés, and people's homes, anywhere that writing takes place. It also puts us in touch with real people living their lives, people with differences of race, class, gender, and sexual orientation, people having bad days or good weeks, people with jobs or with hobbies, people in a hurry to have their voice heard and some reticent to share what they have to say. It brings us into mindsets and worldviews, ideologies and dogmas, flights of whimsy and moments of dire urgency. The site of production, in short, opens up questions of authorship to include literary works and e-mails, vlogs and poems, collaborative wikis, and individual school assignments. It forces us to consider what fuels the fire of youth cultural production and how and in what circumstances youth write. The role that cultural life plays in conditioning youth writing is the significant caveat to a naturalistic assumption of writing as a simple reflection of interior thought. Rather, we are attendant to the notion that youth (and all of us) to some extent are ventriloquists of the ideas and assumptions circulating around them (us). We feel strongly that culture—in all its assemblage of formal and informal circuits of communication—plays a key role not in determining, but in inflecting youth writing.

A foregrounding of text and audience is not a revolutionary consideration. We focus closely on text and feel that audience plays a key role in determining what youth choose to pay attention to and the manner in which they do so. Close readings of text enable us to identify some of the tropes of youth consciousness at the turn of the century. In general, youth writing is not as polyvalent as more mature writing. Youth tend to mobilize strong opinions, drawing on what Kieran Egan (1997) calls the philosophic mode of discourse. They are able to make sophisticated, synthetic arguments, but often stop short of Egan's ironic mode of discourse, that capacity to consider two or more sides to an argument and express contradictory lines of argument in the same utterance. In short, youth have a tendency towards dogmatic renderings of complex issues. They use their capacity to communicate to an audience to express deeply held opinions. And that audience plays a key role in how they structure their arguments. In effect, we identify three dominant modes of address, based on the nature of audience. Peer-to-peer communication is the most ambivalent of the three, requiring lightheartedness, humour, and the eschewal of earnestness. Here the key function is demonstrating a recognition that a good joke or wisecrack will always trump heavy-handed seriousness. The second mode of address is youth to adult. Here the focus is on performance and mirroring back to adults what they wish to hear. Elizabeth Soep suggests that youth often mobilize "crowded talk" (2006). Their voices in crowded talk are always already inflected by the wishes of their audience for naïve and earnest expression of teacher talk, whether the audience member be a teacher, a community organizer, or a parent. The third mode of address, and the one which we feel is most revelatory of youth social consciousness, is the hybrid, public audience of peer and adult. It is when youth feel that the audience is real, that their voice can make a difference, change an opinion or attitude, that they mobilize their strongest opinions. We have found in our own work with youth that they do have serious concerns that they will express if there is some possibility that it will be taken seriously. In the projects in which we were directly involved, Young People's Press and the performance poetry course, we witnessed youth telling it like it is to hybrid audiences, mobilizing their deepest fears, desires, and hopes in expressions about the most important issues of the day.

Cultural Studies and Education

What is needed (is) to give young people a sense of hope in the future based on learning how they, individually and collectively, have within their reach the power to make a difference.

—Shaun C., Young People's Press

Cultural studies has come to the field of educational research relatively late, and educational researchers still struggle to make a place for themselves within cultural studies. Education only merited one seat at the table of the "Cultural Studies: Now and in the Future" conference, accorded to critical pedagogy in the figure of Henry Giroux. This modest inclusion should be considered surprising given cultural studies' commitment to research which matters "on the ground" and to its roots in adult education. Giroux has been identified as the only education go-to guy in many of the biggest cultural studies forums.[1] Giroux (1994) has been haunted by the question, "what is it about pedagogy that allows cultural studies to ignore it?" (p. 130) and over the past 20 years has written and edited an impressive number of books, book series, and journals at the crossroads of cultural studies and education. Broadly defined, his work has focused on youth cultures, identity (border cultures), policy and politics, and media studies. While Giroux has done much to try to mend the fences between the theorists of cultural studies and the presumably more practice-oriented domain of education, he seems to do much of his theorizing about youth without actually talking to them. In fairness, Giroux has never positioned his work as ethnography or empirical sociology. Nonetheless, his work is highly influential and often is seen to define the field of research on education and youth in cultural studies. The lacuna in his arguments to take youth concerns seriously is the lack of youth "voice," something that is apparent to us whenever we read, in particular, his work on youth and youth cultures. There is a leap of faith that occurs through some of his critical readings of the popular, where textual readings of media representations stand in for ethnographic voice. For instance, Giroux (1996a) writes:

> How youth are seen through popular representations becomes indicative of how they are viewed by mainstream society and points to pedagogical practices that offer youth themselves images through which to construct their own identities and mediate their perceptions of other youth formations. (p. 23)

The site of reception and the many often contradictory ways in which youth do, in Paul Willis' words, "necessary symbolic work" (1990), is theorized by

---

1. Other critical pedagogues who draw explicitly on cultural studies include Joe Kincheloe and Shirley Steinberg (1997) and David Trend (1992). While cultural studies has been most vocally taken up by critical pedagogy, Carlson & Dimitriadis (2003) point to its influence on two other "subfields" in education, the reconceptualist curriculum movement (in works such as Marla Morris' (2001) Curriculum and the Holocaust: Competing Sites of Memory and Representation) and the social foundations of education (see, for instance, Edgerton, 1996; Yon, 2000). Recent collections in the field of education grapple more generally with the implications of cultural studies for educational research and practice (e.g., Carlson & Dimitriadis, 2003; Gaztambide-Fernandez, Harding, & Sorde-Marti, 2004).

Giroux, usually quite accurately, but it is nonetheless untested in the streets of everyday life. Giroux (1996a) does point to the importance of studying the "reception and use of various texts, and how they are used to define diverse notions of self, values, community, social relations, and the future" (p. 51), though that work has been for the most part outside his project.

While much of Giroux's writing is absent of youth "voice," he does argue persuasively for a reconsideration of writing as a form "of cultural recovery in which the production of knowledge, subjectivity, and agency can be addressed as ethical, political, and pedagogical issues" (1994, pp. 127–128). He takes up youth "voice" in the classroom, and talks of writing as an opportunity to get "students to theorize about their own experiences rather than articulate the meaning of other people's theories" (1994, p. 135). Writing about personal and collective experience allows students to position themselves in the chronotope they inhabit and empowers them to go to the next level, challenging convention and established verities. States Giroux:

> ...writing [is] not merely used as an ideological marker for locating specific biographical interests and forms of identification; it [is] also viewed as a rupturing practice, as an oppositional pedagogy in which one pushes against the grain of traditional history, disciplinary structures, dominant readings, and existing relations of power. (1994, p. 135)

This speaks to the heart of what we are trying to accomplish in this book. Youth writers, we have found, tend to develop a strong passion for their writing when embarking from personal experience. In voicing their opinions, youth can be intimidated by existing power structures and hierarchies, but, when given a chance to tell it their way, they can cut to the chase on some issues in a manner reminiscent of the old fable, *The Emperor's New Clothes*. *Reading Youth Writing* works to complement studies of youth representation within mainstream media-driven culture through a focus on practices of youth self-representation. Rather than envision pedagogies that offer youth alternative images with which to identify and make sense of themselves and others, we reflect upon pedagogies which make space for youth to create, share, and test out those images themselves. We argue for the importance and challenge of listening to what youth have to say, and make this argument through careful engagement with the stories youth choose to tell when given a hybrid audience of adults and peers.

Cultural Studies Meet the New Literacy Studies

There are a number of theoretical and methodological convergences between New Literacy Studies (NLS) and cultural studies. Like cultural studies' rejection of high art/low art hierarchies and its commitment to exploring popular culture and everyday life, NLS research counters the traditional model of "literacy" as consisting of value-neutral reading and writing skills with its assumption that literacy is always a social practice whose meaning lies in the specific ways it is mobilized and used by particular people in particular contexts (Street, 1995). Both fields are interested in questions of agency: cultural studies in the active production of culture, or "what we *do* with the cultural commodities that we encounter and use in daily life ("practice") and thus what we *make* as culture" (Frow & Morris, 2000, p. 331) and NLS in how language is lived and in what people do with literacy. Street's (1995) argument that "autonomous" models of literacy are inaccurate for representing literacy practices that are always "ideological" gets reflected in cultural studies' understandings that the study of culture requires the analysis of power relations. Raymond Williams (1976) notes that "culture" tends to designate "material" production within archeology and cultural anthropology and "symbolic" production within cultural studies and history: a distinction, Williams argues, that wrongly obscures "the central question of the relations between 'material' and 'symbolic' production" (p. 91). The notion of literacy as social practice explicitly takes up the relation of the material to the symbolic: how is literacy used and how does it mean in specific contexts for specific purposes? However, NLS' roots in anthropology and socio-linguistics have meant careful attention to what people *do* with language, oral and written, and less analysis of how people *are shaped* by forms of representation such as art, media, and literature.

Key to cultural studies is the concept of representation broadly defined to include the languages of the word, the image, the body, and social formations. A cultural studies lens focuses on how identities and social relations are made within, through, and against available representations. And cultural studies pays particular attention to the role of popular and media culture within contemporary social communication under the semiotic, political, social, and economic conditions of everyday life. It provides a lens for reading pop culture as central to student knowledge, skills, and interests—and to literate practices and identities in the rapidly evolving present, given that the popular both drives and reflects the evolution of culture more generally. Popular culture is transient, shifting, contradictory, and multifaceted, and academic frameworks will always be ten steps behind, struggling to keep up. Cultural studies embraces the chase, alert to the changing shapes and directions of the popular, and thus is a crucial framework for educators committed to understanding and engaging, rather than reifying, adolescents' out-of-school literacies. Also particularly useful for the study of adolescent literacy practices and not typically present in NLS is cultural studies' radical interdisciplinarity and the multiple traditions it mobilises in its close reading textual strategies. Street (1995), writing from the perspective of NLS, singled out the usefulness of cultural studies' text-analysis for understanding "'the cultural attitudes, sentiments, values, and traditions'" (CCCS publicity document, cited in Street, p. 59) of a particular place and time, what Raymond Williams, from within cultural studies, has called "textures of feeling."

Both the study of literacy practices and more general cultural practices are at the same time studies of identity, for literacy practices reflect and require certain ways of being in the social and the making of symbolic culture is also the making of identity. The self emerges in part through processes of identification in relation to and against available narratives and representations. Drawing on Hall's description of the postmodern subject, Yon (2000) explains that although this process of making identifications is "constructed and open-ended" (p. 13), these representations serve to "anchor" the subject in the social world (p. 14). Hall contrasts this postmodern theory of identity with the theory of the Enlightenment subject with its unfolding "autonomous inner core," and that of the sociological subject produced through symbolic interaction with the social world. Unlike the coherence and stability offered by the latter models, postmodern identities multiply, fragment, become contradictory, and remain unresolved (Yon, 2000, p. 13) and "subjects are no longer perceived as fastened to cultures and external social structures" (p. 14). New literacy studies and contemporary cultural studies reject the essentialising tendencies of an "autonomous" model, whether of literacy or identity. The postmodern notion of multiple and fragmented subjectivities is not an abstract construct; instead, in the words of Luke & Luke (2001), it "appears to have strong experiential and phenomenological, empirical, and even experimental corroboration" (p. 94). Adolescents participate in a culture whose "intellectual, laboring and signifying capacities...are in flux" (p. 93) as a result of

> unprecedented and seemingly irresistible global and borderless flows of human laboring and thinking subjects, of capital both symbolic and material, and of information, discourse and texts having immediate and palpable impact on social formations, on cultural practices, and indeed, on human development. (p. 93)

Luke & Luke's (2001) description of contemporary culture under conditions of globalization moves us closer to the final section of this chapter which maps out in greater detail the "contemporary youthscapes" within which youth are writing. We begin this exploration by thinking about the concept of cultural change from the perspective of Raymond Williams' model of cultural co-existence.

What Makes Something "New"?

Key to understanding the present cultural moment and the media and messages that are part of its fabric is an awareness of processes of cultural change. Where are we now, where were we, and where are we going? In chapter 1, we introduced the two contexts of new literacy research which frame this book—"new" as in theoretically and methodologically different from traditional literacy research and "new" as in literacies which are chronologically new. Here we work to complicate the question of what makes something "new" by examining the early cultural studies work of Raymond Williams (1977) on the blurred stages of cultural change, and the coexistence of residual, dominant, and emergent forms in a given cultural practice or historical moment. According to Williams, the dominant forms are those which in a particular historical cultural context are dominant, normative, hegemonic, and understood as "common sense." We know that dominant forms evolve and thus carry a residue of the past and the capacity to continue transforming in the future. Williams' (1977) definition of residual and emergent forms is worth examining:

> The residual, by definition, has been effectively formed in the past, but it is still active in the cultural process, not only and often not at all as an element of the past, but as an effective element of the present. Thus certain experiences, meanings, and values which cannot be expressed or substantially verified in terms of the dominant culture, are nevertheless lived and practised on the basis of the residue—cultural as well as social—of some previous social and cultural institution or formation...By "emergent" I mean, first, that new meanings and values, new practices, new relationships and kinds of relationship are continually being created. But it is exceptionally difficult to distinguish between those which are really elements of some new phase of the dominant culture (and in this sense "species specific") and those which are substantially alternative or oppositional to it: emergent in the strict sense, rather than merely novel. (pp. 122–123)

Changing communicative practices do not emerge on a conveyor belt, one neatly following the next. Williams' description of the dynamic internal relations which shape culture recognizes that cultural change is a complex and layered process in which old and new experiences, meanings, and values (based in social and cultural formations and institutions) coexist and conflict. It can therefore be difficult distinguishing between residual, dominant, and emergent elements. This is particularly relevant to literacy research informed by a strong sense that new theories of literacy are needed in order to catch up with practices; Williams' model confirms that culture is continually evolving but also warns us that determining what is new and how it is new is difficult. In our rush to understand contemporary literacy practices we need to be wary of overstating their emergent qualities and overlooking the residual. For the residual is a fact of life, just as in human genealogy. There is a cultural lag time after the introduction of any new technology or media as people invent new practices on the backs of inherited forms.

This is the point that Michael Clanchy (1979) makes in relation to the introduction of written contracts in the English Middle Ages. It took over 600 years for people to really accept that a written signature could mediate a formal agreement. Residual forms of contract—the exchange of blood, the plunging of a sword into the ground—continued for centuries. The same point is made by Larry Cuban (2001) in relation to the introduction of computers in schools in the Silicon Valley in the 1990s. Residual forms of practice—typing an essay, filling in an assignment sheet—continued despite the great potentials the new machines had for horizontal learning, collaborative engagement, and networked communication. Clanchy's England and Cuban's Silicon Valley are miles and centuries apart, but the story remains the same. The difference is what Paul Virilio (1986) calls the historical phenomenon of "speed" in modern culture. It is not change itself that is new today, but the pace of change. Another great example of cultural lag time is the case of early network television which took all of its cues from the theatre and vaudeville. It has taken television years to know itself and most of us have grown up with it, literally becoming new selves alongside the new projections of our selves on the television. It is difficult to notice that television has grown up because we have been busy growing up alongside it all the while.

The residual and the emergent are woven into the tapestry of everyday life in a relatively seamless manner, more often than not incorporated in (or in the process of being incorporated into) evolving versions of the dominant forms. Like Johnson, Williams (1977) commits us to considering questions of cultural production in relation to power relations and to particular political, social, and economic structures, and how culture as a "whole social process" operates to maintain relations of dominance and subordination. He thus signals the importance of understanding whether the emergent or residual cultural practices function to reinforce the dominant culture (or perhaps extend it into a new phase), to provide an alternative to it (ushering in something different), or actually oppose or challenge it in counter-hegemonic ways. While it is beyond the scope of this book to usher forth a detailed argument on the economy and polity of the new public/private spheres where much youth writing is finding a home, we warily watch as the new times unfold under political and economic conditions that are as yet unresolved. In fact, it is the conditions of flux and uncertainty that make the "dominant" far more elusive than it was when Williams was writing. The continuity, of course, is the profit motive of an increasingly globalized capitalism. The discontinuity, or rupture, is the move from the modern to the postmodern, from Fordism to post-Fordism, and from the mass media to the new multimedia. In brief, we are dealing with a world of uncertainty, where knowledge is multiperspectival and multicultural, economies are increasingly global, the consolidation of capital into fewer and bigger private corporations continues, where cities are replacing nations as nodes of global economic power, and in which the one way flow of a primarily corporate media has been supplemented by a diversity of voices occasioned by the broadcasting and publication potentials of the Internet, particularly now in its Web 2.0 incarnation. This is a time of reshuffling and reorganizing of cultures, economies, and means and modes of communication: an era where the residual and the emergent are writ large as new and old forms mix, meld, and transform. We start mapping out some of these contexts in the concluding section of this chapter.

There are important implications of Williams' model for understanding and paying attention to youth cultural production. One response to the near impossibility of keeping up with new literacy practices is to give up trying, just as many parents and teachers can't make sense of and hence stop listening to or watching youth popular culture. But there are residual cultural elements in the new forms. For example, blogs are home to a type of literary discourse inherited from the private side of the letter form and the public dimension of Op/Ed journalism. The explosive growth of the blogosphere has brought the energy channelled all these years into personal diaries, journals, and creative writing into the public sphere. The texts, sometimes introspectively personal, sometimes outwardly didactic, are works in progress in historical terms, blended genres of new youth writing. These blended genres, or transitional discourses, have homes in both new and old cultural forms. Identity text writing intended for real and imaginary peers online intersects with institutional text writing for teachers and other figures of authority. The e-mail blends with the class project, and the essay melds with the blog. Like the rest of us, young people are inhabiting the liminal in-between spaces of technological innovation and changing literacy practices. There is no established form, nor ur-text of the new era, just a lot of people writing a lot of the time. This means that some of the sorts of strategies used in the past to read youth writing are still relevant.

In their most recent inquiry into "new literacies," Lankshear & Knobel (2006) also critique the notion that literacies "displace" one another, arguing instead for an evolutionary model in which various forms of new literacy are understood as being on the ascendance; some of these eventually become so normalised that they are part of the mainstream (as in the ubiquity of e-mail). We build on their model through Williams by arguing that the new literacy practices in question can also be hybrids of residual and emergent forms. Also valuable for our argument is Lankshear & Knobel's (2006) disaggregating of the "new" into parts: ontologically speaking, the "new" in new literacies is made of both new technological stuff, driven by the digital revolution, and new "ethos" stuff out of which new mindsets emerge. These new mindsets are facilitated by the new technologies and share the features of what Gee (2004) calls "affinity spaces" which "instantiate participation, collaboration, distribution and dispersion of expertise" (in Lankshear & Knobel, 2006, p. 82). This description of new mindsets has important implications for paying attention to contemporary articulations of youth voice. They suggest that listening should also involve participating. Rather than peeking voyeuristically into spaces of youth cultural production, we need to actively participate in them. If these spaces are characterized by the distribution of expertise, one of the sources of such expertise should be teachers and parents. Engagement means moving beyond both the rejection or dismissal of new literacy practices and their attendant identities and the uncritical celebration of them. Following Heath (2004), we caution against romanticising youth voice, and indeed, notions of voice more generally. This problem is not new to cultural studies. The next section of this chapter turns more specifically to the study of youth, and examines the branch of British cultural studies most preoccupied with studying youth culture, subcultural studies. Its researchers have also had to grapple with some of the dangers of romanticizing youth in their quest to value and understand the everyday lives of young people.

Reading Youth Subcultures

So I would suggest that the portrayal of my entire generation as wasted space (slackers) is a conscious attempt to keep us down and prevent us from attaining power.

—Nicole D., Young People's Press

As any socially-conscious teen will confirm, today's concerns go far beyond what kind of jobs are waiting when we're finished university, or whether women will get equal pay for those jobs. Past these shining causes are those beasts which lie at the feet of my generation. In an age where the middle class is vanishing to give way to a massive lower class, an elite upper class, and a huge gap in between, the warriors of the next century will have to deal with more economic problems than just their own.

—Samantha B., Young People's Press

Regardless of the popular characterization of North American youth as consumption-mad slackers, driven more by the need to fulfill their self and group identities in popular culture practices than to care about their social and environmental conditions, the reality is far more optimistic. If anything, youth coming of age in the information age have access to a broader range of data and opinions about the world than ever before. Examples abound of youth activism, or, at minimum, emergent consciousness, even if some pro-social and pro-environmental attitudes coexist with the same consumerist mentality that is part of the problem to begin with. It is not our intention to paint a romantic picture of an active culture of resistance on the part of youth, but to register some caveats about too pessimistic a reading of the cultures of youth. What is required in this context is a more flexible way of conceiving social change, a more inclusive emancipatory agenda, which does not turf the uninitiated out on their ears for not living up to prevailing political orthodoxies. For this purpose, and in the tradition of cultural studies, we will adopt Andrew Ross' (1989) term, "impure criticism," to describe an approach that refuses "any high theoretical ground or vantage point" and instead launches itself into the contradictory terrain of everyday life. An impure criticism starts from the premise, familiar to readers of Antonio Gramsci (1971), that "all men [sic] are intellectuals," that people are not mere hostages to a dominant ideology, but that instead they are knowing and sentient beings who do things for reasons (even if not always for good ones). Impure criticism resists preachy disdain and instead looks for the sites of possibility in seemingly contradictory political worldviews.

This type of approach strongly informed the work of the CCCS subcultural studies scholars in the 1970s such as Angela McRobbie, Dick Hebdige, and Stanley Cohen who paid serious attention to the lives and meaning-making practices of subculturally identified young people such as punks, mods, and teds, working to better understand what Hebdige (1979) called the "meaning of style" and the functions of subculture. Contesting simplistic discourses of youth deviance and romanticized notions of a post-war generationally distinct "youth culture" that had transcended class barriers, subcultural theorists argued that subcultures were oppositional working-class youth formations. These historically specific formations purposefully and spectacularly deviated from the normative ideals of mainstream culture, cultivating styles that subverted and transformed the typical meaning of objects, such as the safety pin or the Edwardian suit. This "resistance through rituals" (the title of the 1976 CCCS volume of collected papers on subculture) constituted what Phil Cohen (1972) calls a sort of magical or symbolic solution (in Hall & Jefferson, 1976, pp. x–xvii) to the contradictions of dominant culture and the problem of disjuncture from both the dominant as well as the parent culture (a British working-class culture whose worlds of work and sets of family and neighborhood relations had been profoundly unsettled). Theorists such as those assembled by Hall and Jefferson (1976) concluded that while subcultures claimed public space and leisure time for the young, they did not open up sustainable life pathways for young people, nor did they translate into a potentially politically transformative class strategy of resistance.

The subcultural studies published by the CCCS have been much critiqued on a number of grounds, including the practice of reading for resistance, biases towards the countercultural and the spectacular, false binaries drawn between cultural authenticity and incorporation, and a lack of attention to young women and people of color. That said, the CCCS tradition of subcultural studies incorporated critique from the beginning (see for instance McRobbie and Garber's chapter on girls and subcultures in *Resistance through Rituals*). And many of its methods—critical, semiotic, ethnographic—and a commitment to better understanding youth cultural expression in light of larger social, political, and economic processes and conditions (the dynamic interplay between "structures, cultures, and biographies" (Crichter, 1976) remain foundational to (post) subcultural studies (Huq, 2006; Muggleton & Weinzierl, 2003). These perspectives certainly inform this book, and the many Hip-Hop identified youth in Bronwen's study can certainly be thought of as part of a subculture—stylistically distinct and oppositional (though "impure," given the increasing corporatization of Hip-Hop and the contradictory representational politics of both Hip-Hop and North American mainstream culture). Though Hip-Hop is often referred to as a culture rather than a subculture in the literature, emphasizing it as a whole way of life, it has many of the qualities Weinzierl & Muggleton (2003) attribute to postmodern subcultures, such as its global nature, its multifaceted relationship to the cultural mainstream (which is itself fragmented and fluid), its divisions across distinctions of class, race, and gender, and its entrepreneurial spirit. About the latter, Weinzierl & Muggleton (2003) write, "subcultures today are also complicit in the (niche) marketing of their own identities. There is a vivid role for subcultural-related practices as an entrepreneurial engine for the new media, fashion, and culture industries" (p. 8). This is especially true for Hip-Hop, which has offered some economic opportunities for black and other youth as rappers, fashion or accessory designers, concert promoters, video-makers, writers, youth workers, cultural critics, webmasters, etc. While the notion of complicity with the market stands in tension with the notion of resistance, it also means potential job prospects for some of the youth in our study. That said, many of the youth we worked with and whose writing we read here are not part of spectacular subcultures and might instead be classified as "mainstream" by early CCCS scholars; we read the work of, for example, "middle class kids with modems", in light of Clarke's (1990) critique that such individuals are also negotiating identities in relation to complex realities, and sometimes taking part in more mundane subversions (such as manipulating a school uniform). A primary distinction of our work from the subcultural studies research tradition is our attention to youth writing, for none of the early subcultural studies work examined written expression, nor does much of the contemporary writing on youth subcultures. For example, the very comprehensive *Subcultures Reader* (2003) includes but one article on Goth writing on the Internet (as well as studies of writing more broadly defined such as graffiti tags and tattoos).

The concluding section of this chapter begins to map the socio-cultural and economic context within which contemporary North American youth are writing and making sense of themselves and the world. This frames our subsequent analyses of texts and programs and classrooms within the bigger picture of adolescence under contemporary conditions of globalization.

Contemporary Youthscapes

The epochal, ruptural shifts in the global economy are being lived by north American youth in contradictory ways. On the one hand, the global realignment of industrial production away from the nations of the north has created the conditions where, for the first time in the post-war era, young people in North America must face diminishing economic expectations (Hoechsmann, 1996). On the other hand, the increasing centrality of consumption as the motor of domestic economic growth in the nations of the North interpellates these same young people as a powerful new consumer force (Hoechsmann, 1996). For theorists, activists and educators, this period of rapid change presents a unique challenge and opportunity. While the walls of a manufacturing empire crumble around us and the nation state loses its sovereign distinctiveness, our attention must be firmly fixed upon the emergence of new ways of life. In this era of globalizing economies and cultures, rapidly changing technology, and a reshuffling of workplaces and working conditions, it is increasingly difficult to develop a clear sense of purpose and belonging—two key elements of identity formation for young people. The rhetoric of lifelong learning, multiple career changes, and contract work are predictable outcomes for relatively privileged folk; for those less privileged, the circumstances are even more dire: economic insecurity caused by diminishing social safety net, the flight of nationalist capital, and an increasingly ruthless socio-economic polity. In this context, youth performing imaginary selves in media and consumer spaces is a natural response.

Though North American youth may not have a collective voice, they do share a common experience, albeit in multiple and hybrid ways, which is the historical moment. Paul Willis makes a provocative case for an impure critical perspective on youth consumption practices, proposing that they should be seen as "necessary symbolic work" (Willis, 1990). Willis argues that despite the "hidden-selfish, blind, grabbing-hand of the market...commercial cultural commodities are all most people have" (Willis, 1990, p. 26) and that perhaps ironically "commerce and consumerism have helped to release a profane explosion of everyday symbolic life and activity" (Willis, 1990, p. 27). In an era when work futures are increasingly uncertain, when the instability of youth self- and group- identity formation is exacerbated by a changing global economy, youth are more likely to invest their identities in their consumptive futures. For Willis, "we are all cultural producers in some way and of some kind in our everyday lives" (Willis, 1990, p. 128). That commercial culture makes up much of our symbolic terrain is a fact of our contemporary condition. Nonetheless, buying in to the pleasure and desire of consumption practices to some extent does not preclude developing or maintaining a critical perspective towards the culture of consumption and the corporate interests which enable it.

It is important to emphasize, as Grossberg (1992) does, that "youth is a cultural rather than a biological category" (p. 176). Just as in language change, where youth are the primary source of innovation, in cultural change too youth are a force to be reckoned with. For example, young people born since 1973, the year commonly cited as the watershed between the epoch of contemporary capitalism called Fordism and the new "post-Fordism" (Harvey, 1989, p. 145), are 35-years-old and under today. While in the short term the roughest and rudest awakenings to these "new times" will be experienced by middle-age workers who are summarily dismissed from long-held jobs in the manufacturing and resource extraction sectors, the attitudes and actions of young people present the most prescient beacons of what is to come. For instance, youth, or more precisely, the representations of youth, have been at the heart of the electronic media industry since its inception. As Stuart Ewen (1976) has documented, youth were seen as the key innovators of social change by the advertisers of the 1920s who set out to win that future generation over to the ethos of the culture of consumption. Youth were first identified as a "target market" in the post-war economic boom. Larry Grossberg (1992) argues that despite "sociological differences...and the cultural diversity of its tastes and styles,...this was the first generation isolated by business (and especially by advertising and marketing agencies) as an identifiable market...[and] by 1957...was worth over $30 billion a year" (p. 173). Families were encouraged to have children in order to produce "more consumers." A cover of *Life* magazine in 1958 spelt out this need for new consumers: "Kids: Built in Recession Cure. How 4 million a year make millions in business" (cited in Grossberg, 1992, p. 172). Not only were youth identified as a generational category and a consumer force in the post-war period, but the representation of youth became central to the media text.

Images of vibrant, visually appealing youth have been used to sell virtually every consumer product imaginable, but particularly those which are identified with pleasure (as opposed to drudgery). Dick Hebdige points out that when youth are represented in the media, they tend to be portrayed either as "youth-as-fun and youth-as-trouble" (Hebdige, 1988, p. 19), the former concentrated in the advertising text. Identifying and empowering youth as a consumer force has led to a genie-out-of-the-bottle effect: youth are seen as a "market" and the new leisured youth, or more precisely those left out of the leisure class demographic, are also a "problem" (Hebdige, 1988, p. 19).   In the first chapter, we described how the representation of youth—particularly youth of colour—as "problem" in the news media, has provoked many a moral panic and has served to focus sociological and journalistic attention on youth. On the flip side, youth continue to represent "fun" and pleasure in the advertisement text, and while self and group identity is increasingly tied up in those interpellations of "youth," in a changing global economy, North American youth straddle a contradictory space. They are contingent consumers, in general one of the most materially blessed generations in human history, but for whom economic decline looms as a real threat as they prepare to enter shrinking job markets.

This is particularly the case for the African-American students in Bronwen's classroom study. Distinctions are regularly drawn between the Civil Rights and the Hip-Hop generations. Kitwana (2002) describes the latter's members as the first generation of African-Americans who have grown up in post-segregation America, but whose experiences are shaped by high unemployment rates, the proliferation of low-paying jobs in the service sector (the McJobs phenomenon), the increasing criminalization of young black youth and disproportionately high incarceration rates, and the deterioration of public schools. He argues that this generation is influenced less by the traditional purveyors of black culture, family, church, and school, and more by entertainment culture. And they share different values than the civil rights generation; members of the Hip-Hop generation rely upon themselves, their peers, and mass mediated commodity culture for direction (Kitwana, 2002). This might mean that members of the Hip-Hop generation disregard censure by these institutions—or capitalize upon it in order to reject and distinguish themselves from traditional sites of authority.

Moreover, those for whom struggle is an everyday fact of life might not have the luxury to even question the circumstances. Lalo Lopez (1994) makes this point in "Generation Mex":

> For the Gringorder, there's gotta be baby boomers and thirty-somethings, Generation X and slackers. I'd like to be a slacker, but my family would kick my ass. A poor Mexican worrying about esoteric emotions like angst? Get a job, "mijo." (p. 134)

In a social fabric riven with injustice and difference, one walks delicately when trying to make meaning from complex and contradictory contexts. Thus, the objective of listening to youth voice and taking it seriously can run aground on the politics of difference. And it is not a question of either/or. We must attend to difference, whether grounded in historical conditions of class, race, gender and gendering, or in spectacular forms of youth subcultures and resistance. But we must also look beneath the surface at those youth who are suffering silently, regardless of whatever privilege they may have.

Writing of youth as a generational category is an enterprise fraught with contradictions, given the historical biases of youth scholarship towards normative projections of white, middle class male subject positions, the actual complexity of youth cultures that are marked by class, race and gender differences or by subcultural practices, and the transitory nature of this stage of life which can never be more than a temporary condition. Nonetheless, as a historical marker—a synchronic sampling of diverse people and groups who share many of the same changing social, cultural, economic, and technological conditions—the category of youth plays a useful heuristic role. There are, after all, some shared tropes being mobilized by North American youth and there are hybrid new forms of identity and sociability which speak to the changing cultural conditions these youth face. Cultural studies has straddled this fence throughout its history, whether in positing subcultures as essentialist and non-contradictory (Clarke, 1990) or in over-enthusing the role of the subject, subjectivity and identity. Says Paul Gilroy (1996):

> ...The concept [identity] has also provided an important site for the erasure and abandonment of *any* political aspirations. Clarion calls to comprehend identity and set it to work often suggest that mere politics has been exhausted and should now be left behind in favour of more authentic and powerful forms of self-knowledge and consciousness that are coming into focus. (p.225)

Gilroy (1996) argues for a return to political engagement as a vehicle for social change, grounded in our mobilized cultural identities: "In this way, we may be able to make cultural identity a premise of political action rather than a substitute for it" (p. 238). That imperative for social change has fueled much of the best cultural studies work. It is, then, paradoxical that the cultural studies work in Education has had a relatively low profile. Educators are fueled by the telos of change. And, of course, most practitioners and theorists of cultural studies spend considerable amounts of their energy teaching, primarily in colleges and universities. Whatever the case, it is with haste and urgency that we should take our pedagogical energies and apply them to the living, breathing aspirations of young people.

We do not intend for this chapter on cultural studies to stand as a *corrective* to work in New Literacies Studies. Rather, we have attempted to map out some points of convergence between cultural studies and New Literacies Studies and to show how cultural studies can productively contribute to some ongoing debates in New Literacy Studies. For one, we mobilize Johnson's conceptual structure to synthesize a variety of topoi of social, cultural, and literary analysis. We feel that this heuristic enables us to keep in tension and relation various aspects of the reading and writing process. We also draw upon William's work on cultural formations to describe cultural change in order to raise the question of what makes something new. Along the way, we have begun to undertake the task of reading *youth*, reading *youth writing*, and reading youth *writing*, ultimately, the project of this book. In this chapter, we also set the stage for later chapters by presenting the contemporary context that fuels youth writing: the changing social, economic, and cultural conditions that structure and inflect real lives. We turn now to closer readings and closer analyses of youth writing in a variety of spheres and circumstances. In the next chapter, the readings and analyses serve primarily to make an argument about some of the challenges of reading youth writing and about some of the limits of "self-representation" and "voice" as concepts for understanding youth expression. It does so in relation to a series of documentary films in which professional filmmakers give youth cameras and ask them to tell their own stories.

CHAPTER 3

Says Who? Video, Voice, and Youth Self-Representation

Bronwen E. Low

Once the dispossessed and powerless have access to the means of information they can no longer be misled by Establishment bullshit. And that in itself is a revolution.

—Patrick Watson (1970, p. 20)

Video and Media Revolution

The critique is well worn: the mainstream media are major players in the representational politics of anxiety in which young people, embodiments of the future and so ready targets for social anxieties about cultural change, get cast as symbols of fear rather than hope. Activists hoping to intervene in media discourses of youth violence, desire, and disaffection have turned to the possibilities of Watson's information revolution by giving youth the tools to fight back and to tell their own stories. The 1990s saw the proliferation in the United States of community-based media production programs aimed at youth. Hopes for more democratic processes of self-representation and of political engagement have been particularly high for video. Compared to film, video has low production costs, is readily available, and is easy to use, factors which spurred on the development of non-profit media arts and video collectives in the 1960s, the community-access television movement of the 1970s, and school-based vocational media programs in the 1980s (Goldfarb, 2002; Goodman, 2003).

Hopes of "giving voice" to the disempowered have also long driven documentary film production more generally. Recent decades have seen this commitment take the form of increasingly participatory structures in which filmmakers give cameras to those who have traditionally been objects of others' representation and interpretation. Much of this work takes place within community-based media programs in which the education and empowerment of the filmmakers-in-training is the foremost objective. The participatory videos produced in such settings tend to be low- (or no-) budget productions whose audiences are rarely larger than the participants' local communities (Fleetwood, 2005). (Exceptions include some of the New York- based Educational Video Collective's documentaries, which occasionally get broadcast on major networks; one short film made by youth through the EVC about military recruiting became part of a documentary entitled *Why We Fight* (Jarecki, 2005), which won the Sundance American Documentary Award that year). Here we explore a number of what we are calling "professional participatory documentaries," which also work to give voice to youth by giving them access to video cameras but which have relatively large budgets, equipment infrastructures, and intentions for broadcast and distribution.

Because of their sometimes sizeable viewing audiences, these professional documentaries help shape the popular construction of the "true voice" of youth. We examine them in order to grapple with the implications and challenges of Watson's information revolution for youth "writing" through video production, but also for the reading of this writing. We argue that in his assumption that access to the "tools" is automatically empowering, Watson's vision is utopian. The vision glosses over the intricate politics of representation, of speaking and of listening, which inevitably shape all forms of cultural production and reception. This chapter works to complicate the conversation about youth voice and self-representation by tackling these tricky politics head on. It analyses the finished products, and also draws upon interviews with two of the filmmakers of the documentaries in question, in order to better understand some of what happens when adults ask youth to self-represent. Drawing on Johnson's heuristic for cultural studies, this chapter grapples with texts (the documentaries) and, to a lesser extent, production (through the interviews with two of the filmmakers about their processes) in order to enrich our understanding of the dynamics and challenges of another site on the circuit, reception.

We start with a discussion of what might be the earliest example in Canada of the "giving the camera to the voiceless" genre, move to a U.S. documentary produced by the Discovery Channel, and then turn to three other recent Canadian documentaries, in part or wholly funded by the National Film Board of Canada and set in Montreal. They give a glimpse into the local context within which Bronwen and Michael are writing this book, and expand our inquiry by offering another specially located site of youth writing. We end with a brief discussion of some of the implications of the discussion for understanding community-based participatory youth media projects, a problem we will take up in greater detail in the fifth chapter, "What's On Your Mind?"

Filming the "Real": Challenge for Change

The Canadian National Film Board (NFB), arguably the institution which has most shaped the documentary genre world wide, has a long history of support for film and video as a means of fostering greater democratic participation and citizenship. In the late 60s, the NFB developed a "Challenge for Change" programme designed to increase media access and participation for members of marginalised Canadian communities by having them be filmmaking partners rather than objects. The prototypes were made in 1967 on Fogo, an island off Newfoundland whose fishing industry had been destroyed by corporatization. The inhabitants were to be relocated by the government, a plan which they resisted, and they used the films as a means of communicating with each other about this. The videos consisted of a series of minimally edited interviews with members of the isolated island communities, on topics they chose, which would then be screened to other members whose reactions would also be filmed. Members could choose to edit out sections from the daily rushes which they did not think represented them properly. Marchessault (1995) offers an analysis of both the program, which quickly gained international attention, and these early instances of community video, and points to potential limitations of documentary projects which work to "give voice." In particular, she asks us to pay careful attention to how the "real" gets constructed and framed. Challenge for Change's commitment to minimising the influence and perspective of the filmmaker in favour of transparent community self-representation took shape, in part, in a kind of authenticity of representation evident in the documentaries' aesthetic (or anti-aesthetic):

> the formal characteristics of community video were delineated in opposition to art and the mediating subjectivity of the auteur. Video was an antidote to indeterminacy; the more ordinary and transparent, the more authentic. (Marchessault, p. 141)

The video documentaries were imagined by NFB director Colin Low as a "collective mirror" of the real (cited in Marchessault, p. 136), as pure conduits for the voices of the dispossessed rather than complex mediations of the perspectives of real people. And as Marchessault argues, the aesthetic obscured the structures of authority of both the filmmaker and the NFB, which meant that these could not be challenged. From the study of a number of these documentary projects, she concludes that they were largely confined by the mainstream, nation-building imperatives of their sponsoring federal agency and that they worked to contain and package cultural difference and to "defuse direct action" (p. 143) via the display rather than actual practice of political participation. They delivered media access without any real agency. One could argue that "the Establishment" continued to "mislead" despite Challenge for Change's rhetoric of opposition and revolution by obscuring the films' structures of representation and power.

Marchessault's analysis sets the stage for the readings of contemporary projects which follow. It makes clear the central role played by those who initiate participatory video projects in determining what the product, and "the real," look like. It suggests the importance of asking questions about the projects such as who produced them, who funded them, and for what audiences they were intended. It also makes clear that the complexities of representation and power can never be side stepped, regardless of the intentions of the producer.

Re-presenting Representation

The very word representation enacts some of the tensions embodied in Challenge for Change's video for self-representation project for it collapses two very different meanings: representation in the political sense, as in "standing in for," and representation in the larger aesthetic sense. In her oft-cited essay "Can the Subaltern Speak?" on the project of "giving voice," Spivak (1988) explains how these two senses are lexically distinguished in German as *vertreten* and *darstellen*, the former that she associates with "speaking for," the political and legal representation required by liberal democracies, and the latter that she reads as the "re-presentation" in art or philosophy (pp. 276–277). Linked to performance and art, *darstellen* suggests the making visible to another mind or eye an idea or creative impulse. While both senses of representation involve substitution, the functions of *vertreten* can be more restrictive than *darstellen*: whereas political representation requires a simplification and temporary reification of a group or class interests for purposes of social action, *darstellen* can be dynamic, fluid, and contradictory. Like "representation" in English, the concept of "authentic voice" also seems to collapse *vertreten* and *darstellen*, which means that the interplay and difference between political and aesthetic representation—as in the connections and tensions between issues of authority and accountability and then style and genre—cannot be explored. This is what seems to happen in Challenge for Change where the artistic re-presentation of a population's stories is seen as the same as their political representation and the complexities of that re-presentation get glossed over under the guise that video mirrors or is the proxy of the real. In this same essay, Spivak (1988) also reminds that the dilemma of self-representation is as much one of listening as of speaking. This is a crucial argument for a book which is about reading youth writing. She makes clear that speaking and listening (or reading and writing) is a transaction mediated by such things as gender, class, history, and global relations of political, economic, and cultural power, as well as by the desires and interests of individual subjects. This means we need to move beyond thinking about the politics of production to include the politics of reception, and to ask questions such as who the representation's audience is, how the audience is addressed, and what the audience is hoping is to hear.

Framing Youth: *Harlem Diary*

The production we examine first is *Harlem Diary: Nine Voices of Resilience* (Williams, 1995), made in the U.S., and broadcast on and produced in conjunction with the Discovery Channel (and which had the largest audience of the documentaries discussed here.) It powerfully enacts some of the representational challenges and contradictions facing the professional participatory documentary genre: directed by Terry Williams, a professor of sociology at Manhattan New School for Social Research who seems deeply committed to the voices of a group of urban African-American youth, the documentary remains more about the needs and anxieties of its producers and audience than about the youth themselves. Henry Giroux (1996b), one of the most vocal and powerful critics of Hollywood's representational politics which "demonize" youth, acclaimed the documentary in a critical review of the controversial film *Kids* (1995). Giroux describes *Kids* as a classic case of mainstream representational politics which cast black youth as threats to eliminate, white working-class youth as problems to contain, and youth in general as driven solely by their libidos (p. 32). He then contrasts *Kids'* "conservative pedagogy and politics that fails to rupture dominant discourses about subordinate youth" (p. 35) with *Harlem Diary*'s stories which reveal domination's "contradictions, cracks, fissures and how within such spaces teenage youth fight domination and racism rather than simply yield to it" (p. 35).

The story behind *Harlem Diary* is one in part of reading youth writing, traditionally defined. Terry Williams started a "Writer's Crew" of Harlem youth who wrote in journals and shared their work. The group depicted in the documentary are members of the third Crew; in an opening shot of the documentary they are given video cameras and told by Williams:

> We have a visual representation now, we have the cameras, and we want the stories to come from you now, in a different kind of way. If you chose to write, that's great, we want you to write. But we want you also to visually put this together. We want you to use the cameras in a way to tell the story of your life, at this moment in your life.

The documentary is the video compilation of these stories, comprised of on-camera interviews with the Crew, pieces of Crew footage, and Williams' direct address framing each tale. *Harlem Diary* challenges mainstream media representations by giving voice to those usually spoken for, and yet, we argue, does so without critically examining some of the dilemmas of representation and power this project entails.

Williams clearly states that his goal is to counteract the stereotypical representations of black youth as either criminals or passive victims with "remarkable examples of good" and so provide "possibility and hope." Yet the subtext of the project seems to be to reassure the viewer that such youth are not a threat to the existing order. *Harlem Diary* was produced in conjunction with the Discovery Channel, whose audience is predominantly male and upwardly mobile. The viewership's socio-economic bracket helps explain why Williams seems to address viewers who are not from Harlem and have no similar experiences. He acts at points as tour guide facilitating middle-class America's entry into Harlem streets. For example, take his closing words:

> and though their surroundings and experience may set them apart, young people in Harlem are in many ways no different than those elsewhere in this country. Their desires and their dreams are the same: a good life, safe and free of trouble, a decent job, a nice place to live. They yearn for the chance to believe in possibility both for themselves and for the larger community.

Williams seems here to be saying that these voices are not disruptive ones. Perhaps they are resilient rather than revolutionary, less voices of protest than voices of accommodation to middle-class notions of respectability. They are also mostly male: of the "nine voices of resilience," only two are women's. While the Writer's Crews originally included more women, most are not part of the documentary. And the stories which have survived the edit seem conventionally gendered: the men worry about striving towards excellence, educating themselves, and finding careers, whereas the women are concerned with friends and family.

Williams also reinforces the status quo in the framework which pieces together the different narratives. Many of Williams' commentaries stress typical middle-class and capitalist values, especially the belief in formal education, discipline, and ambition as the only means of making a "better life." The youths in both the first and last sequence of the video commit to college. The last sequence begins with Akida Bailey leaving Connecticut College, saying it is

> a predominantly white college...catered for white people for a specific economic class—both of which I wasn't part of. Towards the end of my stay in that world, I wasn't being me, therefore I had to leave.

After experiencing the workforce and limited opportunities available to him without a college degree, Bailey decides to return to school and in the final shot makes his way back to the ivy-covered red brick campus. School emerges as *the* path to success, a way out for which the self ("being me") might need to be sacrificed. And the critical implications of Bailey's comments about education as the site of social reproduction do not get addressed.

A lack of focus on the larger political, social, and economic conditions which shape the youths' narratives means that the streets of Harlem in *Harlem Diary* are cast as a problem without a context. For example, when Williams outlines some of the youths' challenges, "the discipline of not engaging in drug use, the discipline that it takes to maintain an interest in school, and to carry out the business of being a young person in a world where temptation is everywhere," he does not situate these struggles within the fabric of a racist, capitalist society. And in the one interview (with Kahlil Hicks, associate producer of *Harlem Diary*) where Williams does mention "racism, discrimination, and stereotyping" as stressful forces, he never examines their systematic exclusions.

In contrast with Williams' claim in the opening of the documentary that these figures of resilience "have also managed to give back to the community," the struggles and terms of success are largely individual ones. Jermaine Ashwood announces that his motto is "strive for the top...or you'll be average." Another youth, Barr "Star Dragon" Elliot, is a rap singer who wants to produce "nothing but hits." His sequence ends with him singing "I'm a champion man..." While Giroux indicates that the youths' videos facilitate dialogue, no dialogue is included in the documentary—most of the footage features the individual teenager, perhaps accompanied by Williams. Of the nine sequences, only two explicitly involve community: the first a group of women who put together a mural commemorating a friend lost to "the streets," and the second a visit with some of the Crew to an underground community, a tunnel housing over 100 people "living in the shadows of the city and [able to] find dignity there." The group is guided underground by Bernard Monte Isaac, articulate and able to challenge materialistic understandings of fulfilment and success. Asked what material things he misses he replies: "only the luxury of taking a hot bath every night." His eloquence is undermined by the sequence's ending: on top of footage of people huddled together in the tunnel, Williams' voice-over says: "when I see the shattered lives of lost souls, I wonder if any of our group will fall prey." While this might have been included to avoid romanticising poverty, these words also serve to dismiss the underground city as a viable alternative to success in surface society.

Despite Williams' intervention, Monte Isaac's message comes through, as frames shape but do not completely determine their contents. Can the same be said for some of the other sequences? *Harlem Diary* asked the Crew to tell their own stories using visual and oral rather than textual representations; the final product incorporates some of their video footage taken with Hi-8 cameras. In a heavy-handed visual clue for the viewer, footage from the Crew's cameras is black and white, despite the fact that the cameras supplied to the Crew must have been colour (black and white video recorders being obsolete). The black and white is a post-production effect which comes to signify the voice of Harlem youth, and conveys both the gritty illusion of authenticity and perhaps, the naïve amateurism of youth. (The "rough cut" quality of the youths' footage also signifies a black street authenticity, given the series of films about gang life and drug-dealing such as *Menace II Society* (1993), *Boyz in the Hood* (1991), and *Clockers* (1995), which use this aesthetic). However, in a strange manipulation, included in the black and white "youth footage" are black and white sequences shot by a professional (thanked for Hi-8 camera work in the credits), making it impossible to determine whose footage is whose, despite the emphasis placed on authorship. The odd manipulation is particularly evident in one example in which one of the Crew decides to film a sunset from his apartment window—in order to better capture this moment, the editors revert back to the original color.

The issue of authorship takes on an ethical dimension for some of the images. Although Williams is working against a tradition which vilifies and sensationalises black urban centres such as Harlem, much of the footage uses backdrop images of suffering that serve to titillate the voyeur/audience (e.g., a woman stumbling through traffic in tight clothes, a man pushed against a police car who then drops to the ground). The most invasive of the images is that of the stricken and emaciated corpse of one of the Crew's mothers who has died of AIDS, and which raises a number of ethical questions: Did the youth bring his camera into the hospital room? Did the filmmakers? Should they have? To what purpose? On top of the fact that some of the black and white footage is professional and therefore "faked," the black and white scenes make up very little of the documentary. Most of the film is professionally shot (on film rather than Hi-8), showing glossy, colour interviews with Terry Williams on location in Harlem. This is not surprising, for much of the Crew's footage which is included has a rambling narrative and unclear, poorly focused images—what one would expect from inexperienced videographers, but not necessarily the stuff of engaging storytelling. Access "to the means of information" is only a first step towards meaningful self-representation, for it seems here contingent on representing oneself well for the Discovery Channel. This raises the question of whether meaningful self-representation is ever possible in the context of a corporate entity like Discovery whose main interest is its profits.

Terry Williams' project has a particular history. As Bailey (1999) writes, "It must also be acknowledged that everywhere African people have picked up movie cameras, the impulse to tell the 'untold' true stories, stories that have been suppressed or misconstrued by others, has been one of the first priorities" (p. 100). It is within a context of stereotypical representations of black youth that the multidimensional and even ambivalent stories of the Crew—of struggles and successes, but also setbacks, disappointments—are framed or altered into stories of hope and resilience. *Harlem Diary*'s political imperative or *vertreten*, its need to "counterbalance" bad representations of black youth with "remarkable examples of good," confines the structures of feeling, the *darstellen* the Crew express. In its refusal of any contradiction, Williams' framework of "hope and resilience" often seems inadequate to the Crew's experiences. One example is Damon, just out of Riker Youth Correctional Center. In his segment we learn that his mother has just died and his father, from whom he is estranged, is recently out of jail. He also has a serious blood condition for which he is hospitalised during the course of the film. Although trained as a cook at Rikers, he decides he does not want to work in the restaurant industry. He suggests he will go back to school, but how and to do what are not made clear. In one seemingly staged segment, Damon exercises with his father; this, the voiceover suggests, implies the beginnings of a relationship. And yet their conversation has no sound of its own, other than an "alright" from the father. While Damon's story is compelling it is not necessarily hopeful and he is too laboriously presented as a symbol of resilience. Similarly, Rasheem Swindle, the promising boxer, avoids practicing for weeks before an important match and loses the fight. In his interviews he seems less certain about a career in boxing than do his coaches and the filmmakers. As designated spokespeople for black youth, the Crew bear the burden of "good" representation.

Constructing "Cool": *The Year Before*

A recent NFB documentary entitled *The Year Before* (McKenna, 2006) offers additional insight into the challenges of "giving voice" to youth. The documentary, directed by Caitlin McKenna, follows the lives of four boys in their senior year of high school. At one moment during the filming, McKenna decided to give the boys cameras. In an interview, she has described to Bronwen her rationale for this decision. First, McKenna wanted the boys to have a greater sense of participation in the film, to see themselves as part authors rather than just subjects of the film. She also hoped to democratize the filmmaking relationship by giving these youth the opportunities to self-represent. And McKenna worried that by filming in school she was missing out on much of the boys' extracurricular lives. She was certain that in the boys' "downtime" their relationships with friends and girls were paramount, something her school footage did not demonstrate, but thought that trying to "muscle her way" into these weekend lives would be difficult and awkward. If the youth were doing the filming perhaps they'd be more natural, less aware of the camera being around. She ran the idea by them to enthusiastic response. McKenna first wanted to put the boys through a video training session before they started shooting for she knew that filming viewable footage was not easy. But when she started her tutorial explaining "principles of framing, holding the shots for a minimum of 40 seconds, etc," she "could feel their eyes glaze over." So she wrote and gave them a manual which she thinks helped the ones who read it.

The manual is very chatty and colloquial. Here are some excerpts from it:

WHAT TO SHOOT

I want you to feel free to shoot *whatever* you want, so I am giving you guys **FULL EDITORIAL CONTROL over anything on these tapes**. On this part of the film alone, you decide completely what's OK to use.

So...what to shoot? It's up to you. **If you have something to say** to the world, this is your chance to do it.

If you haven't got much to say, but have some mad tricks or talents or pranks to show off, go for it (Mom note: DON'T hurt yourself or others, pls).

The idea is to show the parts of your **personality** or **your life** that I've **missed** in the film, or **haven't asked** about. It can be fun stuff. Ugly stuff. Creative stuff. You can **introduce your people**—family, friends, girlfriend. You can be serious.

This is your chance **to tell your own story**.

SHOOT IDEAS

RANTING: Think of it as your own Speakers' Corner. Turn the camera on yourself and talk about what's on your mind. Pissed off at school? Obsessed with a new album? High and happy? Tawk to me.

NFB CRIBS: Tour your room/house. Why did you pick the posters, Cds, DVDs, clothes and other stuff that you do? Why are they so great? What do you like about them?

BUS, METRO, WALK... You've done it enough times...show how boring and/or exciting it is to be you, on the way to WHS in the morning.

ASK A GIRL: *"What do you think about a film on guys? Why do you think Katie chose me to be in it? Do you love me?"* And other important questions that may come to mind.

PARTY: Pahtay! Don't forget the camera at the end of the night.

MY CITY: When it gets warmer, go out and introduce your hood. We live in an awesome city—what do you like about it? Where do you hang out?

McKenna speaks the youth's language here by drawing upon some familiar genres from youth culture—*MTV Cribs* (where celebrities offer tours of their homes) and *Speakers Corner* from the Canadian Much Music program (a 24-hour-video "soapbox" from which certain selections get aired)—to stimulate their imaginations as filmmakers. She uses humor to help engage them ("Do you love me?") and phrases and terms from popular culture ("pahtay," "tawk to me," (from *Saturday Night Live*'s "Coffee Talk") and "the hood").

McKenna was disappointed by much of the footage for a number of reasons. She explained:

> The vast, vast majority of the footage I got back was unusable: the content was actually often really funny and revealing, but the camera would be shaking, or the audio inaudible, or the person talking was off-camera. These problems were compounded by the fact that the tapes were filled with timecode breaks which occur when you shoot something, rewind the tape to watch it, and then start recording again from a different point, which starts a new timecode (and often cuts in halfway through the previous scene). The reason this happened is that they were obsessed with watching and re-watching (usually with friends) a lot of the stuff they shot: especially any pranks (throwing firecrackers at girls, blowing up Barbies), shots of girls' breasts and butts, and some interview-type footage they shot with girls: "have you ever...?" etc. Sadly I didn't get to see a lot of the most interesting stuff because some of the guys also became masters of editing in-camera: rewinding and taping over anything they didn't want me to see and/or use.

Despite their crash course in video-making, the boys' footage was plagued by technical problems, a common challenge facing those working with youth as amateur videographers. And the youth took McKenna at her word, assuming "full editorial control" and determining what they wanted her to see or not. While this is one of the rights of self-representation, McKenna felt what got taped over was probably the "most interesting stuff." What the footage does do is give insight into how the boys want to be understood.

Much of the youths' footage reads like constructions of cool, portraits of how and who the boys wanted to be. McKenna noted of the boys that

> I definitely don't think they cared if I thought they were cool. I think they really imagined that this footage could be used in the film, and finally they were going to be able to present themselves however they wanted: I'm sure this was for their peers, or people they'd never met, more than for me.

And these self-portraits mostly relied on a narrow template of what adolescence looks like, much of it drawn from MTV "reality" shows about youth. While McKenna thought that mentioning *Cribs* would give the boys a structure to work within, she hadn't anticipated how the structure could also limit the narratives they developed and shared. That said, the boys would probably have drawn on these popular genres anyway given that they are what they watch and admire. Even when we are holding the camera or pen, our stories tend to take shape within given narrative and aesthetic conventions. And MTV now sets many of the terms for North American youth and culture more generally in terms of what adolescence looks like, and in particular adolescent "hip" and "cool." As McKenna told Bronwen, the first comment made by one of the boys after the director gave them the cameras was "Great! Girls Gone Wild!" In turn, there was a good deal of focus in the footage on girls' bodies.

The MTV aesthetic shaped parts of the footage from all of the boys. Stefan (a white, middle-class boy) adopted a "hip-hop" (read black and "street") TV show-host voice as he walked into a friend's party: "Yo, let's go see whas goin' on." Another youth gave an *MTV Cribs*-style tour of his suburban bedroom, saying of his bed, "this is where the magic happens," but then laughed self-consciously, aware, perhaps of the limits of the cliché. And all of the boys would take turns freestyling (improvising poetry) into the camera with hand moves drawn straight from music videos. That said, some of the freestyle footage offered the greatest spontaneity of expression, especially from two black youth, Mike and Nate, who were skilled freestylers. They also played an engaging word association game. And the most troubled of the youth, Mikhael, who eventually gets kicked out of school for a string of violent confrontations in and outside of class, makes a first-person video diary where he talks directly to the camera and confesses to feelings of confusion. However, the diary segment also seems calculated when Mikhael rolls a joint, constructing the "druggie" image he thinks makes him popular.

In a telling twist, while the documentary as a whole offers a nuanced and complex portrait of four young men as they grapple with important questions like the place of family and religion in their life choices, the nature of political justice, what counts as sex, what it means to fall in love, and what it might mean to be a success, the footage from the boys mostly reproduces what seem to us to be cultural clichés about adolescent males. This is not to say it is thus any less "real" than what they revealed to McKenna over a year of interviews and through their filmed interactions; instead, their footage reminds us that self-representation is a complex business given the fluidity and performative nature of identity. The boys experience and think about themselves in relation to what they listen to and watch, but these are not the only factors influencing their identities. And they have party selves and more serious selves. Particularly of interest to us here is how the serious, thoughtful self is what they generally offered to McKenna while she suspected the lighter fun was directed at their friends. As we began discussing in chapter 1, our data on youth cultural production suggests that youth often work to be funny, parodic, or shocking with their peers, and serious and contemplative with adults whom they think are listening. This is both a reminder of the role of audience in determining the style and content of expression but also of the importance of adults opening up and/or supporting youth literacy spaces which value complex explorations of thought and feeling. The boys' footage in the context of *The Year Before* complicates the notions of authenticity and voice that drive many participatory video projects, an argument we will return to at the end of this chapter.

The Art of Storytelling:
S.P.I.T.: *Squeegee Punks in Traffic*

Documentary filmmaker Daniel Cross found it very difficult to access street kid subculture while making *The Street* (Cross, 1997), a film about homelessness in Montreal, until he met insider Eric Denis (Roach), a self-proclaimed Anarcho-punk. Roach agreed to participate in the project, using the "RoachCam" to share his experiences as a "squeegee" (car windshield-washing) kid who has lived on the street. This footage became the basis for its own feature-length documentary, *S.P.I.T.* (Cross & Roach, 2001), which is co-directed by Cross and Denis. Roach's footage is complemented by professional footage. We hear a great deal from Denis, and the documentary reads as a very truthful account of his experiences in the margins of the city, at risk of violence, struggling with drug addiction, working to forge an alternate community of youth, and participating in protests against municipal crackdowns on squeegee kids. The project also seems to have benefited him: as he narrates his experiences, he becomes their author. He assumes the identity of filmmaker and uses it to garner greater respect from people like the police. He works at points as boom-operator for the professional crew, recording legislative sessions in Queen's Park, and interviewing politicians and police officers. And he then goes on to make another documentary, *RoachTrip* (2003), through Cross' production company (www.eyesteelfilm.com), about the cross-Canadian "punk highway."

At the same time, *S.P.I.T.*'s strength at facilitating Denis' "voice" is also at points its weakness as a documentary working to illuminate the lives of street youth other than Roach. While we are introduced to other characters, including Denis' girlfriend, we don't get to know any of them (and in fact his girlfriend is silent throughout the piece). There are very few voices in *S.P.I.T* other than Roach's, and while committed to and enthusiastic about the role, he is not always the most insightful narrator. While he makes frequent critiques of capitalism and the fascist police, he offers few explanations for or solutions to the problems facing those kids who no longer live in homes or go to school. This limits his effectiveness as the *vertreten*, or political representative, of homeless or street-involved youth. At the same time, *S.P.I.T*'s *darstellen*, or aesthetic representation, can be alienating to the viewer. Like the boys' footage discussed above, Denis' film is often very shaky and strains the eye, particularly when he is drunk or high. However, this DIY anti-aesthetic might really appeal to him as particularly Anarcho-punk—anti-professional, anti-corporate, and as discordant as the grinding punk soundtrack provided by Deadly Pale. On the other hand, judging from a few clips of her footage, Roach's equally "punk" girlfriend is quite a conventionally good cinematographer. Image stabilisation became an important value within the history of cinema for good reasons. All of this raises some questions for consideration in relation to professional participatory documentaries: Is the subject a good filmmaker? Is the filmmaker a good subject? If the project is designed primarily for the education and empowerment of the subject/filmmaker, these questions might not be relevant ones. However, these questions are relevant if the project also works to empower a *group* of youth. And if the professional participatory documentary is to have a viable broadcast future, they are necessary ones, though the questions also bring us back to the dilemmas of audience and producer expectations that plagued *Harlem Diary*. *S.P.I.T.* also raises questions about some of the limits of filmmaking in the context of video surveillance: are the truly alienated here wary of the potential panopticon effects of being filmed? Those who have to deal with the police on a daily basis might not want voice in this form. The video camera brings with it both the democratizing of filmmaking processes and a culture of surveillance in which public places and the individuals who spend time there are increasingly monitored and policed.

Fact and Fiction: *The Point*

The final project discussed here, *The Point* (Dorsey, 2006), takes many of the conventions of documentary and reinvents them into a hybrid new genre that defies easy categorisation, a sort of professional participatory docu-fiction feature film. Like *Harlem Diary*, it grew out of a writer's workshop that director Josh Dorsey developed for youth in a community centre in the culturally diverse and historically working-class Montreal neighbourhood of Pointe-St-Charles. The setting is urban, gritty, decaying, and the neighbourhood is at the bottom of the slopes of Montreal, both literally and figuratively in the economic margins of the city. It seems neglected, like the youth who live there, who are relatively unsupervised by adults, and roam the dead-end spaces of condemned buildings, alleys, and gulleys, often at night. The plot centres on the interconnected stories of a group of teens, a number of whom are struggling with the unresolved disappearance of their friend Kyra. Her closest girlfriends work secretly at night on a giant graffiti tribute to her that proclaims "Kyra was here" and which adorns the top wall of an abandoned factory whose inner walls are already covered in Kyra and her crew's artwork. Another girl throws a party at her mother's house while she works a nightshift. A 13-year-old boy is running drugs for some of the local dealers and gets himself in trouble when he insults a depressed young woman who beats him up and takes the drug money. In the process, he loses his marijuana, which gets found by a group of young men who spend the night smoking and philosophising. It is a hard-hitting portrait of young people and their friendships, desires, hopes, and frustrations. Sometimes they are loyal, generous, creative, even wise; other times they seem petty, jealous, or short-sighted. At points in the film, the youth treat each other in selfish, even cruel ways; for example, one girl takes her frustrations out on her ex-boyfriend's old girlfriend, confronting her as a "slut" at work and graffiti-ing the word on her home door. At other points, they work to help and protect each other, though this usually puts them at risk. The drug-runner's young friend jeopardises his own job in a pet store and his safety by "borrowing" some money to pay back the violent dealers and then confronting them. One girl recently out of juvenile detention reluctantly fights another in order to "watch the back" of her friend. The youth live in a world in which adults are indistinct, peripheral, and very ambivalent figures: part-time service job employers who are sometimes fair, sometimes not; police officers who get in your way, harass you, but who get called in to help as a last resort; a mother who is a "bitch" but who advocates for you in front of your neglectful, absent father. The youth often seem unsafe. They get high, drunk, pregnant, and mixed up with gun-waving drug dealers. And they seem to get beat up or hit almost as often as they get touched or hugged.

The Point redefines the participatory documentary. The process was developed by Dorsey over a number of years working in the community centre, an initial project that culminated in the production of a short film. The film garnered enough attention for Dorsey to get the NFB and others to produce a feature with a million dollar budget. It is a remarkably ambitious film with a cast of 40 teen actors and several professionals playing the adults. The only prerequisite for involvement in this film was that the youth, in Dorsey's words, "commit to me and to themselves." The youth generated individual narratives, which the director and story editors crafted into one story, which was then developed into a screenplay by a professional writer. They acted in the film, along with some professional actors, and were filmed by a professional crew. Despite the script, much of the acting is improvised, for Dorsey found this to be the best way to get natural performances from the youth. The film makes no claims to being a documentary. However, the youth shared stories that came from their own lives. As Dorsey explained to Bronwen, each week he asked the youth participants to write a story they felt was *both* "real" and "intense": he explained that stories which are just real can be boring and that stories which are just intense can be dumb. Dorsey feels that some of the value of the process for the youth was in thinking about their lives as art or narrative; this move could offer them some distance and enable critical self-reflection. And the youth act in their own and others' narratives, delivering performances which are almost always good and often great. The smaller vignettes, drawn from the youths' own stories, which make up the larger narrative, frequently seem very real, and they avoid the moralising tone of the after-school television special as well as the glamorisations of both wealth and poverty found in Hollywood portraits of youth. At times, though, the intensity feels repetitive and unrelenting, which is not necessarily real. The youth are often angry, usually melancholic, and almost always tough. There are, for instance, three different scenes in which girls are fighting—each other, a stepmother, and a younger boy—which, while a refreshing change from the usual gender dynamics portrayed around violence, is an extreme swing of the pendulum.

The film was clearly a powerful and empowering experience for the youth involved. Alyssa Kuzmarov, a social worker with a long history of work with adolescents, was one of the script writers on the film and was amazed at how deeply the youth invested in the project and at the self-confidence many of them developed through the process. Deeply inspired by *The Point*'s participatory method, she has since started a non-profit organization with Jean-Michel Sauri called Productions Oracle, which teaches film production to youth-at-risk. And Dorsey has described to Bronwen how powerfully youth audiences respond to the work; at a screening in Halifax to hundreds of youth, many commented that it was the best film about teens they had ever seen. However, while the film screened successfully at a series of festivals, it is not getting as wide a distribution (Seville Pictures) as its creators hoped. This lack of commercial success might be attributed to some of the tensions between *vertreten* and *darstellen*: while the experience of participating in the film benefited and even empowered many of the youth involved, the final product lacks some of the narrative characteristics of more marketable films. The size of the cast, for instance, made the process very inclusive, but also meant that the film has trouble developing the characters. And the stories the youth chose to tell about themselves as "real and intense" lack some of the range and subtleties of other accounts of adolescence (see, for instance, the independent films *Show Me Love* (1998) or *George Washington* (2000)). That said, the film is a strong testament to participatory creative processes involving youth, and shares these at a website designed for teachers and filmmakers (www.nfb.ca/webextension/thepoint/userguide.html).

Fantasies of "Authentic Voice":
Community Participatory Documentaries

The final section of this chapter briefly examines some of the literature on community-based media projects which suggests that these are also often dogged by notions of the "real" and of "authentic voice." Campbell et al. (2001)'s review of grant applications by community-based media programs as well as academic writing on the effects of such programs makes clear that the trope of "voice" is central to both discourses (cited in Soep, 2006). Soep (2006) notes that "the opportunity for young people to 'tell their own stories' and 'find their own voices'" (p. 201) is both a stated primary objective of the programs themselves and an "overwhelming focus" in studies of the "emotion and identity benefits" (p. 201) of the programs. However, there are some critics who do point to the potential dangers of concepts of voice which romantically assume that all self-expression is necessarily liberating and students' voices should never be challenged by teachers, and which ignore the power relations which work against free exchange in places like classrooms (Soep, 2006). For example, Fleetwood (2005) argued in a study of one project designed to serve urban youth that an emphasis on "realness" ironically served to reproduce the sensational portraits of urban life that the projects hoped to work against by privileging "experiences that racialize and sexualize participants as outside normative, white adult culture" (p. 156). The template of the urban real, embodied in films like *Menace II Society*, limited the youths' expression by setting up narrative conventions for what was possible. Fleetwood found that fantasies of "authentic" expression particularly shape projects that serve urban youth of colour, who, along with "at-risk youth" more generally, tend to be the targets of youth media programs in North America. As in Challenge for Change projects, the language of authenticity can obscure the structures of power that "maintain social, economic, and political imbalances" and the simultaneous hypervisibility and disenfranchisement of the population they are designed to serve, in this case youth of colour (p. 172).

In his discussion of the work of the Educational Video Collective, Goodman (2003) has also raised questions about projects whose principal objective is to facilitate youth expression. Goodman noticed that the strengths of documentary projects in which youth draw upon their life experiences, as in a film which explored community violence, can also be limitations: he regularly observed the way that experiential evidence of the "way things are" gathered by the youth on the streets could mitigate against their researching why they are this way, and how they might be otherwise. The authentic here trumps any move towards making changes in the "real" conditions. Goodman also argues for the importance of youths' intellectual growth, including "developing their knowledge base and critical habits of mind" (p. 58) so that gathering data that documents social conditions is not in itself enough; the youth need to build on what they already know and learn to start thinking differently about themselves and their social contexts.

A detailed analysis of the challenges and possibilities of alternative media activism through documentary production, or more generally, is beyond the scope of this chapter. That said, we feel strongly that community-based media organizations can be important sites for facilitating youth expression and cultural production, as we explore in chapter 5's in-depth examination of one such organization, Young People's Press, and in chapter 8's discussion of what media education inside school might learn from media education in community settings. And we are very excited about the broadening range of representations of and by youth and the increasing possibilities available for self-representation through technologies such as video, particularly in the context of video distribution and networking Web 2.0 sites such as YouTube, examined in the next chapter. However, we must be suspicious of the revolutionary language and fantasies of authenticity that can haunt these projects, and cautious about the spell of technology and the way it gets cast as saviour. This romanticization particularly occurs with the video camera, which has been imagined as implicitly revolutionary since its introduction. We should ask not only who speaks in youth media projects but also who listens, as well as who profits from the speaking. And we need to take seriously the job of listening by submitting the products of these projects to the close critical attention we think they deserve.

CHAPTER 4

I'm Speaking to You!
Cultural Production and Audiences
in the New Media

Michael Hoechsmann

It's a story about community and collaboration on a scale never seen before...It's about the many wresting power from the few and helping one another for nothing and how that will not only change the world, but also change the way the world changes...We're looking at an explosion of productivity and innovation, and it's just getting started, as millions of minds that would otherwise have drowned in obscurity get backhauled into the global intellectual economy...And for seizing the reins of the global media, for founding and framing the new digital democracy, for working for nothing and beating the pros at their own game, *TIME*'s Person of the Year for 2006 is you. (Grossman, 2006, pp. 14–15)

As we move away from the old monolithic one-way flow mass media to the new interactive environment of Web 2.0 platforms such as social-networking sites MySpace and YouTube, and knowledge-sharing sites such as Wikipedia, there has clearly been a shift in the conditions in which having a voice in the public sphere is even possible. Young people no longer need to participate in documentary film projects organized by adults or to labour through long apprenticeships in media production to tell their stories. Changes in access to technology have facilitated new conditions for young people to shoot, cut, and mix multimodal texts, and the emergence of the Internet as a convergent multimedia vehicle and a hang-out for a global audience has enabled youth to communicate both across borders and across the street. Much of the new online cultural production by young people is in new media forms, which forms the focus of this chapter, but a tremendous amount of old-style writing is also taking place in the blogosphere and in knowledge-producing and sharing sites such as Wikipedia. While there is a great temptation to view the wildfires of cultural production in online habitats as innovative examples of ruptural cultural change, we instead focus our attention in this chapter on continuities between new and old literacies, on the hybrid nature of change where the emergent shares strong elements of the residual. We undertake this analysis through a focus on audience as a necessary component of the circuit of communication, and a consideration of how assumptions about audience fuel youth cultural production in the new and old forms.

The phenomenal growth of this activity prompted *TIME* magazine to name us–or more specifically "you"–the Person of the Year in 2006. Although there is a tendency to overstate the case and imagine that young people didn't do any writing or video production before the advent of blogging, podcasting or vlogcasting, it is no doubt true that access to the means of production and even more importantly, to control of distribution, and the fracturing of the mass audience into niche markets, has created an intense period of cultural production and communication by previously excluded and marginalised young people. While new digital divides are increasingly apparent, a great number of young people, including primarily middle- and upper-class kids with modems and those of lower economic status who get involved in youth media organizations or media education in school, have the capacity today to create sophisticated media and to share it. That is an extraordinary development and cannot be minimized. Power is a scarce resource for young people and if we consider social, political, economic and cultural arenas of power, then we must recognize that laptop- and camera-toting young people have an extraordinary advantage over previous generations of a comparable demographic. While some corporations are making a fortune producing and selling the new relatively low-cost hardware and software for the hypermedia generation, the reality is that the costs of production and distribution have dropped so low that millions of young people can join the new virtual studio, some becoming instant celebrities and many others just having the potentially feel-good moment of being a part of the hypermedia world.

These new conditions have allowed for an outpouring of youth expression, a channelling of already latent youth voice, now redoubled with the potential of making a difference, changing someone's mind, or making a mark on society. It is evident from the frenzy of activity in the Web 2.0 domains that a seismic shift in the means and modes of communication is taking place, but the pace of change is so quick that even recent statistics on participation may lag behind actual practice. The Young Canadians in A Wired World study (Media Awareness Network, 2005) reported that 30% of kids in Grades 6–7 had their own Web site and that 12% of them regularly write and post a blog.

The number of young people hosting a Web site in Grades 10–11 was down to 26% but the rate of blogging was up to 18%. This is a significant participation rate and given that the study was conducted before the biggest gains in traffic to MySpace, YouTube, and Facebook had occurred, these numbers are quite high. The study claims that 94% of kids have Internet access and that by Grade 11, 51% of them had their own Internet-connected computer, separate from the rest of the household. In the U.S., the numbers are similar, yet the findings distinct. For example, the Kaiser Family Foundation found in 2005 that more than half of online teens in that country had created content for the Internet (including creating a blog or personal webpage, or sharing artwork, photos, stories or videos online). It was estimated that 87% of U.S. teens were using the Internet and half of those were online daily (Kaiser Family Foundation, 2005).

Given the unprecedented flow of new cultural production, it is an opportune time to pay attention to youth cultural production. However, the vast torrent of material appearing online daily, which would exhaust even the most prolific reader or viewer, ensures that much will be left unread, unseen, unheard. This is where an active audience plays a part in what would formerly have been the selection and distribution of content. The new conditions of reading and writing the Web occasioned by the Web 2.0 innovations have radically transformed the conditions of audience research. To undertake audience research today, we need to indicate the more active role the audience presently plays in determining the production of content. The new "folksonomy" is determined by arbiters of taste: viewers and readers who, with a click of the mouse, determine a v-log's popularity or a blog's selection and increasingly decide what will rise above the rest. A folksonomy is a system of data selection and management from below, a manner of organizing knowledge not driven by experts but by people or users whose authority derives from an active interest in or affinity with the material in question. Wikipedia, a user-driven content system, defined it in this manner on May 19, 2007:

> The term folksonomy is a portmanteau that specifically refers to the tagging systems created within Internet communities. A combination of the words folk and taxonomy, the term folksonomy literally means "people's classification management": "Taxonomy" is from the Greek *taxis* and *nomos*. *Taxis* means "classification" and *nomos* means "management," while "folk" is from the Old English *folc*, meaning people. (Wikipedia, 2007)

In practical terms, a folksonomy works through a series of classification tools available to Web 2.0 users: viewing, tagging, favoriting, linking, commenting, discussing, responding and bookmarking. Each of these actions plays a minor role in distinguishing one piece from another. Once multiplied by millions of users, the sum of these simple key strokes ensures the prominence of certain pieces over others.

While we should remain sceptical of *TIME* magazine's (2006) assertion of "the many wresting power from the few," the grassroots "seizing [of] the reins of the global media" (pp. 14–15), there is an element of truth to it. Certainly we did not take over the profit-making, corporate control side of show business. Nor did we make the big decisions about mass media content, far up the corporate ladder. But we did begin to make multiple small decisions about content on a daily basis, both while producing and consuming it. These small decisions began to add up to major influences on what content rose above the rest. This chapter is about the production of content and its consumption. Today, the most popular Web site, v-log, or blog is determined by the number of people who visit it, view it, write a comment on it, rate it, link to it, and follow it on their RSS feed. Marketing has not disappeared, but has become a more inexact science, relying even on the very vagaries of viral communication used by people in everyday interactions. The audience has come into its own in the new environment.

Of course, audience incorporation–Audience Inc.–is of necessity always already a part of the circuit of communication. The Web 2.0 innovation was to incorporate readers as writers, allowing readers to write/produce their own texts/shows. While an active audience in times past has been one that uses its imagination, critical faculties, and capacity for sharing with others, the new Audience Inc. is also a generating audience, an audience of writers or producers. The inherited tradition of an active audience in an era of one-way media flow was of taste cultures (Bourdieu, 1984). From the scientific audience capture of Nielson ratings to the soft science of water-cooler-buzz marketing, the audience of the past exercised its power by selecting from given choices and ever so subtly inflecting cultural change upon the media by letting its evolving attitudes and worldviews be known. The audience relation to media production in the new environments is far more intimate and the effect is much more immediate, increasingly embedded or incorporated into the message itself. Much in the manner a flash mob assembles—a real world gathering of people who use IM and cell phone technology to bring a large group of people together quickly—the new denizens of the Web 2.0 mobilize audiences to quirky new v-logs, blogs, and webpages.

For example, when P. Diddy launched his YouTube channel in partnership with Burger King in October 2006, he had 750,000 views within a week. A culture jammer called Lisa Nova produced a spoof of Diddy's v-log the next day that was seen by over 650,000 people in a six-day period. Four months later, Nova's mockumentary had been seen by a total of over one million people, but the biggest buzz occurred relatively spontaneously in that first week. A great part of the success of v-logs such as this one lies in the active audience functions of social-networking sites such as YouTube, where audiences vote with their mouse clicks to launch the most popular v-logs and directors of the week or of all time. The empowered audience has emerged as the newest actor in the mediasphere, helping to determine and create content and seemingly balancing out increasing corporate control, the other major development in our mediascapes. Incorporated into all of the stages of consumption and reception, the audience appears to have unprecedented power to shape and determine media content. We will argue that differing conceptions of audience—incorporated into the act of media creation—produce different outcomes, and that there are strong residual communicational and cultural elements in contemporary "participatory" media production. Thus, as young people are drawn into new forms of media practice, they also draw substantially on a pre-existing repertoire of cultural meanings.

As we race to understand and respond to the new literacies required for the new media, privileged young people—middle-class kids with modems—are involved in one of the most extraordinary peer-to-peer learning experiments in human history. This is a just-in-time pedagogy environment involving millions of people with access in real time to what one another are saying, where the activity of learning to play and playing to learn is supplemented by the use of cheat sheets, queries to peers, and the consultation of resources offered by Web 2.0 sites, as well as the Web at large. Rather than a predetermined, standardized curriculum, just-in-time pedagogy on the Web is learning on demand, user-centred, task-driven and immediately applicable. Jim Gee (2003) describes the just-in-time principle among 36 learning principles that he derives from the learning communities developed by video game players: "The learner is given explicit information both on-demand and just-in-time, when the learner needs it or just at the point where the information can best be understood or used in practice" (p. 211). Of course, every student who has ever raised an arm in class to get clarification or elaboration on a question has taken advantage of just-in-time pedagogy, but the point is that the online world treats teaching and learning as activities virtually always undertaken mid-task; hence, just-in-time pedagogy is an operating principle. One does not read an entire user's manual before using an application or a technology. Rather, one tends to boot up and follow intuition as far as possible before seeking out instruction. The learning community Gee describes is marked by motivation, flexibility, teamwork, and agency. It makes room for different learning styles (and speeds), it pushes learners without overwhelming them, and it weaves together action and reflection. And while the gaming environment is marked by the complexity of tasks and learning curves that require far greater dedication than what is needed by the average Web 2.0 audience member, the domains of the Web 2.0 offer tremendous opportunity for growth and development. The potentials are there to move from tagger to producer, from viewer to creator.

The Pledge. You Will Learn Nothing Useful Here: Peer-to-Peer Youth Media

Web 2.0 harnesses the stupidity of crowds as well as its wisdom. (Grossman, 2006, p. 15)

The pledge. You will learn nothing useful here. (Slogan on Smosh T-shirt available at www.smosh.com)

Enabling youth expression is a good thing, but it is wishful thinking to assume that an outpouring of unadulterated youth voice will yield copious samples of enlightened interventions against the stereotyping of youth or the multiple injustices some or all youth face. If anything, youth online cultural production is profoundly ambivalent, dependent on audience and occasion. Youth voice is always inflected by some assumption of the expectations of the audience, whether an active peer audience of frivolous pranksters, a niche market of well-meaning adults, or some hybrid of the two. Take, for example, YouTube's #1 most viewed youth production, the Pokemon Theme Music Video (#2 over all)[2]. With over 20 million viewings in just over one year, this video has made its 19-year-old producers Anthony Padilla and Ian Hecox among the early success stories in the new world of grassroots media production (www.smosh.com). An earnest display of lip synching and amateur dance moves, this video is endearing and silly, perhaps a testament of yearning nostalgia for lost childhood, but more likely just a couple of guys hamming for the camera. Their notoriety has increased traffic to their Web site, a promotional and commercial vehicle for smosh shirts and hoodies. Winners of a recent contest at smosh received iconic t-shirts with the logo, "The Pledge. You will learn nothing useful here." Not to detract from the determined good fun of smosh productions, their appeal is to an audience of leisure seekers, apparently the majority audience of Web 2.0 sites such as YouTube. But the youth audience is a hybrid one. Not only does the audience include a spectrum of shades of difference, but individual viewers/participants can draw on an array of video resources, some frivolous, some deeply serious. Indeed, it is an audience willing to learn, as long as learning can be made fun.

---

2. Postscript: This video has fallen victim to the copyright battles that are beginning to heat up over unliscenced YouTube content. In June 2007, the video was removed from YouTube after Shogakukan Production Co. Ltd. threatened YouTube with legal action over copyright infringement despite a parody fair use claim by the Smosh auteurs (The Utube Blog, 2007).

On a more reflective, serious note is *One World*, the #1 most responded video on YouTube. This video by MadV uses graffiti written on hands to spell out a message. A total of 2179 video responses appeared at YouTube in just three months. Compared to the numbers that viewed the *Pokemon Theme*, this might appear a modest sum, but given that each response is a new video produced and posted in response to the first, it is a strong showing. This is the sign of an active, participating audience, incorporated right into the circuit of consumption and production. Typical responses are unspoken with music in the background, positive slogans or words written on the palms of hands. Love and peace are the predominant themes. As examples of media production, the *One World* responses are simple and innocent webcam testimonials. They are impressive in their sum, in the collective energy of more than two thousand people having their say about a conflicted world. While even the *Pokemon Theme* video appears scripted and produced alongside these quick little testimonials, they are powerful in their brevity.

Reading youth writing in the new online habitats is thus a hit-and-miss affair. To approach this with the raised expectations of being exposed to the true feelings and deep insights of young people is to court disappointment. Yet to dismiss playful, foolish, and even hurtful representations as somehow inauthentic is to miss the point. Young people will fool around, and expressing themselves among peers often means having a laugh—sometimes at the expense of others—and couching anything serious in light and frivolous tones. The quick cam moments of cell phone foolhardiness demonstrate some of the excesses of the new cultural production, as do the often unrehearsed, narcissistic, static shot webcam testimonials. Cell phone cams have proven a mobile tool for the prankster and the cyberbully, to the point where schools and school boards are beginning to have to contend with banning them outright from school premises. At Ecole Secondaire Mont-Bleu in western Quebec, a student deliberately provoked a teacher who then lashed out in anger. The exchange was videotaped on another student's cell phone and was later uploaded to YouTube. The teacher took stress leave and the students were suspended from school (Sandoval, 2006). Cell phones are notorious tools of cyberbullies, who can shoot video of students in compromising positions and circulate them rapidly to audiences of thousands. Some of the more notorious uses of quick cams are for capturing school yard fights or locker boxing, the latter an instance of hockey violence where teammates take each other on in the locker room wearing only gloves, helmets, and light clothing. Young people are not only filming these encounters, but also quickly uploading them to the Internet. Schools are taking notice of the emerging and ongoing problems of quick cam abuse, and board and school administrators in many jurisdictions are undertaking policy reviews with the intent of nipping this perceived problem in the bud, but they are limited to banning cell phones and blocking Web sites.

The affordances of the new capacities of Web 2.0 communication have caused an institutional crisis in schools that have historically tried to control the flow of information by students. Incidents at Canadian high schools involving student comments on Facebook have focused public debate on what young people are saying online. Chatter that used to be confined to etchings on the sides of bathroom cubicles and notes passed between friends has become not only public knowledge but also front page news. Nasty and defamatory comments about teachers have been broadcast for all the world to see. Facebook, a social networking site originally designed for university and then high school students, became a public domain in 2006 and its popularity skyrocketed, particularly in Canada. What is said on Facebook, and how it is interpreted, is an example of misunderstood rhetorical contexts. Young people think they are venting on an adult-free Web site, and teachers are reading this same site as a public domain. Both are negotiating the new conditions of Web 2.0 communication, but teachers, administrators, and parents who have read student comments are more ambiguously involved. They have peered into Web sites designed for students and found their worst nightmares, kids who dare to complain, to make fun, and even to make viscious verbal attacks. Facebook is threatening, mainly because of its wide popularity. It is important to note that social networking sites like Facebook, MySpace, and YouTube have come to inhabit a central part of our mediascapes, rivaling television in importance.

This is where the old and new media collide in our cultural mindsets. Our expectation, culled from years of television, is that an event becomes more real if it is broadcast. From the Kennedy assassination to the toppling of the twin towers, events mattered more if they were on TV. As we move into a new media era, we carry with us baggage from the past. The difference today is the rise of the citizen blogger and content determined by folksonomies, resulting in a corresponding decline of the traditional gatekeepers of truth in the professional media. While in new media environments such as Wikipedia, the collective intelligence of "smart mobs" can enhance our visions of the world, the reality is that a lot of creepy, crummy ideas and concepts are also mobilized when anyone with a computer terminal can publish or broadcast their views. Youth involved in the Facebook incidents made spurious allegations, usually involving some implication of sexual misconduct on the part of teachers. It is worthwhile to step back and seek some explanation for why students could be so vicious in their complaints about their teachers. The European tradition of carnival, which traces its origins to the Middle Ages, had as its central feature the turning over of social hierarchies. This was a sanctioned time for making fun of authority. Allowing and enabling popular dissent for a prescribed period of time was a way of letting out steam, of giving the disenfranchised a chance to make fun of the powers that be, in order that they would carry on with the established order once the party was over. Young people today, in an era of tremendous liberty and openness, still have to confront rules in school that, although necessary, are sometimes arbitrary and unfair. For years, they have vented their frustrations verbally and in graffiti scrawls. Facebook, and the very public teacher payback enabled by it, has complicated matters. But it is important that we not confuse the medium with the message. Ultimately, it should not be a new technology and a new form of youth communication on trial. What is occurring in the new school-based cultural collisions between emerging communication practices and established authority goes beyond the question of what is written on bathroom walls versus what is published on Facebook.

The nature of communication has changed and schools are not the only institutions or organizations to have to contend with this. With advances in interactive media and technology, communication is becoming increasingly viral. The notion of viral communication derives from the concept of point-to-point contact, an actual one-to-one transmission that quickly multiplies exponentially as more people become involved in communicating a given message or idea. An originary message or idea is referred to as a *meme*, a viral knowledge node that seeks out other minds to propagate itself further (Lankshear & Knobel, 2003). This concept illustrates a type of face-to-face communication that has been around for millennia but that has now been given a technological delivery system and a high speed, worldwide distribution network. Whereas formerly memes could only pass to and from people in several degrees of separation from one another, now total strangers can learn directly from one another. Thus, ideas can proliferate across space and time at a speed and scale formerly unimaginable. Peer-to-peer social networks such as Facebook demonstrate another element of the newly empowered audience. As a meme spreads, more and more people are empowered to add their commentary to the original kernel. The distance between writer and reader has diminished, even collapsed, in these new conditions, and the capacity for the reader to respond at will has enabled a corresponding wildfire of communication.

Whereas in an era of mass media, a small number of powerful corporations controlled the air waves, in this interactive media environment, virtually anyone—the virtual everyone—can at least try to transmit their ideas to a broad audience. And as ideas come into contact with others, new knowledge can form. The knowledge-sharing site Wikipedia demonstrates the great potential of collaboration on a mass scale, where millions of modest contributions combine to produce a collective document that is more substantial in breadth and depth than any broad compendium that came before it. Though Wikipedia is not a youth site per se, it is one of the best examples of "collective intelligence" and "participatory culture" (Jenkins, 2006), a virtual community that leverages the combined expertise of its members. Henry Jenkins draws on Pierre Levy's (1997) work on knowledge culture and collective intelligence to describe the aggregate power of many minds working together to a common goal. Levy writes "no one knows everything, everyone knows something" (cited in Jenkins, 2006, pp. 26–27). Peer-to-peer knowledge building emerges when people are driven to participate in a network, project, or campaign. Jenkins shows how "affective economics," an equation of desire, connection, and commitment (p. 62), comes into play in motivating these contingent communities which are voluntary, temporary and tactical, forming and disbanding with relative flexibility either when they get "beyond the tasks that set them in motion" or "no longer meet their emotional or intellectual needs" (p. 57). This new knowledge culture is one where the affective economics of desire, connection, and commitment combine to produce a powerful motivating force, where things get done because the will is there, and the knowledge and talent of the many is pooled into a task-driven project of knowledge production.

In this context of collaborative learning, social networking sites such as MySpace, YouTube, Facebook, and many other lesser-known sites have come of age. Regardless of its past in community activism, the term *social networking* has become the adopted and adapted term that describes Web sites where people typically post a personal profile with the goal of sharing it with others. MySpace and Facebook are basically virtual online scrapbooks, and YouTube is an online sharing site for streaming video, either home-produced or media-industry produced clips, old and new. There is a tremendous range of other social-networking sites, some of which mobilize affinity groups and some of which enable cultural practices. Affinity groups might take the form of specific demographics (eg., African-American people, wealthy people, students of a particular school or university, etc.) or people with shared interests (eg., fan sites). Some sites center around cultural practices or shared activities (eg., hobby sites, activism sites, profession sites). A common denominator across social-networking sites is a sense of connecting with others, sometimes with flirtatious intentions, but in a broad sense for increasing a virtual sense of community. The virtual relationship is very real to the participants despite the mediation of distance and technology. While there are privacy settings on v-log and blog sites that can limit who will be able to view or read a posting, this just means the poster is selecting to narrowcast to a limited audience. For the most part, the audience setting for a given post is limited only by the number of Internet users with broadband access worldwide. Youth are reading widely and writing to broad, often unknown audiences. Outside of one's local community and affinity groupings, the potential audience for a given piece can be limitless, albeit arbitrary.

And many people can participate, even some who are differently abled and others without economic privilege. The learning curve involved for participation is modest. As learning economies, rather than structured learning environments, social-networking sites function through emulation and peer-to-peer support. There are no manuals to read, nor classes to attend. Pedagogy is just-in-time and task-oriented. Rather than the reciprocal relations of the real world, learning is networked, involving multiple learners with varying levels of expertise at multiple nodes, united by shared interests and goals. In youth subcultures, early adopters are the trendsetters who initially experiment with ideas before they go mainstream. This has not changed in the Web 2.0 environment, but what has changed is the multiple points of contact through which a meme can pass, the difference between taking a virus into a closet or into a crowd. Despite the efficiency of new technologies for viral communication, there is a certain randomness at play as to what will be most distributed, similar to how news or rumours spread in oral culture. Some messages will surpass expectation and spread like wildfire; others will not make it out of the gate. Sociologists might call this the role that the agency of the receiver plays in selecting certain messages from the massive flow of media artifacts in contemporary culture. But there is some chance or luck involved in what makes it into the hands of the receivers and what remains on the cutting room floor. At minimum, there are no guarantees that a given message will survive the circuit of communication.

A look at the most viewed videos of all time on YouTube demonstrates the haphazard nature of viral transmission and the idiosyncrasies of audience-driven content. YouTube features both cultural production by young people and mainstream media content recycled for viewers. Of the twelve videos that had more than 10 million viewings by January 2007, half are what could be described as user produced and the rest as professionally produced. Three of the videos are low-tech webcam v-logs, all featuring a professional music soundtrack, two with lip-synching duos (*Pokemon Theme* and *Hey Clip*), one with real electric guitar playing over Pachelbel's Canon (*Guitar*). *Free Hugs* and *Urban Ninja* are mini-documentaries with a home made visual feel and a professional music soundtrack. *Evolution of Dance*, the most viewed video of all time with over 41 million screenings, is a decidedly low tech, if semi-professional clip of a man dancing to various songs. On the other side of the ledger are television clips from *America's Got Talent*, *Saturday Night Live*, and a Nike ad featuring soccer player Ronaldinho. The other three are a rock video by OK Go and two professionally produced comedy clips, *Real Life Simpsons* and *Shoes*. The fact that these videos stand above the rest is extraordinary and utterly unpredictable with the exception perhaps of #12 which features the world-famous Ronaldinho. The most remarkable of the 12 is the *Free Hugs Campaign*, a real life story of 24-year-old Juan Mann, whose video has had more than 10 million views in just over four months and whose new found notoriety landed him an appearance on *The Oprah Winfrey Show*. *Real Life Simpsons* and *Shoes* are quirky and intelligent comedic productions that might have made some noise in the mass media and the OK Go rock video is a polished buzz-marketer's dream, gaining over 10 million views in just six months. In general, however, the feeling that one gets poring over the top-viewed videos is that they are at best a rather mediocre sample of media in an era of torrential output and dizzying distribution potential. With a presence on both MySpace and YouTube, the *Free Hugs Campaign* is the only video that appears to perform the old-style work of social networking. The video tells the story of alienation and anomie, and has picked up quite a following of supporters around the world.

If anything, the top twelve most viewed videos on YouTube show that a revolutionary communications technology does not a revolution in content make. YouTube is a distribution means, a narrowcast or broadcast channel, depending on the viral flow of the content. But it does demonstrate a prototype form of amateur videography and does showcase some trends in youth authorship in the new digital environment. Amateur videography on YouTube does not depend on high production values. The webcam, the cellphone cam, or the videocam are the most accessible technologies and the results are apparent. Video editing suites, typical to software packages on late-model computers, help to polish up the rough edges on many of these amateur videos. In particular, replacing low sound production values with a pop song soundtrack is an effective and commonplace technique used by these aspiring videographers. While some productions on YouTube are more ambitious, the peer-to-peer learning environment teaches that communication of content is primary, the quality of the form secondary. Content is, for the most part, frivolous and fleeting, true to the nature of the v-log as the new literacy equivalent of the print diary. It is somewhat stream of consciousness, somewhat disposable content, expressive of and in the moment, but redundant and senseless the next.

Webcams can turn any room into a low-tech television studio. Also widely used as sci-fi telephone appliances or surveillance cameras, webcams have come into their own in the era of streaming video as DIY (do it yourself) media production cameras. *Pokemon Theme Music Video* and *One World* are both webcam style productions, whether or not they were shot on webcams. (The style is essentially that of a static camera shot). Scroll through video responses to YouTube videos and you will find that most videos are produced with the webcam shot. Typically, the webcam videos found on YouTube feature one or more people speaking to the camera, dancing to a pirated soundtrack or performing a goofy act or trick. While there is plenty of low-grade content on YouTube that wouldn't make it in the old media world, there is also plenty of clever material, a veritable firestorm of cultural production that picks up momentum daily. The webcam is most notorious for the case of lonelygirl15, the most popular and most subscribed YouTube member of all time. Lonelygirl15 sat in her bedroom and spoke languorously about her everyday life, occasionally joined by her boyfriend Daniel. Her tone was monotonous but cute. She played up the role of a naïve but spirited teenage girl. Ironically, lonelygirl15 was everything that the usual webcam user is not—she auditioned for the part, read from scripts, and was produced professionally with proper lighting, camera, and editing. It turned out that this girl was not lonely, but surrounded by a production team, and not 17, as she claimed, but rather a 19-year-old actress called Jessica Rose hired to create a new online franchise. Despite or because of the notoriety of being outed by her audience, lonelygirl15 was chosen as a spokesperson for the UN Millennium Campaign to fight global poverty and a v-log was posted to YouTube at a second lonelygirl15 channel, *lg15standup*.

Standing up against global poverty might not have been the predicted outcome the lonelygirl15 organizers had bargained for, but it suited their goals of creating and sustaining her brand identity. They counted on the "affective economics" of identification others would have for her. Lonelygirl15 was, for a time, every girl, someone working through her turmoil and problems online, but a legitimate girl like me or girl next door. When the jig was up, when it was revealed that lonelygirl15 was a hoax, the backlash was immediate and massive in scale, but modest in emotional force. The outing of lonelygirl15, that YouTube character that was ultimately too scripted and too neatly produced to be authentic, was international news. Though this event was published and debated more widely than the average flood or famine in the global South, the backlash online was modest and receded quickly. Beyond a certain smugness on the part of some of her online rivals, nobody really seemed to care and it has not stopped her from continuing with her YouTube presence.

The audience wasn't ready to lose lonelygirl15. The needs of this audience for an affective alliance with a reliable YouTube regular was greater than a rational response of anger or rejection. YouTube is a media environment co-created by its audience, a vehicle for the distribution of videos, both good and bad, free of charge and to a potential audience of millions. If there is a prevailing ethos at YouTube, it is one typical of the lightheartedness of the peer-to-peer communication of youth—have a laugh, don't take things too seriously. Fooling around is a residual element of youth culture taking place for a peer audience on a new media platform. It is nothing new; what is new is an audience of thousands and sometimes even millions, an audience that makes choices by viewing, rating and linking or responding to videos. In its broadest strokes, the assumed audience of YouTube is one of peers, among whom one does not appear too serious and sombre. For this audience, the way to make an impression is through competitive frivolousness. While viral communication will occasionally enable a more serious-themed video to get rated and viewed to the point where it is viewed by millions, the random nature of the peer and viral filter ensures that a representative sample of youth cultural production online is frivolous and fun. The audience would not have it any other way.

Another major home to the active audience is MySpace, a site that acts literally as a conduit for the creation of social networks. Users develop a profile, often a multimodal collage of text, sound, and image. Given MySpace's origins as a hub for Los Angeles-based musicians, it is no surprise that music plays a key role. Users upload a favorite song and/or a video, and decorate the page with photos and links. The key component to a MySpace profile is the list of friends who link to the page. These friends become the network that any visitor can follow through the provided links. Enter into a typical page and you are privy then to the people who make up the host's friendship circle. Another networking feature to MySpace is the capacity to send messages to users that are online. Given that the youngish demographic that frequents MySpace is in general more beholden to synchronous communication such as instant messaging than to e-mail, this feature allows them not just to visit MySpace, but to "hang out." Whether just down on the browser bar while doing homework, or on the screen when chilling out, the MySpace portal is a "sticky" one-stop shop. It combines some of the features of the old media (listening to pop music, viewing videos, commercial entreaties) with the functionalities and affordances of the new media.

The page hosted by Tila Tequila, who *TIME* magazine (2006) calls "the Queen of MySpace," demonstrates the cross-pollination of old and new media on MySpace, and the capacities of this social networking site for shameless self promotion. Tila calls herself "the baddest bitch on the block." She has "tramp stamps" (tattoos) on her "bod," but her biggest stamp is on Web 2.0 popular culture. The world inhabited by Tila Tequila is a familiar consumerist one of semi-nudity, DIY pop music, and as much cross-marketing as possible. She is at once one of the most successful new Web 2.0 entrepreneurs and a flashback to every booty-shaking starlet who has risen to stardom through a combination of good luck and heavy promotion. Tila has a lot of assets that can be rapidly assessed on her MySpace page. She has a fashion line, a casino and poker site of her own, a subscription-based Web site, www.tilashotspot.com, a mansion on Second Life, a hit single called "I Love You" that can be downloaded from iTunes, and a Tila Zone map which shows that her celebrity is worldwide. One innovative feature on her MySpace page is the Call Tila function. Viewers can phone in their comments and other people can eavesdrop on their personal messages to Tila. Her notoriety pre-dates MySpace, having posed as the first Asian Cyber Girl on Playboy.com among other modeling gigs. According to Tila, she was invited over to MySpace by its founder, Tom Anderson, and played a role in its success by mass e-mailing 30–50 thousand people who helped to populate that site. Her subsequent celebrity has been noted in features in *TIME* and *Rolling Stone* magazines, and cover shots on *Maxim* and *Stuff*. The symbiotic relationship between Tila Tequila and MySpace has been substantial. By April 2007, Tila had already over 60 million page views and she counts over 1.75 million viewers among her MySpace "friends." According to Hitwise, which tracks Web visits in batches of 10 million, 80.74% of Web visits to social networking sites in the U.S. in February–March 2007 were to MySpace. The closest rival was Facebook with 10.32%. Friendster, which predates MySpace and demonstrates the fickle nature of the Web 2.0 denizens, stood way back with only a .34% share of Web traffic (O'Hear, 2007). Whether Tila Tequila really perfected the MySpace method, or was that lucky someone who was in the right place at the right time, she has borne out the potential of MySpace to launch not just a network, but a career. She might not have the most interesting profile on MySpace, but she has what she needs most: notoriety, celebrity, a community, and the biggest prize of all, a worldwide audience.

Getting and keeping audiences is central to the economics of attention (Lanham, 2006). In a world flooded with information, attention is a scarce resource. And while forms or media of communication are changing, so too is the relationship of author and reader. For better or worse, authorship is no longer the preserve of the educated elite or even of those who have something really striking to say. Rather, authorship has become a democratic right for the world's privileged denizens, an effect of incorporation into a communication nexus of an empowered, incorporated audience. Youth today have at least the potential to express themselves, to try to give voice to their inner thoughts, and to communicate and mobilise with others. They are at the vanguard of a new era of impertinence, of talking back, speaking out of turn, of reclaiming the right to narrate the future. When the potential is present to draw on a hybrid audience of adults and peers, often the result is powerful and heartfelt. But much of the cultural content produced in the informal media production circuits of Web 2.0 environments is frivolous, even foolhardy. This is a world of play, a world at play. While educational institutions—Ministries of Education, university faculties of Education, school boards and schools—scramble to make sense of the new literacies in these new times, youth are using the new tools at their disposal to produce media across modes and genres, not waiting for the educators to catch up. The new economies of attention and learning among young people break from tradition to make learning fun and with goals that are pleasurable. In many cases, youth media organizations have responded to these new conditions more flexibly and effectively than have educational institutions. Here we are not speaking about vocational training programs but rather organizations focused on youth empowerment and capacity building. In the next chapter we examine one such organization, Young People's Press, a youth media project focused on giving youth voice in the mainstream media.

What's On Your Mind? Youth Journalism in/of the Community

Michael Hoechsmann

As a generation, we have been called (and may even have become) passive and apathetic in attitude...We have something to say, and I plan to make a difference. Let our voice be heard.

—Sombra F., Young People's Press

If you're trying to lower youth unemployment rates, doesn't it make sense to get the input of youth? If you're trying to stop the increase of gangs in the city, why not ask young people why they exist? How will anyone know what we need, if we don't speak up?

—Jelani N., Young People's Press

Life isn't about money, having a big house and letting machines do all the work. Life isn't about designer clothes and expensive cars. Life is about joy, love, peace and creativity. It's about learning who you are and not having someone else tell you...When I hear a tune, I'm going to sing...When I feel a beat, I'm going to dance and when I dance, I'll do it with all my soul...When I have something to say, I will say it, and my thoughts will be heard.

—Mai L., Young People's Press

Youth expression, whether in print or other forms of cultural production, is encouraged and developed in a variety of spheres, both formal and informal, encompassing a spectrum ranging from schools and community organizations, to youth subcultures, affinity groups, and solitary endeavours. Within this spectrum, community organizations have played a signal role in cultivating and nurturing interests on the part of youth often engaged in social action of some sort, whether local or global. In such contexts, youth journalism projects have usually been limited to local publication capacities, sometimes small-run local publications, zines, or in more recent times, web publications such as e-zines or blogs. While the reach of these types of projects has picked up considerably with the new publication possibilities of the Internet and particularly the Web 2.0, it is the rare circumstance where a youth news organization has the capacity to provide regular copy to the major newspapers of a nation. As a doctoral student, Michael had the opportunity to get involved with Young People's Press (YPP), a community-based non-profit organization that offers a national newswire service for Canadian youth, 14–24. He continued to stay involved in the organization and eventually took a position there as director of education.

Established in the mid-nineties, the mandate of YPP is to give "voice" to youth, specifically by offering workshops and editorial assistance to fledgling young writers—with a specific emphasis on youth from historically marginalized groups—and by attempting to place articles written by youth in the mainstream press and in a number of YPP social-justice oriented e-zines (electronic magazines). While the tendency in the Canadian print media has been towards increasing control over editorial content, YPP copy was published in over 200 Canadian daily and weekly newspapers and appeared regularly in major newspapers such as the *Halifax Chronicle-Herald* and the *Toronto Star*. Youth represent roughly 27% of the Canadian population, but too often their voices are not registered in the public domain. Youth "as problem" are the focus of a great deal of public debate (i.e., youth violence, crime, drug abuse, education standards, etc.), but ironically these very stakeholders are hardly consulted on issues that directly effect them. The YPP project aims to correct this imbalance as well as to empower youth, develop literacy skills, and generally provide meaningful experiences for them in a non-patronizing manner. The "reach" that these articles had was unequalled by any other similar youth media project. YPP is the only youth/literacy/media project in Canada that operates as a news agency, publishing young writers on a consistent basis in large mainstream newspapers. A non-profit national organization, YPP depends on a mix of foundation and government grants for its existence.

In this chapter, we report on some organizational elements of this project, the pedagogical and participatory process involved in getting young people writing, and on the themes and issues raised in the many pieces of writing generated by the youth writers. In the terms of Johnson's model, we will consider the production context of a small non-profit organization, the textual themes and issues raised by youth, and the reception by youth not of previously authored texts, but of the idea and challenge of writing. Production in this chapter is focused on the challenges familiar to all who work in the just-in-time grant writing and reporting contexts of the non-profit sector, where organizational flexibility can be both a blessing and curse. It is a blessing when mission statements mesh with funding opportunities, when a small organization unencumbered by tradition and bureaucracy can flexibly adapt to new challenges and opportunities. And it is a curse when a small organization finds itself paying the bills by taking on side projects that detract from its primary goals. This is not the production analysis of the big-budget mass media familiar to media theory, but a description of the hand-to-mouth existence of small community projects that tend to come and go with the tide, usually cast adrift on funding currents that either die out or shift with the winds of political, social, and cultural change. This story is one well known to the many who have worked within the non-profit sector, one of grant-writing and projects designed around financial viability, a story of limited budgets and flexible workplaces. It also has its own specificity surrounding the work of developing and securing space in major mainstream newspapers. As well, the chapter treats the other side of production, the production or creation of the texts of youth writing, in this case focusing on collaborative authorship in a teaching, learning, and publishing environment.

Reception, or audience, will also be treated differently in this chapter from what is the currency of media theory. Here we are interested in the reception contexts of young people to the idea and opportunity of writing their stories, of having voice in the public sphere. The treatment of reception is in this case a pedagogical one. To what extent is the pedagogy of an organization such as YPP successful? What works, what does not? How does writing pedagogy differ for distinct groups? Another point of departure that differs from the norm in media theorizing is to treat text, and textual analysis, in a more restricted and literal sense, looking less for hidden and unintended meanings and more for authorial intention. Here we are interested in what young people have come to say, about authorial intention writ large across a large and diverse group of youth. This is a macro-analysis focused on identifying the tropes of youth consciousness. Finally, and drawing on Williams' concept of the residual, we argue that this youth voice project is demonstrative of continuities in literacies that have survived the transition into the present of new media and new literacies. While production and reception contexts have changed, as reported in chapter 4, for the most part the social, political, and cultural themes and concerns mobilized by youth have not been transformed by the arrival of a new technology. Consciousness does not simply change as a reflex of high-speed technological innovation. Rather, it moves at a more glacial pace. A decade of profound technological change has made far less impact on the tropes of youth consciousness than we might believe. If we are really reading youth writing, paying attention to youth voice in all its forms, we will not see a revolutionary sea change of perspectives and opinions in the recent past.

The period that is reported on in this study predates the newest innovations in Web communication that have spurred the development of a blogosphere and the participatory Web 2.0 where youth can have a voice by contributing content or simply tagging it or linking to it. It was, for all intents and purposes, the eve of a genuine revolution in communication, though the architects of Young People's Press were not aware of what was to come. YPP had a Web presence, both a main Web site (www.ypp.net) and a number of electronic magazines (see, for example, www.equalitytoday.org), but the primary vehicle for youth voice in this project was the conventional news media and ultimately a non-conventional intervention, the publishing of 'amateur' youth-written copy. Given that the participants of the YPP project were the same generation that would soon be called "Generation Net" (Tapscott & Williams, 2006), but without the souped-up new Web, this experiment in youth advocacy journalism is revealing for the continuities it displays across communicational media. As much as scholars and theorists wish to emphasize the change that the technological developments have enabled (Jenkins, 2006; Lankshear & Knobel, 2006; Tapscott & Williams, 2006), youth were quite willing, when given a wide audience, to express themselves freely and forcefully. In other words, the new technologies and participatory domains that have followed may be nothing more than audience machines. Of course, we know that they are much more than that, these hybrid, multi-modal, globalizing vehicles of communication. But if they do harness and express a type of youthful energy, we should be wary to ascribe too much determining power to the technologies and recognize that they channel a power that is in many ways already present.

Having worked and consulted with YPP over a six-year period, Michael had the opportunity to work closely with more than one thousand young people and to see many of them publish articles in the various newspapers YPP provides copy to and the e-zines it produces. With a wide-open mandate for youth to articulate what is on their minds, certain themes emerged time and time again: body image (self), anti-racism (culture and society), media (pop culture), education and jobs (economy), relationships with friends, family and lovers (others), and—what shouldn't come as a surprise—a generalized bias towards youth on the part of parents, teachers, government, employers, and the media (generational bias). In regards to the latter, every good story requires a villain, and this one is no different. Youth appear profoundly misunderstood by older generations who they see as anchored to traditions, holier-than-thou, and hogging all the jobs. Issues of the day such as homelessness, global warming, warfare, racism and HIV/AIDS are the curses of the past, haunting those growing up in the present. The ambivalence of the adults' gaze, a mix of indifference and bewilderment to the conditions and practices of youth and youth cultures, often leaves young people feeling ignored and alienated. Of course, gauging youth consciousness is a fickle process at best. Youth is a transitory demographic, and it is intersected with all of the same identity markers as the population at large with the added contradiction of identities-in-process, the necessary ideational and symbolic "work" that young people undertake developing a sense of self in relation to others. Nonetheless, in reading youth writing, taking seriously thoughts and ideas in process, a picture emerges informed by the tropes of youth consciousness in this era of social, economic, cultural, and technological change.

Reading Youth

Generally, people think that teens are trouble. In reality, many youth are capable of being positively involved in society, and making a difference.

—Esther M. & Julie B., Young People's Press

We sometimes get caught up in the clichés that 'young people are the future' and lose sight that they are also very much the present.

—Missy G. & Eric M., Young People's Press

There is no free lunch in this interconnected world.

—Jacob N., Young People's Press

Media by and for youth. Such a simple formula; such a tough sell. For cultural workers attempting to create a space for youth opinions and ideas in the mainstream print media, this concept has usually remained elusive, a dream waiting for the right context. Over a nearly two-year period spanning 1997–1999, YPP had the unusual opportunity to participate in such an experiment when the *Toronto Star*, Canada's largest daily circulation newspaper, provided a space in its now defunct weekly "young street" section (Tuesdays) for copy produced by the news service. Though the final editorial say rested with the *Star*, the editor of the award-winning "young street" section, Vivian MacDonald, gave YPP a wide mandate to go into the community to find out what youth were thinking, saying, and doing, and to bring the resulting copy into the pages of this major daily. In order to attract not only youth writers, but also youth readers, a balance was struck between social justice and pop culture reporting and opinion writing. Three columns that would anchor a weekly feature and one or more soft news stories were developed by YPP. *Very Cool* was a listings column where movies, books, CDs, Web sites, writing contests, and youth events ranging from town hall meetings with the police to anti-racism conferences would be publicized. *Confidentially Yours* was a teen advice column written by and for youth that enabled young people to "just say know" about issues of sexuality, drugs, and relationships with parents and friends. *Youthbeat* was a weekly opinion piece that usually combined personal experience and opinion writing. The "young street" experiment opened the door to hundreds of youth from all walks of life to add their "voice" to public discourse on the issues of the day and for other youth to read their views. It is a model for youth journalism and a window into youth consciousness in the closing years of the last century.

Over this 22-month period, YPP managed to publish 297 articles written by youth in the "young street" section, this in addition to the weekly *Very Cool* and *Confidentially Yours* columns. Youth came into the process with a direct sense of purpose: to be published and to let their voice be heard. Herein lies the key to motivating youth to write: given a broad audience, youth were mightily motivated to put pen to paper. And their output was expressive of a positive, public advocacy for change. A content analysis of the articles published in the *Star* over the almost two-year period revealed a tremendous sense of hope and desire for social change. Of the 255 articles which held opinions about social conditions (the remaining 42 were neutral reportage of events), a full 221 carried within them the seeds of optimism and the potential and desire for social change. The 34 that were pessimistic or fatalistic reflected the values that are commonly attributed to young people: that they are shiftless slackers unwilling to step up to the plate to turn what is offered to them into a hit. The main themes raised by youth were activism and social change (60), body image (38), education (66), global and social consciousness (60), multiculturalism and diversity (59), peers and peer pressure (31), racism (57), sexuality (41), popular culture and mass media (45), voluntarism (31) and bias towards youth (63). Of course there is some reported overlap between these categories, particularly in the social change/consciousness and diversity/racism themes. But the results are significant in their generalized focus on the negotiations of self and group identity between self (body image, sexuality, education and voluntarism) and other (social change/consciousness, diversity/racism, voluntarism and intergenerational bias). Another overarching theme is the role of media/pop culture, education, and intergenerational misunderstanding in overdetermining youth experience. The other themes that emerged but in smaller numbers were the familiar ones of adults' chronicling of youth: crime/law (24), home/family (21), drugs (16), consumerism (17), low-income realities (19), work (15), and youth subcultures (19). That these themes were registered by youth is not surprising, but their lower prominence indicates that young people are aware of what is being said about them, but are not simply beholden to themes not of their own making.

It is difficult to quantify the results of public education, but the "young street" experiment exposed literally millions of readers to youth views, and hundreds of youth were empowered to use newly developed literacy skills to actively participate in the discourses of the public sphere. With a paid weekday subscription rate of over 454,000, the *Toronto Star* has a reach of well over one million readers per day. Youth who had never dreamed they could publish a piece of writing in a major Canadian newspaper have done so and some have become empowered to pursue a life of writing. Like many non-profits, YPP organized its activities around funding opportunities from corporate and government agencies and foundations, normally focused on annual outcomes. This topsy-turvy way of administering an organization favored data-collection models predicated on publication output, not on writer empowerment. Unfortunately, the organization did not set up longitudinal forms of data mining that could monitor the activities of YPP writers once they had left the organization. Only anecdotal evidence remains of how this experience affected the lives of the participating youth writers. Michael has maintained contact with a number of YPP participants spread across various sectors, some in journalism, some in other creative and educational endeavors. The capacity building structured into the experience is one both of professional development in journalism and broader citizenship engagement in general. Of those who did not continue in the field of journalism, many left YPP with the knowledge that they could return to journalistic writing as occasional contributors.

In order to make the representation of youth "voice" as inclusive as possible, tremendous effort was put into reaching out to racialized minority, Aboriginal, street, and LGBT youth. Most significant was the participation of youth representing Canada's racial and cultural diversity. A full 47% of the bylines in the *Toronto Star*, for example, were of racialized minority and Aboriginal youth. (For a broad sampling of this copy, see www.equalitytoday.org). While Canada's news media is attempting to increase its diversity, a study of 41 newsrooms of daily newspapers commissioned by the Canadian Newspaper Association in 1994 revealed that only 2.6% of the staff was of racialized minority or Aboriginal background. A 2004 follow-up by the Ryerson Department of Journalism indicated very little had changed in a decade, having risen by less than one percentage point to 3.4% (Diversity Watch, 2004). YPP's achievements in this realm were to an extent a result of focused outreach, but they also demonstrate that young people are ready for social change: when given the chance to rock the status quo, they will take the opportunity. Many of the articles went far beyond simple platitudes of cross-cultural celebration; recurring themes included cultural hybridity, histories of race relations, and contradictions at the heart of Canadian multiculturalism. One series of articles that stands out in particular was a set of four day-in-the-life pieces—two by black Canadians and two by Aboriginals—that brought readers into the everyday lives of the young writers and featured the use of slang and vernacular common to these cultural groups. At the end of the day, YPP received Awards of Distinction from both the Harmony Movement (2000) and the Canadian Race Relations Foundation (2001).

Youth Space

We are not so far removed from a world where black people were forced to use separate washrooms, gays were banned from public spaces, natives were kicked off their land and women could not vote.

—Amy C., Young People's Press

Homophobia is no joke. It is a rampant social disease that hurts people emotionally and physically.

—Johanna K., Young People's Press

Feminists are not asking for a chubbier Barbie. They are asking for a change of societal values, where people are judged by who they are, not by what they look like.

—Rachel D., Young People's Press

The media portrays black males as thieves, murders and drug dealers. We are rarely presented in a "positive" manner.

—Kirk M., Young People's Press

Asian youth need to know they don't have to be doctors or mathematicians or store owners. If we wait for the media to tell us that, it might not happen. It is up to us.

—Joyce L., Young People's Press

The system made one big box with no breathing holes for us low income folks. They told us to survive on the little we had. Sounds like a project to me—a trap to keep us in our place as society's burden...Do you know that if I'm seen in my neighbourhood with more than two or three people, we're considered a gang?

—Ghetto Princess (anonymous), Young People's Press

Once you serve time, it's easier to serve time again. The courts have little mercy and the police have no mercy for you. It's up to you to not give anybody a chance to ruin your future...It's up to you to open your eyes and see what's been in front of you all along.

—John Smith (anonymous), Young People's Press

Our accents appear to be so cute to North Americans, that we have been portrayed as rodents (Speedy Gonzales) and little dogs (Taco Bell ads). In westerns, the last, treacherous Mexican represented our entire culture. And from *West Side Story* to *Scarface*, mainstream films have portrayed us as sexy yet dangerous gang members. Apparently, we are crazy, passionate criminals who kill for love, honour and drugs. In reality, [the] Latino culture is rich and diverse...We are the offspring of our aboriginal ancestors, Africans brought over during the brutal slave trade, and the Spanish colonialists...To depict us as East Los Angeles "gang" members is absurd.

—Noel F., Young People's Press

I ask myself why you grew so much to hate me, taunt me, beat me or even kill me? How did you become so cruel? What is about my brown skin, my accent and my name that annoys you so?...You will win only when you cause me to hate, if you harden my heart and cause me to shut my eyes to injustice.

—Lesly J., Young People's Press

During the time of slavery, music helped to keep black people's faith alive for a better day to come: a day when we would all be free...That music is in our blood and soul. After slavery was abolished, musical forms like the blues, gospel and jazz flourished among the black community and beyond. Through music, the gap between white and black people started to get a little smaller. Blues, gospel and jazz speak a universal language that sees no colour, therefore making it acceptable for all to enjoy.

—Jennifer T., Young People's Press

The beat send chills down the spine and warms the heart. The song takes listeners to a different place, a different time...We are a generation who almost lost a beautiful culture—a beautiful way of life the Creator gave us as a gift. But native people have struggled and will continue to struggle to keep our culture alive. The drum is part of that struggle, an expression of our culture which is both joyful and sorrowful.

—Eddy R., Young People's Press

The writing that YPP facilitated opened the door to the expression of some powerful and evocative words by the young participants. It appeared that given a space to have voice and the possibility for that voice to travel widely, young people were willing to speak forcefully and courageously. These were not wishy-washy words of bored youth, young slackers with a gift with words. Rather these were the ideas and insights of youth from a diverse spectrum expressed in the broadest of public spheres. The opportunity that YPP had, especially in the "young street" experiment, to open a space in the media edifice was unusual in the world before Web 2.0, and continues to be more often a potential than a reality in the new circuits of youth communication. We now turn to the question of production, as it is experienced in the non-profit domain of this one youth media organization, a chronicle that is typical of other such organizations. Two primary tensions tug at one another in this context: keeping the doors open (financial survival) and keeping it real (remaining true to the mission statement and goals of the organization). Keeping it real seems to be one thing youth media organizations will go the wall to protect. Typically, those of us in community organizations who make the commitment to produce youth-media copy develop a commitment to the writers themselves. The process becomes one of capacity building, empowerment, and support. As well, community youth media organizations generally recognize that a connection must be made between the loci of youth culture for any meaningful connections to be made.

It was a summer job that first brought Michael to YPP, and it was to the streets that he and his coworker turned to seek out youth copy. Given a rather open mandate for that first summer's endeavors, Michael and Brian McDonald decided to take a table out into the streets to try to "sell" writing and youth voice to young people much like a street merchant hawks goods. While their goal was to enable "authentic" manifestations of youth voice, they adopted an "impure" critical stance to the project. As they hoped the young writers would do, they attempted to "buy in" but not "sell out" to mainstream culture. First, they re-appropriated the traditional sense of "Speakers' Corner" from its Canadian incarnation as the name of the Much Music (Canada's rock video station) video booth. Thus, "Writer's Corner" was born, a mobile unit with a staff of two that would set up in areas of high-volume pedestrian traffic around Toronto. Second, they organized a contest, "Youth in a Changing World," and set about soliciting corporate sponsors such as Much Music, SONY, and the Gap to provide—in the words of one of our judges—some "corporate swag." Third, they sought the participation of three young, progressive, successful—but "cool"—judges (journalists Naomi Klein and Avi Lewis as well as York University professor Rinaldo Walcott). Fourth, they shamelessly solicited any media attention they could get. Fifth, they negotiated to get a high-profile site for an awards ceremony, the *Toronto Star* tent at Toronto's "Word on the Street" literacy festival. And finally, they tried to project some "attitude" when soliciting youth.

As with any such project, they hit some road bumps along the way. "Writing" and "youth voice," quite frankly, were hard sells on the streets of Toronto. Certainly, they met their share of extraordinary youth, some of whom were already very accomplished writers. But they soon learned that the questions "do you write?" or "what are your thoughts about 'x'?" just do not inspire much interest on busy city streets. Further, because they positioned themselves on streets where most solicitors were selling actual goods, they were in double jeopardy, suspected as merchants and rejected as literacy advocates. Thus, they adapted their message to fit the hustle and bustle of the streets of a culture of consumption where "what do you think about 'x'?" does not compete well with "how would you like to have an 'x'?" By the end, their patter was the following: "Hi. We're running a writing contest for youth. We have prizes from SONY, the Gap, Much Music, etc." The trick was to collapse syllables as much as possible so that "prizes" followed a split-second behind "writing."

By commodifying writing, they reduced their practice as editors and educators to the lowest common denominator of the culture of consumption and were rewarded for it. Youth would write it (an article) in the hope that they would get it (a prize). Nonetheless, they achieved limited success until they were able to piggyback their message onto the promotional vehicle of consumer culture, the commercial media. Getting media attention for grassroots causes, as activists and community organizers well know, is a hit-and-miss affair involving press releases, phone calls, and desperate pleas and entreaties.   After numerous unsuccessful attempts, they were pleasantly surprised when Toronto's City TV/Much Music came calling. A brief feature on a local City TV newscast was repeated to a national audience on Much Music. Most impressive was an appearance on Much, book-ended by brief features on Van Halen and Bono (the U2 lead singer). Immediately, their fortunes looked brighter. The YPP office was swamped with calls and other local media (the *Toronto Star* and *Now* magazine, Toronto's free entertainment weekly) printed contest details.

The contest resulted in several hundred articles submitted full of insights on the changing conditions of youth in a period of a globalizing economy and culture going global. Much of it has since been published (the two grand prize winners were published in a feature article several days later in the *Toronto Star*). Everyone involved in the contest—editors and judges alike—was swayed by the creativity of the narratives and the poignancy of the arguments. When many of the young writers, who as a group represented the shifting cultural demographic of Toronto, assembled in the *Toronto Star* tent at "Word on the Street" for the award ceremony and a series of "Youth Speak Out" readings, the sense of hope in this celebration of youth voice was palpable. While only the winners got the "corporate swag," the material goods were outshone by the visible elation of young people seizing the floor to have their voices heard. That this outpouring of "authentic" youth expression occurred through the auspices of the culture of consumption seemed not to matter; rather, as we would argue, the "impure" critical stance adopted from the outset enabled this dialogue. In this case, the "necessary symbolic work" of youth identity formation in the culture of consumption coalesces with the expression of critical youth voice on some of the pressing social and cultural issues of the day.

YPP has had to downscale its operations in recent years and has a single base in North Bay, Ontario. The organization came into being at a difficult time for non-profits. There had been a move away from core funding models to project funding, which makes 'sustainability' and long term survival much more difficult. The organization tried to commercialize its operations, a goal that would be reached if a big part of budget could come from newspaper contracts, more fee-for-service arrangements. A number of meetings were held with the bigger Canadian news wire services, but it proved difficult to make long-term, sustainable arrangements. Most often YPP would provide the publishable copy for free or for a nominal fee just to fulfill its mandate to give youth a voice. This was the double-bind YPP found itself in. In order to give voice and make a difference in the public realm and to fulfill government and foundation targeted outcomes in the short term of a given fiscal year, it had to keep doing what it did best, providing top-notch, polished youth writing to newspapers, regardless of the long-term sustainability of the organization. The operating costs varied depending on the scale of operations in any given project year. Funding levels determined how many people could be hired and the organization would expand and contract within its limited capacity to develop a stable core workforce. In its prime, YPP operated out of a 3-room office in a building in Toronto located at Yonge and Eglinton. The three full-time staff were responsible for outreach, training, mentoring, editing, responding to writers re-drafts and revisions, networking with funders and newspapers/agencies, and preparing copy to deadline for transmission to newspapers and news agencies. The staff members were not certified teachers, but the organization had to be as focused on teaching as on news production. There were a revolving number of co-op students from Toronto high schools who would work primarily as reporters. Some university students, mainly from Journalism or English, came in as interns or as paid workers in the summer. YPP was limited in its capacity to incorporate interns because of the supervisory limitations of the core staff of three, but the positions, paid and unpaid, were highly coveted and helped launch some young people into journalism or public relations careers, and to enable others to get into university Journalism programs.

YPP was supported by a number of grants from funders such as the Department of Multiculturalism (Canada), the National Crime Prevention Centre (Canada), the Trillium Foundation (Ontario), and the Levi Strauss Foundation. In some cases, funding outcomes required some congruence with the relatively narrow mandates of funders (Multiculturalism and Crime Prevention), but these were sufficiently flexible to enable a diverse set of writings. For example, anti-racism and multiculturalism are goals that can be satisfied partially just by getting youth from Canada's racialized minority communities published. Michael and other YPP editors delivered workshops and worked one on one with youth writers in racialized minority community centres and non-profit organizations and also Aboriginal schools and programs. Several young leaders from Aboriginal and racialized minority community contexts were hired to help perform the outreach and to work as reporters. Similarly, crime prevention can be achieved by engaging so-called "youth at-risk" and again helping to get their stories into print. The outreach strategy here involved community drop-ins and youth detention centres. At one point, a squeegee youth was hired by the organization. This young man worked as a YPP reporter, bringing to the organization insights from a population normally reticent to speak to the media.

Private foundations were sometimes trickier to incorporate into a broad strategy of youth empowerment, and hence a lot of funding opportunities were passed over by the organization. YPP was very fortunate, however, to be chosen over a three-year period as one of seven youth projects worldwide in the youth engagement initiative of the Levi Strauss Foundation. The Levi Strauss Foundation left it to participating organizations to develop a strategy of youth engagement and was satisfied with outcomes as long as a large number of youth were involved. In other words, delivering the highest profile publication was not the only objective. Working with many youth on their writing skills was paramount. From this initiative, Writers' Circles were developed and a substantial YPP Writer's Guide was written (more on these below). The Levi Strauss Foundation works in communities where its plants are located, presumably reporting in internal year-end reports how it has made a difference in its communities. That said, the Foundation was explicit that its logo not be used and that any acknowledgments be written in fine print, not trumpeted out. There were no brand tie-ins. No corporate shilling. And alongside the work in its target communities, YPP should be free to work with youth from other communities. Perhaps the single biggest YPP youth outreach accomplishment associated with the Levi Strauss Foundation funding was the work with Aboriginal youth, both on the Six Nations reserve near Levi Strauss' Brantford, Ontario, operations, and in urban contexts in Toronto and Edmonton. (Some of the results of this work can be viewed at www.equalitytoday.org/edition5/voices.html).

Writing Youth

It's time to make our own history, not pass down the old stuff.

—Nina A., Young People's Press

Yes, I know people who squeegee. I have done it myself. I have been homeless. I have slept in vacant building...I have been verbally abused, spit on, pushed around, punched, kicked and threatened so often it doesn't faze me...I'm no different from your kids. I have hopes and dreams. I have ambitions and goals, and I intend to follow them.

—Cory H., Young People's Press

Look carefully at a braid of sweetgrass. Imagine that each bundle of the braid represents a person, a nation or an age group. When we put the three bundles together, we become united. When one bundle is taken away from that braid, our unity is broken. The more strands of sweetgrass in each bundle, the stronger and more powerful our braid will be.

                                                —Joni S., Young People's Press

What people need to realize is that no matter what, the rhythm continues. And we, like the beating drums of our African brothers and sisters, will never cease to express that rhythm. Because when the rhythm ceases, it's like stopping the history of a people.

                                                —Ozioma I., Young People's Press

While some YPP participants were motivated by the dream of being a writer or a journalist and could spend countless hours enjoying the buzz of the office, many others were more singularly focused on the prospects of having a voice and making a difference by expressing their views in a large circulation daily newspaper. They came to YPP with not only an intellectual project, but an affective engagement; they came in anger and in joy, frustration and inspiration. In *School's Out* (2002), Glynda Hull and Katherine Schultz have compiled accounts of a number of projects which mirror Young People's Press' engagement with literacy education outside of the school. They argue that it is in "out-of-school contexts, rather than in school-based ones, that many of the major theoretical advances in the study of literacy have been made in the past 25 years" (2002, p. 11). In setting an agenda for analyzing the use of literacy in out-of-school settings, they have been concerned by the incongruency between young people's uses of literacy in the community, versus their success, or lack thereof, in school-based settings. One of the authors in this collection, Elyse Eidman-Aadahl, describes what motivated the young learners in a newspaper project she was involved in:

> ...The old hands stressed that a newspaper ran on love...My future editors, photographers, layout artists, and advertising execs would need to love being on staff, to love the tradition of the paper itself, to love the responsibility, even to love just being in the newspaper office with its distinctive smells and purposeful clutter. Being part of the newspaper would have to fill deeper needs than the ostensible goals of learning to write, thinking critically, to practice effective design. Nothing else would motivate the long hours, the endless rewrites...(2002, p. 242)

For some YPP participants, this description would reflect their experience. Many of these young people had been seeking or dreaming of such a context or opportunity. Many others, however, were less interested in becoming part of a team. They just wanted to use the organization's expertise and capacities to express themselves. These young people would briefly stop by the office, or send in copy electronically. Another large constituency of writers were those who needed encouragement to even consider getting involved with Young People's Press, let alone write an article. For these three distinct groups of young writers, YPP had to flexibly adapt its pedagogy and outreach strategies. For the purposes of this chapter, we consider these as contexts of reception. Reception is not a naturalized category that registers how and who receives what bit of information or instruction, but rather a conflicted set of contexts where pedagogy and learning can make a difference. How is the appeal to have voice by writing a newspaper article received distinctly by different young people? How does a community organization adapt its pedagogy and outreach to draw together an inclusive range of young people? What follows are some of the strategies and approaches employed by YPP.

YPP relies on senior editors who play both an editorial and educational role, but the broad decisions in regards to editorial content—what counts as "news" and how youth are represented within it—are most often made by the youth participants. The concerns mobilized in the project are essentially those of the young writers, though experienced facilitators are in place to enable the work to reach its potential (in this case, publication in major newspapers). To fulfil this objective, YPP developed alternative pedagogies in the area of language and literacy education. Drawing on the principles of rhetoric and composition theory, popular education techniques, critical media theory, and the basic tenets of news writing, these workshops provide youth an alternative view of the writing process, one which empowers them to use literacy as a tool which can enact change in their lives. This innovative approach to writing pedagogy has had an impact on the young writers YPP works with, a significant number of whom came into the process feeling that they lacked the requisite skills. To break down the fear of failure, inculcated by many years of red ink and report cards, requires, in part, a "deschooling" of youth literacy practices. The editors at YPP recognize the need to teach writing as a communicative practice, not to teach writing as a set of rules which set up failure, but to empower young people to view writing as a simple extension of human communication.

The primary innovation used by YPP is the emphasis on writing as storytelling, a form of communication basic to human cultures across history and geography. In YPP workshops, youth are empowered to recognize their capacity as storytellers, to first emphasize what they wish to communicate and then to work out how they will do it. This approach reflects the writing process as defined by Aristotle, and demonstrates the resiliency of oral narrative in our literate—or post-literate—times. It emphasizes invention (the idea) and arrangement (how to structure that idea), as well as style (grammar, usage, etc.). By emphasizing the importance of invention for storytelling and news writing, young writers are empowered to recognize the value of what they have to say before being taught how to do so. This approach valorizes youth "voice" over writing competency. Unlike many school writing exercises, the strength of a piece is in what it has to say, not how it is composed. The key is motivation, inspiring young learners to go the extra distance when confronted with the more constrained aspects of arrangement—specifically in relation to journalistic practices—and style. The newspapers involved were interested in "teen voices," so a great deal of energy was put into working in particular with the 17–19 year-old age group. YPP editors were looking for writing that was publishable, not just well composed. Journalistic writing brings together forms of logic, but also storytelling—how to spin a good yarn, how to tell a compelling story. Often those with the best and most compelling stories were those with the least experience in writing. A theme that was repeated in various writing contests was the "school of hard knocks." Submissions that were received in this category were typically poorly composed but powerful testimonies of the struggles of growing up in varying difficult circumstances. Here "voice" trumped scholastic fluency, "story" trumped polished writing.

Given the pressures to submit professional copy on a weekly basis to major newspapers and news agencies, certain sacrifices had to be made in regards to working with a broad spectrum of youth. However, the mandate and institutional ethos of the organization was to try to make the idea of a youth voice as representative and inclusive as possible, so YPP targeted specific demographic groups—e.g., Aboriginal youth, low-income street youth, LGBT youth, and racialized minority youth. Working with some youth at the margins involved a longer term commitment, perhaps several weeks or months to work with their stories until they were ready to go. In the meantime, deadline pressures never relented, stories and columns still had to go out. So the organization relied on the already highly motivated and capable youth journalists with a passion for writing. While it was not the intention of YPP to favor "middle class youth with modems," the organization was not in the position to right all of the social wrongs of society on good intentions alone. Nor did the organization wish to turn a back on young people whose relative privilege enabled deeper engagement in the week-to-week machinations of a news agency for youth. Ultimately, to go from the wish for inclusion to its practice on a weekly basis was a daunting task. The way YPP rose to its own challenge, however, was in the inclusion of racialized minority youth in its core group of regular contributors.

The outreach strategy employed by YPP was varied. Many writers would hear of YPP through word of mouth and either come to the door or get in touch by e-mail. And on an ongoing basis, the organization was able to self-promote through its widely published *Very Cool* column to bring in new writers who were at a geographical remove from the main office. As well, YPP held an annual writing contest with cash or "swag" prizes which succeeded in attracting hundreds of new participants from across the country on an annual basis. Regardless of how thin the prospect of winning may be, this added value appears to motivate many young people to make the effort to sit down and write. On the other hand, street and otherwise marginalized youth are less likely to participate in a contest because they are often cut off from the circulation of the contest details and lack the material conditions of a quiet table and a mailing address. These youth, for whom the culture of consumption—the store windows, the billboards, and the swagger of shoppers—is a constant reminder of their outsider status, can be attracted to a workshop if bus tokens, pizza, and juice are offered. Thus, it is important to cater to two sides of the consumption coin; the fetish of commodities and the survival need to consume the basics of life. And in order not to privilege only the middle class-kids with modems, handwritten copy was often accepted from marginalized youth. Numbered questions are sprinkled through the text by a YPP editor and the piece is returned to the writer who needs only to answer the questions, rather than rewrite the whole document by hand.

In addition to all of the various strategies of outreach, YPP offered structured instruction, along three different models. First was the one-time workshop, mainly offered in high school classes, but also at community centres and drop-in centres. Here the goal was to teach some basic principles of news writing, but primarily to focus on exploring issues of the day: YPP's mantra, "what's on your mind." Participants were asked what they would do if they were given the chance tomorrow to take over a whole page of a newspaper to express their ideas. They were invited to speculate on what the issues of the day should be, not to prove they had the 'knowledge' to back up their opinions, but just to express themselves on issues that mattered to them. The other two structured outreach approaches were similar in intention, but broader in scope. Further, they involved some initiative on the part of the participants. They would sign up for sessions and make the effort to show up on their own. The two-session Writers Institute was run in groups of thirty and was conducted in a classroom-like setting. The Institute facilitators would cover differences between soft and hard news writing, feature writing and opinion writing, as well as how to conduct an interview. All these different genres of news writing were dealt with in more detail than could be done in a one-session workshop. The final approach was a five-session Writers' Circle, limited to 15 people at a time. Here the goal was to create a safe space for participants to develop ideas with some peer intervention, and each session involved the presentation of a new area of news writing so the young writers could become increasingly sophisticated. The YPP Writer's Guide was produced with the Writers' Circles in mind, a five-step module corresponding to the five sessions of the Circle. The Guide was developed to be a youth-

friendly document, to be accessible and less intimidating than a standard
journalism textbook. The Writer's Guide remains online at www.ypp.net and
an abridged version is available in the "How to respond to racial bias in the
media" section of Equality Today: http://www.equalitytoday.org/
edition7/audit.html

Editing with writers took primarily two forms, face to face and by e-mail.
When working via e-mail, YPP editors would rework the structure if necessary.
A common discovery is the "buried lead," an evocative bit of text that works
well to introduce an article. YPP editors did not consider the reorganization of
the text to be an intrusion. That element of rhetorical composition that
Aristotle had called "arrangement" often needs an experienced mentor/editor
to intervene. Over time, writers who worked with YPP developed a greater
capacity to follow journalistic conventions of composition. The other key
element was to embed questions and comments in capital letters before
sending it back to the writer. Participants were asked to elaborate on ideas,
change wordings, and add important details, but were normally asked not to
play with the structure. The challenge was how to stay really sensitive to a
writer's voice during this process, which was a delicate balancing act. The goal
was always to work towards guiding the writer to fit generic characteristics of
journalistic writing, without losing the particularity of the author's style, the
images evoked, their own turns of phrase, etc. YPP editors try to impart to
youth the notion that writing in non-school circumstances is a collaborative
process. They had to work to break down assumptions that the help of an
editor constitutes some kind of cheating. Youth participants were encouraged
to understand that in real work situations writers do not just come up with
works of genius, but rather they develop a draft, get feedback, and return to
completing the task. In regards to learning on the part of the youth
participants, YPP editors were able to identify certain takeoff points. Young
writers, usually by age fifteen, were clearly more able than their younger
cohorts to write at an abstract level and utilize sophisticated grammar and
diction. By age seventeen, many accomplished young writers are using more
complex reasoning and demonstrating higher level thinking (e.g., markers of
this are: the ability to grasp several strands of an argument and integrate them,
as opposed to the unifocal argumentation seen in younger writers).

News writing is both familiar and strange. On the one hand, it shares with
school writing the emphasis on a thesis statement and arguments that support
it. On the other, it shares conventions with conversation and personal
diarying. It is a form of storytelling that requires attentiveness to actor, scene,
and agency. The writer is the eyes and the ears of the reader and must transmit
elements of a context that enable a reader to see and feel. In this sense, it is
much closer to everyday discourse than is the impersonal academic essay.
Writers provide thick descriptions referred to as "colour" in journalistic

parlance. Providing colour involves imparting image-rich text, the need to appeal to and engage the eyes and ears of the reader. As well as providing an affective and visual referent, a journalistic writer must tell a story that flows. Unlike academic writing where a point can be left for future elucidation, a journalistic piece must flow from one sentence to the next. News writing proceeds like walking down a path. In terms of the arguments that are developed, one moves from point to point. The key here is transitions, sentences that weave together narrative bits. While on a conceptual level there is a potential for repetition, on a narrative level there is not. A well-crafted story goes full circle. It ends where it began.

Teaching in a news room environment is of necessity constrained or determined by outside deadlines and demands. In a face-to-face editing context with an impending copy deadline, YPP editors would try to explain structures of news writing to the young writer with the intent that the participants master generic conventions over time. But if the copy had to go out that afternoon and the writer has left things to the last minute, there are real time constraints that affect the teaching and learning relationship. YPP editors let the young writer have the final opinion on certain changes and speak their minds about the way a piece is developing, but this is not a moment where there is a lot of active engagement on the part of the learner. To some extent, in these moments it is like a watching a mechanic fix a car and listening to explanations as to why s/he is making certain decisions and choices. But ultimately, the conventions and formulas of news writing are less complicated than the workings of a car engine, at least for YPP participants who usually self-identify as writers before getting involved. For them, it is a matter of just opening the box, providing a formula. They are taught to read news writing for structure and not just content. Most youth writers begin to get it after a short time and their writing matures quickly.

As stated above, the YPP project continues today, if in a diminished capacity. Its flagship Web site—www.ypp.net—is a publishing hub and copy continues to be provided to newspapers across North America (Scripps Howard News Service provides YPP copy, free-of-charge, to over 300 newspapers across the U.S. and the *Toronto Star* Syndicate does the same to a smaller number of Canadian papers). When the *Toronto Star* mothballed the youth section, "young street," it was initially replaced by a cooler-than-cool, hyper-than-hype section for young adults called "Boom!" And the newspaper has subsequently developed a new section for "tweens" (9–13-year-olds) called *Brand New Planet*. When YPP's weekly arrangement at the *Toronto Star* ended, it was claimed by a *Star* editor that the copy was not up to journalistic standards. Of course, such a claim flies in the face of reader response and audience studies which show that readers bring varying expectations to differing reading contexts. It also insults the many young writers who had written tremendous stories and ignores the fact that YPP was providing almost twice as much content as usual in the two months leading up to the change. But, more significantly, it disguises a differing vision for what counts as youth copy. YPP's final "young street" cover prior to the change was a politicized, critical feature story on HIV/AIDS education and support programs within Toronto's racialized minority community. The following week's 'youth' feature was an adult staff writer's piece on the relative legitimacy of unauthorized Pokemon cards for young people. In the aftermath of the dismissal of youth YPP articles from the *Star*, the paper offered a meandering array of articles pitched across an age spectrum of 9–35, a wandering section in search of a demographic, written mainly by *Toronto Star* staff writers. It appears that the capacity to develop meaningful youth copy in a mainstream newspaper ends when the decisions revert to the newsroom and an organization forsakes the streets and contexts of living youth culture. Schools too run the same risk of falling off the map of relevance for some youth if spaces are not opened up for the living, breathing aspirations of young people. We take up one school's sustained response to this problem in the following chapter.

Slammin' School:
Performance Poetry
and the Urban School

Bronwen E. Low

Thirty high school poets compete in a poetic "mock Olympics" in which they perform original pieces, ranked on a scale of 1 to 10 by judges picked randomly from the audience. In keeping with the principles of slam poetry, the poets use neither props nor musical instruments in this war of words, relying instead on the expressiveness of their bodies and voices. No performance can exceed the 3 _- minute time limit. The teen poets parade on and off the stage, dreadlocked and ponytailed, braided and buzzed, some squeezed into stretch pants and baby T-shirts, while others, in the words of poet Patricia Smith (2007), are "drooped as drapery" (p. 49). Iolet, headwrapped and regal, tells of police brutality. A boy from New Jersey dedicates his poem about being "surrounded by a raging sea called heterosexuality" to "anyone who's ever felt left out of society's categories, or been to a really boring sweet-16 party in Westchester county." There is a poem about Puerto Rican nationalism, an ode to a mother, another to a brother locked up, and many tales of sex and heart break. The crowd hollers its approval and disagreement with the judges' scoring. Asheena McNeil, who writes her poetry on the 125th street bus to and from school in Harlem, won the slam with a perfect score for her "125th Street Blues." She cites as inspiration Maya Angelou and her grandmother who "lives poetry rather than writes it." And like most of the other student poets, she credits rap music, and Hip-Hop culture in general, as having made poetry "cool." As we heard from the Bartenders rap crew in chapter 1, rap music opens up an important space of communication and expression for many youth, including and even especially for young men.

This auditorium packed with youth going wild for poetry at New York's inaugural Teen Slam was the tip of the iceberg of a popular resurgence of interest in poetry which has important implications for youth writing in the here and now. Slam poetry is one manifestation of "spoken word culture," a category used to describe forms of poetry and performance in which an artist recites poetry, often to musical accompaniment which might range from a jazz ensemble to a bongo drummer. The 1960s coffee house reading is back, and most cities feature "spoken word" poetry nights and series in bars, cafés, and community centers. But this is poetry reading with a difference. In the early 90s poetry went mass market and mass media as MTV and Much Music began to televise clips of poets performing their work in between music videos. Performance poetry also hit the road, touring with the music festival Lollapalooza. In 2001, HBO began airing *Def Poetry Jam*, a half hour of spoken word poetry hosted by well-known rapper Mos Def and orchestrated by famous rap producer Russell Simmons. Performance poetry is gathering media interest, much of which is focused on the dynamic and competitive slam poetry movement. Started in the mid-80s at the Get Me High bar in Chicago by poet and construction worker Marc Smith, poetry slams now take place across North America, and culminate each year in the National Slam. Each is held in a city in the U.S. before audiences of thousands. In August 2006, 73 teams from cities across the United States (and teams from Canada and from France) met in Austin, Texas, to vie for the title of Grand Slam champions. While performance poetry and its implications for education are just beginning to garner academic attention (Fisher, 2005; Jocson, 2005, 2006; Low, in press), community-based organizations which offer spoken word programs for youth have been going strong since at least the mid-90s. The largest of these, Youth Speaks, was founded in 1996 in San Francisco, works with 45,000 youth a year in the Bay area, has partner organizations in 36 cities, offers a wide range of programs including after-school and in-class writing and performance workshops, and hosts the yearly International Youth Poetry Slam festival (see their teaching guide, *Brave New Voices*, 2001, and their Web site at www.youthspeaks.org).

Spoken word has a passion for language. At odds with the rhetoric of literacy crisis which pervades popular representations of education, youth—and in particular the urban youth usually deemed most at risk in the rhetoric—are embracing cultural forms in which language matters a great deal. This fact has largely escaped mainstream education's attention. This oversight is beautifully represented by the opening of the movie *Dangerous Minds* (Smith, 1995). White teacher Louanne Johnson, played by Michelle Pfeiffer, peers into her new classroom and sees a group of African American students "freestyle" rapping, improvising rhyming verse to a beat, while other youth listen and dance to rap music. "Noisy bunch," she comments nervously. After realizing that she's going to have to "rewrite" the curriculum in order to engage her class of disenfranchised black and Hispanic adolescents, she develops a poetry assignment in which the students compare the songs of Bob Dylan to the poetry of Dylan Thomas. The students rise to the challenge of interpreting poetry through their engagement with Ms. Johnson's 1960s "popular culture," a plot point that insists they were without poetry (and popular culture) to begin with, in contrast to the poetic force of the freestyle scene.

That certain forms of poetry are now alive and well, even cool, among youth may come as a surprise to many language arts teachers; in this chapter we examine this popular resurgence of interest in poetry and argue for slam poetry as a powerful conduit for youth expression. In order to think through some of slam's implications for youth writing, we describe and reflect upon a high school performance poetry course which Bronwen developed in conjunction with a creative writing teacher and a spoken word poet. This chapter therefore engages closely questions of pedagogy. This investigation of slam pedagogy places a priority on three of Johnson's (1996) four moments in the cycle of a cultural form: the processes of production or authorship, including the conditions which were set up to facilitate a culture of student writing and performance in these classrooms; the texts the students produced; and lived culture, for the data we draw upon includes hundreds of hours of audio and video tapes of classroom life as well as interviews with teachers and students.

Slam as New Literacy

Even more so than rap music, slam complicates discussion of adolescent literacies as chronologically "new" because it is a "low tech" genre, requiring only a stage, performers, and an audience. Slam draws on some of the most ancient forms of entertainment: competition, pleasure in language, storytelling, and self-expression. Central to the appeal of slam poetry to youth is performance, a return to the oral traditions of the bard or African griot. Here slam draws upon African-American musical traditions in which performance is central; as Frith (1983) describes, "Black music is immediate and democratic—a performance is unique and the listeners of that performance become part of it" (p. 17). The emphasis on performance in slam also revives 1960s and 70s interactive avant-garde arts scenes and phenomenon such as dada *soirées* and "happenings"; in these, notes oral poet Jerome Rothenberg (1981), performativity broke down the boundaries between art and life, the arts and non-arts, music and noise, and poetry and prose.

At the same time, slam is a creation of its technologized context. The live, intimate communion between poet and listener in slam is awash in contemporary communication technologies including Web sites and chat rooms that publicize slam events and share slam's history, such as www.poetryslam.com, www.poetry.about.com, www.e-poets.net/library/slam, www.slampapi.com; Web sites for the yearly National Slams such as www.austinslam.com; and, international sites such as the German www.estradpoesi.com. Spoken word record labels, including Kill Rock Stars and Mouth Almighty/Mercury, produce recordings. Feature films *Slam* (1998) and *Love Jones* (1997) and the documentaries *SlamNation* (1998), *Slam America* (2001), *Slam Planet* (2006), and *Poetic License* (2001) translate the intimacy and immediacy of slam's storytelling onto screen and into larger dramas. TV journalism reports expand slam's audiences and communities of participation and interest. Algarín (1994) gives a sense of slam's imbrication in contemporary culture when he writes that the extensive media coverage of slam means "that it is now possible to cull from the endless articles a sense of the poetics that is being created in midair from one article to the other as these poets are made to think about content, quality, and craft" (p. 22). This is a poetics of the moment, forged in cafés and bars as well as in the pages of *Newsweek*, and within which poets learn from journalists. Granted, despite the media attention, slam is still largely the stuff of grass roots and community forms of distribution and promotion (an instance of the Internet fulfilling some of its democratic promise), and of independent film production companies, recording labels, publishers, and documentaries. Many teachers are not yet familiar with slam, nor are their students. However, as noted above, slam is but one manifestation of a growing spoken word scene that includes the Def Jam poetry series on HBO and is intimately related to massively influential Hip-Hop culture. Slam might be considered the "B side" of increasingly corporate rap music, and given some of the limitations of the genre conventions and formulas structuring contemporary Hip-Hop culture, slam poetry is opening up some important possibilities for youth expression.

Why Poetry?

> I've always enjoyed poetry as a way of reading and thinking...the language and methods of poetry have always seemed right to me; they push at the boundaries of thinking; they play in the noise and excess of language; they upset and they surprise. To write critically I've always written poetry. (Fred Wah, 2000, p. 1)

Poetry is a powerful form of youth expression that bridges the past and the present in new literacies. The term "poetics" stems from the Greek *poesis* or "making." Through-lines in theories about the work and importance of poetry are its ability to make language both new and strange. For instance, Shelley's 1840 "Defense of Poetry" argues that poetry revitalises language by disrupting conventions of expression and by building fresh associations between the word and world, especially through metaphor. The Romantic poet warns that "if no new poets should arise to create afresh the associations which have been thus disorganized, language will be dead for all the nobler purposes of human intercourse" (cited in Richter, 1989, p. 325). The idea of making language strange, what the Russian formalists called *ostranenie* or "defamiliarisation," argues that art "exists to recover the sensation of life...to make the stone *stony*" (Shklovsky, 1917, cited in Richter, 1989, p. 741); for the Formalists, poetry estranged reality in order to disrupt literary and aesthetic conventions but also to open up a space of social critique. Poet Fred Wah's sense that poetry is a place to push at the boundaries of thinking and language provides a contemporary articulation of *ostranenie*. Given the close ties between thinking, language and identity, the defamiliarisation and renewal of thought and language works also to make the subject new and strange. Poetry can open up a space of creative possibility for the self, disrupting fixed models in favor of a theory of identity as evolving, experimental, and dynamic. Committed to renovation and making strange, poetry celebrates the limits of what we know about language and identities and so can be the grounds of curiosity and surprise about the world, the self, and others.

Why Slam?

Slam poetry and contemporary spoken word more generally are not the work of the poet-hermit, isolated from society in contemplation. Instead, slam poets tend to see themselves as embedded within and responsible to particular communities and the poem comes to life in its performance. At the same time, writing is also a space of introspection, and so slam lies at the intersection of the personal and public. The importance of the national Grand Slam poetry competition to the scene means that poets associate with venues and cities, and poets end up representing specific places (for instance, New York City is usually represented by a team from the Nuyorican Poets Café). And slam is populist and accessible; as slam poet Miguel Algarín (1994) describes there "is no discerning of 'high' or 'low,' all in the service of bringing a new audience to poetry via a form of entertainment meant to tune up fresh ears to a use of language as art" (p. 16). Given the importance of audience appeal to the judging process, slam poets work to make an impact, to get noticed. This means that slam poetry is often funny, irreverent, and sexy; it is also frequently personal, sometimes hard hitting and even raw, a vehicle for exploring painful life stories. The confessional quality of much of the poetry performed at slams has been a source of criticism, as in the question posed by *Sixty Minutes* reporter Morley Safer to teacher Gayle Danley: "Isn't slam poetry, then, really therapy?" Her ready reply, "Yes," and the question she writes on the board of the middle-school classroom in which she is teaching slam poetry, "Have you dug deep?", suggest that poetry as healing self-expression is not a designation shied away from by slam poets (cited in Hewitt, 28/11/1999). However, slam poets are just as likely to speak out against social injustices as they are to explore their own feelings, and the confessional and critical modes are often connected, the ties between the personal and political writ large. For all these reasons slam poetry appeals to adolescents who see it as a space for explorations of self and society, within which to express anger and sorrow, and to entertain and educate.

Slam in the Classroom

New Literacy Studies examinations of youth literacy practices in out-of-school contexts have convincingly demonstrated their complexity and the ideologically driven disconnect between these practices and schooled forms of literacy (Gee, 1996; Heath, 1983). Also made clear are ways the split between academic and home/community literacies furthers the social marginalization of racial, ethnic, and language minority youth (Luke & Freebody, 1997). As noted in chapter 1, Hull and Shultz (2001) ask, in response to such findings, "How might out-of-school identities, social practices, and the literacies that they recruit be leveraged in the classroom?" and, "How might teachers incorporate students' out-of-school interests and predilections but also extend the range of the literacies with which they are conversant?" (p. 603). One significant barrier to the incorporation of non-academic literacies into school is the deficit model that characterizes many teachers' attitudes towards such literacy practices, particularly those that stem from black popular culture. The performance poetry course which Bronwen helped developed and teach took up Hull and Shultz' challenge of both leveraging and building upon the interests and skills students brought with them from their literate engagements in out-of-school contexts. It also worked to challenge deficit models about Hip-Hop culture by placing rap music within the larger genres of spoken word and performance poetry, and situating it within multiple artistic traditions.

In the spring of 2002, Bronwen began collaborating with a high-school English teacher and a performance poet involved in arts education at an urban arts school in a mid-sized, northeastern U.S. city, helping to develop and lead a performance poetry or "spoken word" unit for two senior English classes. The school's district has the highest poverty rate among the state's largest districts, and 88% of its students are eligible for free/reduced priced lunch, with 50% of the schools at a 90% or higher poverty rate. The teacher, "Tim," is a middle-aged European male, and the performance poet and arts educator,

"Rashidah," is a black woman in her early 30s. Tim, Rashidah, and Bronwen drew and built upon student interests in rap music and freestyle oral poetry and the class culminated in a competitive poetry slam. The students were all 17 or 18 years of age. Bronwen was actively involved co-teaching and researching the course in 2002 and in 2004; we will draw here on poems performed in the slams in those years as well as audio and video recordings of full-class discussions and performances, students' in-class writing, and one-on-one interviews with the students and teacher. We will also examine the pieces performed in the slams in 2003 and 2006 in order to discuss some recurring themes in the students' writing over the years—46 poems in total. The student poems included here are copied with as much fidelity as possible to the hand-written and typed versions students submitted. As with the Young People's Press articles, we will discuss some of the recurring themes in the students' poems. This chapter also discusses whole and parts of student poems, an important part of taking youth writing seriously.

The spoken word curriculum was first offered as a six-week unit in Tim's two senior English classes. One of these classes, the "boys' class," was designed as an alternative to the academic college-level English class and was composed only of male students who chose to be in a same-sex class. Their teacher called them the survivors—students who have not traditionally done well in English, but who have managed to persist into their senior year. More than two thirds of the boys were black, the rest Hispanic and white. The other class was an Advanced Poetry class (which I'll call the "AP class"), which attracted some of the top academic students in the grade including most of the creative writing majors. It was co-ed and most of the students were white. In 2004, the term-length course was again offered to "English IV," the alternative to the college-stream class, composed that year of young men and young women who Tim felt were the weakest group academically of the three years the course had been offered. All the students in the class had had to write the state wide English Language Arts exam the previous year and more than half had just passed it with a 55%. The class shared the racial demographics of the boys' class but was co-ed.

Due to the popularity of the courses and to the repeatedly high quality of students' poetry and performances, spoken word poetry has now been institutionalized in this school as part of the middle school creative writing program and as a senior English option. The school's graduating class regularly votes the poetry slam as the "best school event," no mean feat in an arts-magnet school with a continual roster of drama, dance, creative writing, and visual arts productions. Students clamor to get into the spoken word classes and attendance is consistently high. Fisher (2003) argues that spoken word poetry series in the black community act as "African Diaspora Participatory Literacy Communities": these communities are shaped by respect, audience engagement and participation, explorations of identity, and learning. Tim, Rashidah, and Bronwen tried to develop within the classroom a community of poets similar to those found outside of school. During the course we immersed students in spoken word forms through videos, CDs, visits by local poets, and a series of workshops in which students developed and rehearsed their own poems. Students also brought in examples of rap music, jazz poetry, and other spoken word forms that moved, interested, or challenged them to share with the class. In the first year of the project we examined various contexts in the history of poetics for thinking about rap's experiments with word and sound, including dada sound poetry, Stein's modernist decompositions of language, jazz poetry, and blues poetry. In 2004, led by a literature professor from the local research university and Rashidah, we explored some of the history of black poetics: spirituals, the blues, and poetry from the Black Arts Movement. However, more time was dedicated in class to writing and performance workshops, in part because this second group was much less interested in the more academic investigations into poetry than the two classes in 2002. Always integral to the course are journals within which students freewrite to various creative writing prompts, write drafts of poetry to be workshopped in class, and respond to texts and audio and visual recordings of poetry as well as to their classmates' performances. The course culminates in a poetry slam at the end of the school year in an auditorium filled with all of the senior students, selected classes of juniors, and some invited members of the community. Judges are picked based on a formula in which 2 or 3 are selected from inside the school, such as teachers, librarians or current students, and 2 or 3 are from the larger community, including local artists, parents, and school alumni. This formula strays from the original slam rules in which judges are picked randomly from the audience, but this move was designed to increase the possibility of balanced and disinterested scoring in a high school context.

Reinventing Language: "We are the Public Enemies Number One!"

Near the beginning of the project in both years, the film *Slam* (1998) was screened; it became central to the students' interest in and understanding of the genre. *Slam* (1998) tells the story of Ray Joshua, spoken word poet and subsistence-level marijuana dealer, and his experiences with both the criminal justice system and the redemptive force of poetry. Largely improvised and shot on location in the Washington, DC, city jail, the Anascostia "Dodge City" housing project, and a genuine poetry slam at the Nuyorican Poet's Café, the film, a "drama *vérité*" in the words of its makers, uses inmates and project residents as cast members and extras, and stars actual spoken word poets Saul

Williams (Grand Slam national champ in 1996) and Sonja Sohn (now of HBO series *The Wire* fame). The filmmakers' commitment to working with extras and actors playing close versions of themselves as well as to shooting in real settings is not only a product of their limited budget, "guerilla" shooting-style, and *cinéma vérité* aesthetic, but is also a marker of the relationship rap and slam poetry—and by extension the film—have to the "real" conditions of the lives of the disadvantaged. The film shares its emphasis on authenticity with the genre of spoken word, and with Hip-Hop culture's insistence on "representin'" and "keepin' it real" in relation to the lived conditions of the urban blacks and other minorities who have traditionally been rap music's thematic centre.

In an early scene, Ray (Saul Williams) hears a fellow inmate, Bay, drumming and rap freestyling in the adjoining jail cell. Ray joins in the rap, and the two voices rise in conversation, weaving a freestyle tandem to the rhythm which Bay drums and Ray strengthens as he whispers under Bay's lyrics—"Ba bam, ba bam bam. I had to be strong, I had to be real." The rappers finally stumble, laugh, and stretch their hands through the bars, holding a handshake from cell to cell. "That shit was tight, mo," says Bay (in the film and out, a seventeen-year-old convict about to find out if he is jailed for life) to Ray. Of their rap, the screenplay notes: "the symmetry and rhythm are the culmination of two centuries of slave chants, prison work songs, and blues; a modern, Hip-Hop slave song for the 90s. And as long as they can hold it, they're free" (Stratton & Wozencraft, 1998, p. 200). Locating this rap within a tradition of black aesthetic resistance, the writers suggest that the scene encapsulates *Slam*'s larger theme of the power of poetry to help the socially marginalized temporarily transcend the prisons that constrain them: the prison of a political and economic system that discriminates against minorities and the poor, the prison of an individual's life circumstances, and, in the moment of synchronicity with a fellow prisoner, the cell of the self.

The power of spoken word to reconcile and transcend is taken to its extreme in a later scene in the jail in which Ray defuses a confrontation mounting between himself and two rival gangs in the yard by blazing forth with his poem "Amethyst Rocks," a diatribe against the system which ends with the lines, "i am the sun/ and we are the public enemies number one!/ one one one!/ one one one!" Here spoken word announces itself as the poetry of the disenfranchised. The poem literally stops the jail-yard gangs in their tracks in the film and is one of Williams' best-known works (he gave it as title to his first spoken word album). Evident in the poem is the poet's freedom of reference, as he builds a collection of classical allusions that coexist with references to rap group Public Enemy and singer Prince. This creative freedom might also be considered a characteristic of slam poetry, for as Algarín (1994) insists, there is no discerning between high and low art in slam.

Viewing the film was a powerful experience for the students for a number of reasons. The jail freestyle scene opened up a discussion in the boys' class about freestyle poetry, a genre Tim had not yet heard of. In response, two black young men, the school's most gifted freestylers, performed for him individually and in a "cipher" in which they stand in a circle and each improvise poetry in turn. One of these freestyle poets, Gerard, the subject of the Talent Night Rap in chapter 1, has gone on to some celebrity: he reigned as freestyle champion for seven weeks on BET's nationally televised freestyle battle show, *106 and Park*, opens for rappers at local shows, has toured campuses, and produced his own rap album, which is available for download on the net. Tim was very impressed by the freestyles and that moment seemed to confirm for the students that this was a class in which their skills and interests were greatly valued. Carlos, one of the most enthusiastic supporters of the project, had hinted at some of the students' talents when Tim mentioned the course the previous term. Carlos had requested a tape recorder to start chronicling some of the poetry action in the hallways, saying "there's a lot going on in this school that teachers don't know about." After watching the freestyle scene in *Slam*, the students were asked to compare and contrast the two different styles as a way of having students pay close attention to questions of form and content. Saul Williams' style is particularly metaphoric, abstract, and philosophical, while Bay's is more direct and colloquial, ridden with "fucks." The students reflected upon these differences, often associating the first with education and the second with the "streets." Saul Williams and his more literary style and intense, often frenetic flow (or style of delivery), became a poetic role model for a number of the Black male students, evident in some of the performances in the slam.

The film was also used to introduce students to the role played by various communicative modes in the production of meaning: students first read, then listened to, and finally viewed different versions of "Amethyst Rocks": the written text, Williams performing the poem on his spoken word CD by the same name, and finally the scene from the film. After each version, they were asked to journal about and then share what they were getting from the text. Their journal entries make clear how the students' interest in and understanding of the poem grew as the audio and then visual elements were added; in reflecting on the slam many of the students observed that the performances of their poetry were less likely to be misinterpreted than written versions of them. This seemed to be very reassuring to them.

Opening the Floodgate

The spoken word course continually opens floodgates of student writing and creativity. This was especially striking with the weaker English IV group who were generally less engaged in the class discussions than the previous groups, but who Tim felt produced as a whole the highest quality of performance poems. For instance, on the second day of class Clayton, a student who was very shy and had not once spoken in class the prior term, came to see Tim in the morning to show him a poem he had written and wanted to read for the group. By the third morning of class, Tim was surrounded by students with open notebooks and had started a performance sign-up list with six names. Pablo, an English IV student who was on the brink of failing English and who rarely showed up for the first half of term, began actively participating when the focus turned to producing and workshopping poems for the slam. He performed a powerful poem at the slam called "Just Another Baby Dad"; when Rashidah ran into him in the hallways of the local community college two years later, he told her that since the slam he had been doing "nothing but writing." The first year of the project, Jaz, one of the few blacks in the AP class, was the slam's Master of Ceremonies and also won the slam. He was a creative writing major, unlike the majority of the students in all three classes, and felt that the course "rekindled a fire in me to write more, it just got me excited and I just started writing crazy and, like, I wake up in the middle of the night writing poems and stuff. It's got me excited again about writing." He added that he felt that this passion for poetry was improving his writing more generally, even his essays which "really needed some work," but within which he now finds he can "still put a sense of poetry in it, the way you use the words and the way to be figurative." He added that he wished that the slam had been at the beginning of the year for it let people know that he writes poetry and just "opened so many doors" because now he knows about "other people writing poetry" and can have conversations with them about their work.

Jaz's thoughtful slam poem and impassioned performance had some of the intensity of Saul Williams' work:

> Continually I shadow box
> silhouette soldiers
> defeated
> I'm beaten, but naked
> until I bleed infinite
> beads of blood
> the world shows not its own love
> the streets gives not hugs but through
> drugs delivers amphetamine slugs
> slow like forest I try to outrun the streets
> escape its heat but these braces that bind

> my feet won't bust
> fallin unconscious I get caught in my sleep
> my lion roar subdued to a
> simple hush
> Hush somebody callin my name
> a once confident brother downsized to feel in
> pain
> Broken down hollowed out like an
> abandoned window pane
> this my major pain my daily
> growing pain
> My new white suit with a baby's kool-aid stain
> my five heartbeats like Big Daddy Kane
> and nights like this I wish raindrops would
> fall, and christen my dome
> I click my heels close my eyes
> there is no place like home
> There is no place like home
> there is no place like home
> But once awakened there's no Kansas for me
> No scarecrow no tinman or cowardly lion as far as the eye
> can see
> Just darkness
> and pissed off family
> cause I interrupted their
> sleep

Jaz creates an evocative scene of a man at night in his bedroom fighting his demons—the drugs and unemployment, the streets and despair which drag him down. He dreams of being transported away into the world of Oz but is (screamingly?) jolted back into the realities of his life. The poem is powerfully imagistic, filled with sound and color and stark contrasts between the lion roar and the subdued hush, the kool-aid stain on the white suit, the fire of the heat, and the rain on the roof. Like the narrator in "Amethyst Rocks," the one in Jaz's poem figures himself as at war, and this war also involves drugs, bullets as "amphetamine slugs." Jaz's performance greatly complemented the poem: he accentuated its use of repetition, imagery, and alliteration by varying his speed and volume. It was a symbiosis of poem and performance that brought to life the struggles of the poem's persona.

Getting Students to Write: "I'm Reading Off the Top of the Head"

The performance poetry students' enthusiasm for writing poetry stands in sharp contrast with the feelings of many about writing more generally. One of the reasons Tim makes journaling a central piece of the course, including its assessment (50% of the class grade is usually based on their journals) is that he wants the students to be constantly writing. Classes often begin with "writing practice" about which Tim says, "Don't edit yourself. Be adventurous with your language. No talking." The students write to specific prompts, such as William Carlos Williams' "Men die everyday for what they miss in poetry," "Poetry heals the wounds inflicted by reason," and "Write down the words for a song or poem you wish you'd written. Then explain why." One year, the morning after the Oscars, the prompts included phrases from the broadcast including "And the winners are_____" and "Outcast no longer." The students are also given the following series of sentence openers to help them to start formulating in writing their "first thoughts" about something: "I don't understand/I noticed/I wonder/I was reminded of/I think/ I'm surprised that/I'd like to know/ I realize/ If I were/ The central issue here is/One consequence of_____could be? If_____then_____/I'm not sure/Although it seems." While Tim's prompts are engaging enough that the students usually do some writing to them, they are also often very reluctant to read what they have written. This is particularly the case for the black men in the classes.

In the second year of my involvement in the course, one male student started to paraphrase what he had written during the writing practice, saying "I'm reading off the top of the head." Tim responded, "you need to read what's on the page," to which the student replied, "then I don't want to do this." In conversation with Tim and me after the class period, Rashidah explained that regularly in her writing workshops with black children and youth the students would share what they "wished they had written" instead of what they actually had. Tim explained that he had them read "what's on the page" in order "to put the attention on their writing" for they'd eventually be writing poems. He also did this to keep the class focused, for students can "ramble on" in discussions. Tim tried to grapple with students' anxieties about writing up front, and on day two of the English IV class held out a cup in front of one of the students and told him to "spit in it." He then asked him to drink it, which the student laughingly refused to do. Tim surmised aloud that this refusal stems from our sense that what was once now private is public, that it has been exposed to others but also to ourselves, and then drew an analogy to writing in which we are usually our own worst critics, censoring ourselves for fear of being exposed. Rashidah next emphasized to the students that they should think of their writing as a performance, not to be scared of it as some kind of permanent record but to allow it to remain imperfect and in process.

Students' fears of exposure shone through in year three as soon as they began performing their work in class. One young woman prefaced her performance by saying, "I don't want people to talk too much about it," to which Tim responded that the authors should specify in advance the kind of feedback they are looking for. At another point in that class Jamir worried that he didn't "get" one of his classmate's poems. During a discussion about the group with Rashidah and Bronwen, Tim suggested that these generally low academic achievers would be particularly plagued by worries about the validity of what they have to say. For many of them, English classes had been deadly places where they had learned to get by playing the rules of the game; these don't generally involve taking creative risks. He pointed out that Jamir's "I don't get it" epitomizes how students have been taught to respond to poetry: to mistrust their own instincts in favor of the teacher's "true" interpretation. In order to help change this dynamic, Bronwen regularly read through the students' class journals and validated their responses by putting selections on an overhead for discussion. And Tim offers the students concrete strategies for responding to each other's work. One is the concept of pointing, where the students write down words and phrases that jump out at them from the poem. He also recommends that they initially structure their responses around the following prompts:

> I believe your poem because_____
>
> I doubt your poem because_____
>
> When I hear your poem what goes through my head is _____

These prompts ask the students to be specific in their feedback and so help them avoid simplistic judgments about something being either good or bad. They also make clear the personal and subjective nature of all responses.

Poetry as Cool

This context of anxiety and low-achievement makes the poetry the English IV students performed at the slam and all term all the more remarkable. In order to explain this, we need in part to revisit Asheena McNeil's comment about Hip-Hop having made poetry cool. One valuable aspect of rap music for literacy educators is its commitment to linguistic skill, with rappers proudly proclaiming themselves as word warriors. The links between rap and the other spoken word forms we explored in the course redefined what counts as poetry in school; in the words of one male from the boys' class, "I think people really like poetry they're just afraid to admit it." In all of the classes, many students wrote poetry and/or shared it publicly for the first time. This was consistently a source of surprise to the students. For instance, one student in the boys' class, Darren, spontaneously wrote a poem in class and then performed it, inspired by Rashidah's first visit to the class. His poem began: "My notebook is my horse and saddle/With this/I ride/I ride into the creativity of my emotions and embrace them as one would their child....My thoughts laid out on piece of paper/for all to see/ for all to see that through me/you can see/that I myself/Am poetry." A classmate expressed shock that Darren and others wrote poetry, "because I didn't see that part of him and I was like oh—well they deserve my attention because this is something that I didn't know about." In the Advanced Poetry class, one male announced, "I've seen things come out of people that I didn't know they had in them, and like we've been together since the ninth grade." In this same class, Jaz, commenting on his powerful invective that won the slam, said, "I didn't know I had that in me" and later in conversation added that "a lot of people found a lot of things within themselves."

Seven of the forty-six slam poems reviewed took poetry and/or writing as an explicit topic (these were not a topic of any of the YPP articles). These explorations of the significance and importance of writing and poetry in the students' poems work in the tradition of rap music, which is often self-referentially about the importance of writing and rhyming. Clayton, the shy young man discussed above whose poetic voice erupted in the course, performed a piece at the slam about the power of poetry which included these lines:

> A poet opened my ears to poetry.
> A diva like no other
> she reminded me of hip hop.
> Like her I'm often told me that I sound white
> cause I can't flow to the beat of my block.
> It's cause I'm misunderstood.
> Don't get it twisted though,
> me and you parked in the same hood.
> A poet spits knowledge.
> Knowledge—she's not from college
> but damn she's the truth.
> ....
> At a time when my life was ticking away,
> I was bound to be a statistic too.
> Who knew rhymes could enter the solitary crevice
> of an unanswered question?
> Thank you bringing culture into me
> at a time when I had drowned
> in the sea of preconceived notions of a life
> once known as the black man's struggle. . .
> ....

Clayton's ode to poetry and to one poet in particular contains themes which reccurred in many of the students' poems: the problem of social misperception and stereotyping and the challenges of being a black man. For instance, his classmate Aisha's poem "I write" also addressed some of these themes and in its final lines drew on pieces of the language from Clayton's poem, putting these works into conversation:

> ....
> I write about naked minds
> and twisted allusions
> of the so called American dream.
> Naked minds
> filled with empty aspirations
> and preconceived notions of the life and times of a Black
> man.
> In a time when people in America are just a technicality
> on a piece of paper
> I write.

Aisha's powerful refrain, "I write," punctuated the poem throughout and offered a strong argument for the urgency of written self-expression in the face of a culture of deception and alienation.

Making Selves Strange and New

Contributing to the widespread sense of surprise about the poetry slam and course more generally, students in both classes took significant risks with their poems. Many seemed to experiment with different identities, making themselves strange and new to their peers and themselves. Given that the writers are all adolescents, it won't surprise that adolescent identity was the top theme (found in 15 of the 46 poems). Many of the poets tried on different personae. This experimentation was encouraged by a couple of experiences in the course. The first year, the boys' class had participated in a "many selves, many voices" unit in which they explored the different ways of speaking and communicating that they adopted in different situations in their lives. They wrote a monologue adopting one of their particular voices. In both years, we explored the concept of the persona poem and "mask," and studied a poem by Patricia Smith (1992) written from the perspective of a skin-head. A number of students performed these at the slams, adopting personae such as Pablo's "just another baby dad who leaves his child without a man," an Iraqi civilian, and an American soldier in Iraq. The latter was adopted by Don who dressed in fatigues to add authenticity; when he forgot his lines he was greeted by a chorus of support from the audience whose comments included "alright," "no pressing," and "you tell it," an example of the Participatory Literacy Community in practice. Another persona poem was written from the perspective of a much aggrieved planet Earth, and opened with the following lines:

> Since you were here, I couldn't breathe cause you polluted my air.
> Since you were here, I've bled thousands of times from endless warfares
> Giving me third degree burns from your careless acts
> ripping each single strand of hair right off my back.
> ....

This poet, Jeff, identified strongly as a rapper and mostly dressed in Hip-Hop outfits: baggy clothes, a baseball hat, and a heavy chain necklace. His angry tone and Hip-Hop stance and style made the poem initially seem like a rap "beef" (or complaint); when it became clear that he was speaking as the Earth rather than as a human, the message surprised and then demanded one's attention.

While some students used the slam to publicly explore different personae, others used it as an opportunity to share some aspects of themselves that they previously had not. For instance, one of the biggest surprises for many students the first year, as well as for their teacher, was a poem entitled "Who Can Defeat Me," delivered with force by Clifton, a student in the boys' class known for his soft-spoken, easy-going manner:

> WHO CAN DEFEAT ME
> Inside me
> is an inner me
> that inner me
> wants to be free
> but should I let it free
> therefore releasing
> my enemy
> ....
> is it reality
> to see
> Rodney King join hands w/ his enemies
> after his tragic police brutality
> or to see Afghanistan Refugee
> eat w/ the ones dat made them flee
> ....
> our ancestors wanted to be free
> their spirits live deep in me
> telling me
> "FREE ME" "free me"
> my mind is the key to my individuality
> telling me
> no one can defeat me
> but me.

The poem's ambiguity gets at some of the complexity of this "inner me," at once Clifton's "enemy," the voices of his slave ancestors whose spirits "live deep in me," and his "mind." I read this "inner me" as in part a personification of this student's anger at the injustices of the world, from the treatment of Rodney King to the bombing of Afghanistan. While he fears his anger, he recognizes its source in historical and contemporary racial violence and also its potential for resistance, for working in particular towards the liberation of black people. He suggests that paths towards freedom lie both with the individual, particularly the individual mind, and the community. Clifton delivered the poem with such vehemence and intensity that he was almost shouting, which suggested that this normally reserved student was using the poem as one vehicle for exploring different aspects of himself: part of the journey, perhaps, towards freedom.

Other students also experimented with different perspectives and ways of being. For instance, after the controversy about "Streetlife" at the Talent Night (which was discussed in chapter 1), Tim suggested Gerard write a poem about being labeled and misinterpreted, which Gerard (and other students in this and subsequent groups) seemed to take to heart. Gerard performed a poem entitled "Cry" that critiqued gang violence, and implicitly, models of masculinity that suggest that men have no feelings. "Cry" starts with, "Misunderstood is the definition when a man cry," and ends with the lines, "And you ask why? Why you think I'm crying you bastard?/It's cause I'm at your funeral putting flowers on your casket." The first line takes up the popular theme of misinterpretation, but in relation to a man's tears rather than to generational and cultural stereotyping. "Cry" is a plea for peace in a world of violence. While the poem could still be titled "Streetlife" for it discusses its battles and its victims, Gerard is here the critic and teacher, not the "player." In another line in the poem he writes: "No degree in philosophy but when I talk, I teach." The difference between the two versions of "Streetlife" also suggests that Gerard has in part switched genres, moving from gangsta rap with its playful, hyberbolic conventions to the slam poetry genre, which is often politically provocative, critical, and self-reflexive. However, the poem also draws on some common themes in rap music, especially in its "conscious" renditions: poetry as pedagogy, as tool for healing, and as vehicle for street wisdom.

While the Advanced Poetry students, many of whom were creative writing majors, were already comfortable writing and sharing poetry publicly in school literary events, they also made themselves vulnerable through honest explorations of identity. In year two of the project one young white woman, an accomplished poet who had won several national poetry prizes, performed a love poem to another woman.

> Around the corner from the billboards that the sun rises over
> Is a little take-out place. The manager there has eyes that burn
> Like unattended egg rolls.
> She makes me get mooney-eyed. She makes me go gaga.
> She makes me go and get moo goo gai pan
> At three a.m. I take the bus.
> ....
> I love her spicy wings. I love her breasts
> Served over rice, her legs, her thighs
> The shine of the grease on her arms when she cleans the rotisserie light
> Her simple grin as she brings me my Buddhist's Delight
> I asked her out for coffee one day. Outside it rained
> Dark tea-leaf patterns on the smokestacks and drains
> She leaned close and told me
> that's not what "take-out" means.

Given the widespread expression of homophobia in high schools, unfortunately reinforced by some of the lyrics of a good deal of rap music, this was a very risky poem to choose. The response from most of the audience members was muted and many seemed taken aback by the student's honesty. Only one other poem performed in the slam over the four years directly addressed homosexuality, and it was in a list of people a student wished she could speak for, including "If I spoke for everyone the fearful silence of lesbians bi's and gays would be slain and it would end the pain of their disdain."

While more than 10% of the Young People's Press authors took up the theme of body image, only one of the 46 poetry students did—a white male named Kurt. While the sample of student slam poems is smaller than that of Young People's Press articles, and neither is large enough to warrant the drawing of strong conclusions, we speculate that the disinterest in this topic with the youth in Bronwen's study speaks to the fact that "body image" is still mostly the concern of middle-class white young women, a very small number of whom participated in the poetry slams in this urban school. Kurt's poem, however, also speaks to more general issues around adolescent identity, the most common theme in the slam poems and of love relationships, a recurring theme in both the YPP and the poetry slams (though not one of the most important in the slam poems). Kurt was the class clown in the AP class and wrote a poem about being fat:

A dose of truth
no a large portion.
Some own their blackness
their whiteness
I own my fatness.
But I do wish to sell it
at some lonely garage sale
with its bad memories
but till then that day comes
it is mine
all mine
until I shed its burden
I will never stop striving
to fit in—
to the damn pants.
I can't fit into the pants
that I bought for fifty
bucks cause I said to
my mom they would fit
shit.
A sidewards glance
is all I ask
from one of those
slim girls
those beautiful, elusive girls
with smooth plains for stomach
and golden locks for hair
Is a dance so hard
so difficult to try
maybe they are afraid to see
that I am not a novelty
or a means to a better
rep.

Kurt uses humor very effectively here to both talk about something difficult and to make his classmates laugh. It shows insight into dating relations (the notion that one might dance with or date the "fat" boy in order to try something new or to get yourself a good reputation—as a caring person perhaps?) and also some limits of vision, given that Kurt is also seeking the attention of the "slim"— the girls with smooth stomach plains (from his performance it did not seem that this reference was knowing or ironic).

In an interview at the end of the course, Kurt spoke about the way he normally "bottled things up" that bothered him, erecting a "force field" of humor, and that,

to finally get that out in my senior year, a lot of the things that I just wanted to yell at some people, but to get it out in a way that they won't be offended or they won't be taken aback...if you say it like that and you can get it all to everyone at one time...it was just this huge weight off.

We see here Kurt working, like Gerard, to say something he feels needs to be said without offending his audience; while Gerard's comment suggests some of the difficulties involved with speaking across cultural and generational differences, Kurt reminds that these shape communication more generally, especially in the fishbowls that high schools can be. This repeat theme of misconception is a reminder of how often adolescents feel that everyone is watching and making judgments about them. Another white student in the AP class, Nathan, also spoke to this dynamic when he said that "there are a lot of people that you just don't know, you don't even form a relationship" with and that one can go through school with "tremendous misconceptions about people." Nathan saw the slam as working against this, and argued that the slam demonstrated

> the importance of the individual as not answering to a stereotype, as not being necessarily what people expected, and saying, well, this is me, this is no one else talking. I've been inspired yes, but those inspirations are a part of who I am because my experiences make me. So this is about me the individual...we're all just people and we don't need to be divided by anything unless we decide that we are.

The slam is a space where students can express themselves as individuals, which helps them to move beyond stereotypical notions of each other, and so facilitates the coming together across differences.

While Kurt felt liberated by his performance, he was disappointed by the reaction of one of the judges whom he described as overweight and whom he feels "either doesn't address it or has given up on it." The judge approached him afterwards and

> you know she kind of defended me...to me...she kind of defended me and it was just kind of disheartening to see...she couldn't get over the fact in the poem I was saying that I was fat...she couldn't get past that to get to the poem and if she didn't get to the poem, she couldn't understand what I was saying...so. You know, but she's a teacher, so I just...I took her words and went into class. But it's interesting to see how some people have a shield, have like a force field up when they don't want to hear someone talk the way they do or listen to somebody.

According to this student, his teacher couldn't hear him because of her own issues with weight; whether or not this is the case, it is interesting that Kurt felt that she couldn't even "get to the poem" and that her defense missed the point. This scenario adds another dimension to the dilemma of adults reading or listening to youth: the relationship between adults and young people is burdened by adults' baggage, including unresolved feelings about their own adolescences (Gilbert, 2007).

In both classes that first year we discussed possible reasons for the collective risk-taking in the poetry slam. Several students suggested that they were more willing to explore difficult subjects because performance allowed them greater control over the audience's interpretation of their message. A few students suggested that their risk-taking was in part due to the fact that they were graduating seniors, leaving this particular community behind in a few weeks. One student responded that "freedom" was at stake in their choice of topics, not "vulnerability," and that the slam presented the "perfect opportunity" if "you just want to express yourself."

Spoken Word and Hip-Hop Performativity

The students' experimentation with different styles and identities in school is also very much in the spirit of Hip-Hop performativity, which celebrates the power of what Toni Morrison (1995) calls "word-work" to continually forge new selves, worlds, and meanings. And as noted above, not only has Hip-Hop culture helped legitimize spoken word poetry among youth, but the course also drew upon students' interests in rap music. One important dimension of Hip-Hop's ethos of reinvention is its language: "Hip-Hop Nation Language" (HHNL) (Alim, 2004) is a hotbed of linguistic innovation whose distinct and ever-evolving lexicon, syntax, and phonology draw upon African American Vernacular English (AAVE) word play traditions and then accelerate them through Hip-Hop culture's mass-mediated high-speed networks of distribution and influence. As Alim (2004) has noted, while AAVE is the "cutting edge" of socio-linguistic innovation in the U.S., HHNL is the "cutting edge of the cutting edge" (p. 296). Three mass market examples of this spirit of word-work and self-invention and expression in Hip-Hop culture are the changing identities of prominent rappers: Sean "Puffy" Combs' multiple reincarnations, first as Puff Daddy and now as P-Diddy; Shawn Carter/ Jay-Z/Jigga/and Jay-HOVA, the new God of rap; and, perhaps most infamously, the three personae of the character known alternately as Slim Shady, Marshall Mathers, and Eminem. HHNL embodies a dynamic poetics of the moment.

Making Society Strange

Not only was the self interrogated and reworked through the composition of poems, but so was the social. In every class, students grappled with important issues at the individual, local, and international levels. While adolescent identity was the top theme, it was quickly followed by general critiques of the state of the world, with most poems implicating current politicians and the older generation (13), drugs (13), race and racism (13), and then violence, crime, and gangs (10) and poverty (10). A number of the poems critiqued the American "War on Terror" and the Iraq War (7). Here are some excerpts from two of these:

> "Blinded" (Only to shed a little light on the eyes of the blind")
> The sky is filled with society's pollution that infects our world as a whole
> It was our goal to unite our nations as one but I guess that idea was too far fetched
> Instead Osama Bin Laden gathered some planes together and told the world to catch
>
> ....
>
> How are we the young people of tomorrow when tomorrow's opportunities are no longer?

And

> ....
>
> Yet things are still the same.
> More bombs over Baghdad.
> More innocent victims left sad.
> To everyone who lost someone,
> I'm sorry they had to go out that way.
> But maybe next time
> someone will make the right decision on election day.

One of the most powerful poems on race was by three young women in the 2002 AP class—one black, one white, and one who self-identified as mixed race. They performed a group poem, "Me," in which they interrogated race and racial stereotyping, including being "Too black," "Too white," and "two things combined, intertwined/Through society's eyes blinded by color/ Do I have to be one or the other?" Each poet had a solo section and some group choruses, and they explored the limits of the racialized identities imposed upon them by others, including, "They only see my mistakes as defeat/If I stand up for myself/I am considered defensive/And when I make it to the top/It is considered rare" and "You see my pale skin and think I'm innocent/ My blond hair, you think I'm naïve/ My blue eyes and you think I'm blind."

Several black women wrote poems in which they spoke directly to black men, as in for instance the winning poem in 2003, Danielle's "Stay High":

> Every time I look at you I just want to cry
> You are wasted opportunity
> You are time gone by
> You are unspent knowledge
> You are unfulfilled worth.
> Nigga you are far from a nigga

Ignorance is not what you are
Or were
But now, Shit nigga
Stay high
Stay posted on street corners
Provide me with that high
That fucks me up

....

This poem speaks to some of the tricky politics of representation. It is an undeniably powerful poem, as was Danielle's performance, and was recognized as such by the very high scores it was given by a mixed panel of judges. But it is filled with expletives (five "shits" and two "fucks," which Tim refers to as the "F-bomb"). "Stay High" was the final product of a creative negotiation between the student and Tim, who advises his students to use all "precious pieces of language" with thought and care and not to "cast pearls among swine" by overusing expletives to create sensation rather than meaning. Tim did not want to censor the poem but recommended editing what started out as 14 "F-bombs." And what "Stay High" conveys is both the language of the streets, the speaker's anger, and the urgency of the message. In the four years of slam poems, most of the expletives were used thoughtfully and with impact, as in the line "I wish I was rich, cause living in poverty in America's a bitch," as well as in Kurt's "cause I said to/my mom they would fit/shit."

Race shaped the entire project in very interesting ways, given that predominantly black groups of students (the AP class was the exception) were exploring Hip-Hop and "spoken word" with a white teacher, a white university professor, and a black poet. The contrast between the two classes the first year—one mostly black and all male, the other mostly white and co-ed—brought to the fore some of the usual racial dynamics of the school, and then overturned the usual order of things. The very top academic students in the grade that year were mostly white, and many of them were creative writing majors in the Advanced Poetry class who tended to receive all of the school's literary awards. The boys' class was a less academically successful group with only two creative writing majors—many of the others were majoring in theatre tech. The first year of the project was a particularly surprising one on a number of levels. While one of the creative writing majors from the AP class won the slam, he was black with a strong Hip-Hop style. And many of the students from the boys' class wowed the audience with their work. Two of the strongest students in the school in the AP class spoke of how much they learned from and about the poets in the boys' class who performed. One young white woman, Laura, explained to Bronwen that while she had not "made an effort to get to know the students in the boys' class" (for she hadn't been in their classes and had few friends who were boys) she was very impressed by the way they "expressed emotions and social ideas." Bronwen asked Laura if she noted any patterns of difference between the poems performed by both classes, and she responded that the black students "tend to have a better cultural awareness from being on the other side of the whole dominant culture," giving Gerard's poem as an example:

> his poem, the one about the tears, crying, and he addressed a whole slough of issues
> on racism on different counts, racism against Arabs, and racism against black people,
> and gender issues and all sorts of things. That just the way he talked about this, what
> he knew and his experience of those things. To some degree all of us have known
> some of that because we're all in this school together, but I think that the black
> students understand better.

Laura also speculated that an experience of marginalization meant that many of the black students spoke "straight from the heart" and she pointed to the ways their poetry became powerful through "the type of language, the slang, the kind of the grittiness of the language or the bam bam bam." One of the white students remarked on these differences during the slam performance when he introduced his love poem by saying: "I'm sorry if I'm not angry." This comment can be read as an attempt at minimizing the impact of the black poets' words, or as a recognition, like Laura's, of the very different experiences faced by students who grow up marginalized by white privilege. But these comments also make clear that slam poetry is an inclusive genre that can accommodate different poetic styles; while it is ideally suited for hard-hitting expressions of social critique, it also makes room for more introspective self-analysis.

In contrast with the number of poems which engaged current social problems, only 4 of the 46 slam poems spoke primarily about love, while 2 spoke about friendship. This challenges the common portrait of youth as mostly preoccupied with their romantic relationships and friendships. Why did so many of the students choose to tackle social problems? The spoken word poems such as Saul Williams' which were explored in class might have in part inspired and provoked students to be so socially aware in their pieces. However, Rashidah conducts performance poetry workshops with children and youth around the city and regardless of what they read or watch together finds that her students want to address weighty social issues in their poems. While people tend to think she asks this of them, instead Rashidah feels that her students "just go there, unprompted." That the students frequently choose to tackle important topics in the poetry slam suggests that they crave a venue and permission to take a stand on social issues, in their own language. Or in the words of a male in the AP class, "I think everyone was saying things that needed to be said, but didn't know how to put them, but once everyone said them they were said so eloquently it was amazing." Another pointed out: "racism, terrorism, image, society, love—you can tell exactly what runs through our minds every day." In the boys' class, Carlos put out a call towards the beginning of the project for the group to be as thoughtful as possible:

> cause we think about a lot of things they don't know we think about, you know what I'm saying. We write a lot of things they don't know we write about. So we care about issues they don't know we care about. If we show them that we care about these issues and we learn about these things and we can do it in this creative way of language...with our poetry what I want us to do—me personally—is to have them leave the theatre thinking like damn those are some talented young men and women you know what I'm saying like damn—they got things to say—know something else...that's the future of all of us—we're the future and they got to know that...the things we have to say even though we might say it in a different way, that shit is important.

Carlos' appeal was heard; given the space to share what they think and write and care about, in their own creative language, the students treated their classmates and slam audience with their intelligence, wit, insight, honesty, and emotion. Carlos' comments also speak to our argument that youth are particularly interested in tackling serious issues when "they" are listening, a reference in this context to adults in general and teachers and administrators in particular. This makes a case for the importance of youth writing in schools, for despite many of the students' frustrations with high school (expressed in class conversations and in some of their poems), the committed nature and seriousness of the performances at the slam suggest that these youth still see schools as places where one works to be as smart as possible in the presence of peers but also of adults. Their awareness of an adult audience was made particularly clear in one piece in year three of the project, which began, "All administrators you might want to have a seat with this one" and then proceeded to critique many aspects of the school's bureaucracy and regulations, including what was seen as "learning in city schools." Another powerful local critique was of the city school district's budget crisis and the decisions being made to cut arts and sports program, all within the context of the testing and standardization of No Child Left Behind. Sample lines are:

> ....
> We, and by we I mean we who are coming of age, need to tell the world
> What's what. That we don't give a fuck about color, gay, straight or bi, all
> You need to do is give us the material for wings and we can make ourselves
> fly.
> So don't cut the arts, cause we need to learn to express, don't cut sport
> because without sport we're a mess, the answer here is to spend more
> money on learning, and less money on tests

Learning from Slam

There are a number of elements which contribute to the course's ongoing success. First of all, Tim is a very experienced and talented creative writing teacher who has been working as an English teacher in the city school district for over 20 years, and for the last ten as a creative writing teacher in an arts-magnet school. He is passionate about teaching and writing, and is a published haiku poet. He draws upon many of his creative writing teaching skills such as the freewrite and response prompts discussed above. In interviews, his students shared their awareness that Tim is genuinely curious about them, and willing to learn from them about their lives and culture. He asks them lots of questions and is a careful listener. In illustration of this, Tim proposed co-developing the performance poetry course to Bronwen, feeling that his lack of knowledge about Hip-Hop presented a missed opportunity to engage his students. Tim's students also say that they feel that he is himself with them and shares easily of that self through his storytelling. He is willing to relinquish the role of authority and reject traditional school power dynamics. The students feel that, unlike many of their teachers, Tim isn't on a "power trip" and that he doesn't judge. All of these things help Tim cultivate a lower-risk classroom environment for writing and creativity more generally.

The partnership with Rashidah has also been a key factor in the course's success. She was invited into the course the first year through a local artists-in-residence program so that the students could work with an experienced performance poet; she connected and worked so well with them, injecting a real professionalism and dynamism into the course, that she is now an integral piece of the school's performance poetry program. Rashidah is especially good at helping the students think about the elements of performance and at workshopping their poems. Tim described her as "tremendously talented, a wonderful teacher" who had the "respect and admiration of the kids." She shares the trials and rewards of her own creative writing processes, performing polished works as well as works in progress in class. As some of the students explained in reflections about the course, Rashidah is "poetry." Aside from Rashidah's particular talents, her role in the course speaks to the importance of bringing professional poets into the classroom as resources for teachers who are not usually spoken word poets so that the students have a strong sense that performance poetry lives in the community as well as the school.

Finally, we argue that the slam genre itself is key to the course. Rogoff (2003) explains how our thinking is shaped by the cultural tools we work with. As discussed earlier, slam poetry—vernacular, urban, often politicized, playful, sexy—opens up certain possibilities for thinking, and for trying on new modes of expression and being. Students described some reasons slam poetry seemed like the right vehicle for self-expression and exploration: for one student it is "written and read in the author's own voice" and for another it has "more emotions in it, more of the writer inside the piece." Laura explained that while poetry can seem elitest or pretentious to people, slam doesn't. And central to slam is the fact that it is a competitive performance which brings together the poets and audience into a community of shared engagement in the works. As Laura put it, central to slam's power is "the way the audience reacts to the poetry slam. It's amazing, gave me chills almost as much as the poetry slam itself, but I think it's just that everybody's going to give them a shot, and you get all different types of people who are going to give it a try, and people are funny, and people talk about things that affect everybody." The audience invests in the poems and the poets in vocal and visceral ways, yelling, clapping, stomping feet, laughing, even dancing in order to express disagreement or support for the judges' scores. That said, the competition is one of the contradictions that slam impresario Bob Holman (1994) argues are central to slam's dynamism: just as the audiences tend to be both heckling and attentive, playful as well as very serious, the competition is both important enough to fight about and so insignificant that in his "Slam Invocation," Holman proclaims that "the best poet always loses" (p. 1).

A cultural studies approach to literacy takes youth culture seriously as a resource of creative, provocative literate practices. Given that adolescents might be saying what they have to say in a "different way," the challenge for educators becomes learning how to listen differently. The language arts unit "leveraged" (Hull & Shultz, 2001) the youths' out-of-school rap and freestyle literacies and "extended" such literacies: the students who were accomplished rappers and freestylers experimented with performance poetry, written in advance and performed without musical accompaniment. Experienced creative writers placed greater emphasis on the performance of their works. Some familiar practices were made strange, worthy of analysis; others were situated within the historical and contemporary context of spoken word culture. And given the students' expressions of surprise, not only were the teachers and administrators shown that "we think about a lot of things they don't know we think about" but so were the "talented men and women" in question. The surprise factor speaks to the way "business as usual" in the school was interrupted by the spoken word course. The students were often in the position of knowing more than the teacher. The teacher was collaborating extensively with a local spoken word teaching artist and a university professor, and a range of poets visited the classroom over the course of the project. The school's usual hierarchies of academic achievement were destabilized for none of the winning slam poets were the top students or thought of as the "best" creative writers in the grade. Part of this interruption of the order of things was racial, for in this majority black school, a disproportionate number of the highest achieving students are white; in the poetry slam, the poetic and performative talents of many of the black and Latino students came to the fore and were respected by teachers and peers. In particular, the slams value a poetry of the margins: as Laura described, the cultural insights and hard-hitting social critique of many of the black and Latino students' poems, as well as the powerful, gritty, language and "bam bam" delivery, were what moved and impressed audiences most.

Students in all of the classes practiced important literacy skills as they wrote and performed poems in order to grab the attention of and engage audiences. Many of the poems built and sustained arguments using appeals to logic, humor, and emotion. Some spoke to multiple audiences, hoping to speak to their peers while trying not to alienate the older generations in the crowd. Students had to draw upon all of their expressive instruments—their minds, words, voices, eyes, hands, bodies—and practice the elements of oral performance, including tone, pacing, modulation, and volume. As a result, the course asks us to rethink how even longstanding literacy topics like audience and purpose in writing might be taught. It also asks us to open up what gets valued in school by emphasizing that popular cultural forms like rap music are central to the evolution of culture and communication. At another level, the spoken word curriculum encourages the development of a community of learners who are genuinely invested in each other's work because it makes clear that writing is something to care deeply about. It is a place for exploring what matters most: figuring ourselves out, sharing our worries about the world, getting angry, telling stories, making each other think, laugh, and feel. In this place of exploration, notions of therapy or of healing aren't to be dismissed but instead are integral to the growth of individuals, classrooms, and larger communities. Ultimately, these concerns need to be seen as integral to learning rather than as separate from or counter to it.

Jamming the Signal: Rap Music and the Poetics of Technology

Bronwen E. Low

Following in the well-tread footsteps of academic attention to Hip-Hop culture (e.g., Perry, 2004; Rose, 1994; Sharpley-Whiting, 2007), educators are increasingly theorizing and developing the curricular potential of Hip-Hop and rap music (Morrell & Duncan-Andrade, 2004; Scherpf, 2001). Key to this educational interest has been rap music's potential for better understanding and supporting adolescent literacy practices as well as for building bridges between youth skills and interests and the traditional curriculum, particularly in relation to African-American and other urban youth. Bronwen's spoken word curriculum was very much driven by the former commitment, while recent texts such as *Hip-Hop Poetry and the Classics for the Classroom* (2004) and *Flocabulary: The Hip-Hop Approach to SAT-level Vocabulary Building* (2006) are good examples of the latter. Hip-Hop culture has facilitated an outpouring of cultural production and self-expression by youth traditionally denied a voice in the mainstream, both for the few who become professional rappers and DJs, and for the many others who write and freestyle for themselves and their peers. To echo Asheena McNeil's comments made in chapter 6, rap has made being a poet cool.

Given the emphasis on word-work in rap music, it is not surprising that most of the academic and educational attention to rap has been to its lyrics. But the lyrics are brought to life through performance and are enmeshed in an often dense soundscape or "web of sound" (Toop, 1991, p. 179) produced through technology. In this chapter we take up another dimension of how youth write themselves and their worlds through Hip-Hop culture; we investigate the ways rap music's sound and sense is embedded in contemporary technologies of sound production. This chapter further challenges any fixed distinctions between form and content by asking questions about how and what rap's "technologized" form means, and what it can tell us about the youth who listen to and create it. Engagements with youth writing in the new media age require multimodal reading practices that bring together sound, text, and image; as this chapter will demonstrate, we also need to consider others ways in which meaning is made which go beyond traditional conceptions of sound, text, and image.

Rap music's relationship with technology is, to some extent, paradoxical. Rap stems predominantly from the African-American and Latino communities in the U.S. devastated by the post-Fordist shift away from industrialized manufacturing towards, in part, economies based in new information technologies. And as African-American science-fiction writer Samuel Delany has argued, in an interview with Mark Dery (1994), urban youth are typically positioned as consumers rather than producers of high-tech culture; while they have some access to products such as pagers and cell phones, they are systematically excluded from "access to the formation of those commodities" (p. 193). However, within Hip-Hop culture, rap DJs and producers have seized control of some of the information and communication technologies that participated in the marginalizing of the urban working classes: they have taken technologies, in this instance of sound production, and reworked them into tools better able to express their experiences. Rap music's sound is forged through this reworking and embodies a kind of technologized aesthetic which we are thinking about, in light of the discussion in "Slammin' School," as a *poetics* of technology. We explore this aesthetic in terms of Williams' (1977) theory of the cultural co-existence of residual and emergent forms, drawing here upon Ong's (1982) notion of secondary orality to make sense of the way rap marries, and places in tension, oral traditions with new technologies. This chapter's method is very much informed by the interdisciplinary impetus of cultural studies in that it turns to post-colonial theory, the work of James Joyce, and contemporary and late 1980s rap music in order to argue that rap's sound needs to be read, in part, as an intervention into contemporary culture and communications. The first half of the chapter focuses on the contexts and processes of production and the second offers some close textual analyses of rap tracks, both in the interest of better understanding the lived cultures of Hip-Hop identified youth.

Jamming the Signal

In order to begin thinking about technology and the audio aesthetics of intervention, we first turn to a different time and place. Frantz Fanon (1965) in A *Dying Colonialism* offers a description of a communication technology reinvented in the context of anti-colonial warfare which yields insight into technology as something lived, like language. He writes that prior to the wars of liberation in North Africa, the bulk of the Algerian population rejected radio technology and the French broadcast *Radio Alger*; these were considered to be tools and symbols of colonization, and part of the closed, privileged "world of signs" (p. 73) of the French settlers. During the course of the Algerian war for independence, however, the radio became a central instrument of organized resistance: since reports of the front-line fight of the Algerian resistance were actively censored and distorted by the *Radio Alger* and French-controlled newspapers, the *Front de Libération Nationale* took control of the airwaves through a pirated radio channel, entitled *The Voice of Free Algeria*, in order to inform the people about the daily progress of the resistance. But the French services successfully "jammed" these pirated airwaves, which meant that the broadcasts were usually disrupted, often inaudible, switching repeatedly from one broadcast wavelength to the next. The listeners therefore had to reconstruct, collectively, the information gleaned from the fragments of the *Voice*. This jamming and, consequently, the indeterminate quality of the broadcast messages served ironically to strengthen the listeners' engagement with the liberation struggle by creating the need for a heuristic community which pieced together the information—a collectivity dedicated to debates around the meaning of the battles and of the war. As a result, the Algerian masses were able to insert themselves as participants in the struggle against the French. Fanon describes a scene that illustrates the symbolic power of the broadcasts:

> At the end of the evening, not hearing the *Voice*, the listener would sometimes leave the needle on a jammed wave-length or one that simply produced static, and would announce that the voice of the combatants was here. For an hour the room would be filled with the piercing, excruciating din of the jamming. Behind each modulation, each active crackling, the Algerian would imagine not only words, but concrete battles. The war of the sound waves, in the *gourbi*, re-enacts for the benefit of the citizen the armed clash of his people and colonialism. (p. 88)

Static called attention to the active jamming of the French occupying forces, of the struggle over representation, which was central to the fight for liberation. The Algerians imagined its "piercing, excruciating din" as the re-enactment of the war for liberation within a context in which the key signifier at stake is independence. Static is the sound of the broadcast waves without a signal; a static which *means*, which is read into, takes to the extreme theories of language as absence-in-presence, as difference.

This scene might seem far removed from any discussion of rap music. And yet, while rap's representational strategies and politics take place within a different time, place, and sets of stakes than do those of *The Voice of Free Algeria*, they also involve technologies that are revalued and transfigured within new contexts of use and need by those alienated from and, arguably, colonized by centers of dominant power. And rap's aesthetic shares much with the jammed airwave and static of the symbolic text described here. One of its principle components, the scratch, is the jarring sound of the mistake, of the needle scratching the record. Like static it is a sign of the derailment of the signal, and reminds the listener of the chance quality of the "successful" communication. The scratch also marks the presence of the music's technological production as part of the rap text, just as the static and jamming become central aspects of the text of the *Voice*. As well, rap's frenetic layering of samples, its fragmented movement between one sound clip or byte to the next, is very much the sound of the jammed signal, of the competing interests at work in the war of meaning in a beleaguered field of signs. And the interruptions in rap's sound give it a pirate radio quality, evoking both rap music's illicit origins in the Bronx where DJs like Kool Herc would use public electricity sources to power turntables and speakers and the "underground" status of many politicized rap artists who are rarely played on commercial radio stations. The jam, static, scratches, fragment, and sample—these exist at the intersection of technology and language, and foreground the fragility and embattled nature of information in the communications age.

In "Slammin' School" we defined poetics as making language strange and new, emphasizing the way users intervene into and act upon language, shaping the medium through experiments with it. This concept gets expanded here in relation to sound technologies, which work like language to communicate and which Hip-Hop producers and DJs also make strange and new. We propose that rap music's intentional misuses of the technologies of sound production can be read as poetic ways of acting upon contemporary techno-culture, of flaunting the rules and claiming the space of telecommunications as creative and productive for those who have been marginalized by it.

Rap and the Poetics of Imperfection

Rap's intense, multilayered sound is the product of DJs' unorthodox experiments with the technologies of sound production, what Delany calls, in reference to Hip-Hop youth culture, "a specific mis-use and conscientious desecration of the artifacts of technology and the entertainment media" (Dery, 1994, p. 193). Rap DJs and producers have made their mark on a number of technologies, transforming and reinventing them as users testing and stretching the equipment's capabilities: these technologies include the turntable, synthesizer, drum machine, and sampler. For instance, early rap DJs would link two turntables in order to play duplicate copies of the same record; this allowed them to isolate and then keep playing the "breakbeat" or best rhythm section of a song. And the "scratch" discussed above deliberately works against the turntable's forward movement. Rose (1994) explains how the drum machine was manipulated by DJs like Kurtis Blow in order to produce the lowest possible concentrate booming bass sound. And the sampler, which digitally reproduces any sound, was originally intended to mask the absence of a live instrument in the recording studio. This digital sound reproduction shaped classical and also popular music, as in the work of New Wave bands such as Ultravox who would use synthesizers to digitally sample the string section of an orchestra in order to sound exactly like that same string section. Rap producers "inverted" this logic by foregrounding the fragment, and also went against many of the central principles of music engineering by detuning the sampler and pushing sound meters into the distortion zone. Like the scratch, these techniques celebrate the sound of the mistake; this makes rap a self-consciously flawed and fallible art form.

Mudede (2000) has characterized rap as the apotheosis of the "aesthetics of imperfection," with a production language of error, of "dropping" or "kicking" the beat, of making it "ill" or "jamming" and "breaking" it. Mudede offers three categories of aesthetic "mistake" in Hip-Hop: rupture, the sudden stopping or stutter of the song; incidental noise, the clutter of sounds which periodically and nonsensically enter and exit the track; and wrecking, or the jumbled layers of scratches and sounds in rap. Technology used to create such effects brings to the foreground that which interrupts, interferes with, or modifies the transmission of a sound or a message. If it is human to err, then these uses of technology serve to humanize the machines that structure our environments. They also forecast the future: as Sobol (2002) notes, in the early 80s Hip-Hop DJs and producers were digitally sampling break beats and playing them back through a MIDI-controlled keyboard—predating the World Wide Web and personal computers, in effect "unearthing the cut-and-paste ethos latent in digital culture" (p. 122) before the fluorescence of digital culture.

In an interview with Mark Dery (1994), Rose examines some of the other ways Hip-Hop has reclaimed technology, such as the sound sampling from the 1970s electro-pop group Kraftwerk, and the borrowing of their robotic movement as part of break-dancing's vocabulary of movement—a symbol of African Americans "already having been robots" (p. 212) as the labor for the capitalist engine. The notion of a poetics of technology proposes that such uses of technology can represent interventions into the alienating force of technology in many peoples' lives.

The Sound of the Techno Present:
The Radio and *Finnegan's Wake*

What does it mean for rap's poetics of technology to be engagements with contemporary techno-culture? In a collection on the importance of twentieth-century acoustical technologies to modern literature, Connor (1997) reads Joyce's linguistic experiments, symbols, and structure in *Finnegans Wake* as active engagements with the "wondrous, often mysterious jumble of signal and noise" (p. 20) that characterized the early days of radio in the 1930s. Here the

> radio air was full of noises, wandering signals, high altitude skips, and super-heterodyne screeches, and anyone who listened to it had to gradually attune themselves to a cacophony of voices all speaking at once. (p. 18)

In one intrusion of these wandering signals in *Finnegans Wake*, a sermon weaves its way in and out of some of the novel's other narratives. Interrupting the sermon at one point are words that sound like a flood of static:

> Bothallchoractorschumminaroundgansumuminarumdrumstrumtruminahumptadum
> pwaultopoofoolooderamaunsturnup! (Joyce, cited in Connor, p. 22)

Connor writes that this line conjures the effect of what he classes as the two categories of "static": "generic radio interference, including words and unintelligible sounds" and "that hissing sibilant white noise, close to pure chaos, that is sometimes quiet enough to be ignored, sometimes loud enough to drown out everything else" (p. 20). Joyce's experiments not only mimic in writing the audio qualities of this particular sound field but also reflect the changing theory and experience of language wrought by this new technology: the utterance was understood as reproducible and expansive and so "lost its uniqueness, its singular place in time and space" (p. 20). It was also shown to be malleable, altered by electromagnetic forces along the course of its transmission. And the radio drew the listener's attention to language, and in particular to the sound of language, since it is what McLuhan (1994) calls a "hot medium" which extends only one of the senses: in this case, hearing. According to Connor (1997), these transformations meant "the spoken word was set into the world in an entirely different way" (p. 20). The new and strange status of speech on the radio undermined so-called realistic conventions of consistency and transparency in literary uses of language. Made clear was that words are worth our attention, for there is no saying where they might go and what they might do to us.

If we agree with McLuhan's (1994) claim that technologies have "psychic and social consequences" (p. 4) for they "extend" the self, then Joyce's exploration of the sound and language of the radio is also an engagement with the new social and subjective space the radio helps initiate. As Connor (1997) tells us of this historical moment, radio "changed the way people communicated, the way they lived, the way they thought, the way they conceived of the world, the way they occupied space and time" (p. 28). McLuhan's aphorism, "the medium is the message," advances the idea that these changes to the self and to social relations have as much (or more) to do with the form or structure of the message's delivery as with the content of the programming. McLuhan's thesis and the relationship between Joyce's textual innovations and the radio suggest that rap's relationship to contemporary acoustical technologies of production and distribution, but also to its technologized context in general, is an engagement with the evolving social world, with the new human and communicative relations which these technologies help usher in, reflect, or extend. This relationship in rap is very structural. Raps don't just talk about new sound and communication technologies (although I later explore technology as a theme in one rapper's lyrics), but are forged through them and bear the imprint of their invention. And while rap's technological, communicative context is not Joyce's, the parallels between rap's sound and Connor's description of the wondrous and mysterious jumble of the noise of 1930s radio are striking. This resemblance suggests that rap's aesthetic reflects in part the communication systems of its immediate context, but also some of the reconfiguration of space and time, language and sound, and relations between self and other enabled to a certain extent by 20th-century communication technologies. The rest of this chapter explores two rap albums in order to describe more specifically rap music as a poetics of technology. We first examine some of the work of one of the most influential rap crews in Hip-Hop history, Public Enemy. We then turn to a more contemporary album by a young Toronto female rapper, Michie Mee.

Public Enemy and the "Web of Sound"

One critic describes the impact of Public Enemy's (PE) first album *Yo! Bum Rush the Show* (1987) like this: "It was as though shakin' your ass wasn't enough—the music in some way needed to be analogous to the nervous rush of living in America's decaying urban centres" (Cross, 1993, p. 48). Producing this rush was a combination of "apocalyptic beats" (Cross, 1993, p. 55) and a new level of complexity in layering and sampling techniques. While the hard-hitting black nationalist lyrics contributed to the music's force, the intensity of Public Enemy's sound was also crucial to its effect. PE's sound is that of disruption, of catastrophe, of a war-time air raid. Take, for example, the opening track on *Fear of a Black Planet* (1990), "Contract on a World Love Jam." It begins with a scratch which grates, like fingernails on a chalkboard. It is followed by the opening chords, and then a flood of incidental noise

including honks, synthesized screams, electronic trills, and a wreck of sound
bites, including a couple which sound like they belong to Nelson Mandela and
Martin Luther King, Jr., while others are clips from radio DJs and their
listeners calling to weigh in on the controversies over Public Enemy's politics.
The final words are so electronically modified that the listener cannot tell
whether they are a computer's reproduction of human sound, or human
voices amplified by a computer: "word-or-ord!" and "rap-rap-rap."

Public Enemy's "web of sound" is, according to Cross (1993), "designed to
instruct, to awaken, to energise, to provide catharsis or just to speak" (p. 55).
Although Chuck D's powerful lyrics and "flow" have much to do with this
impact, so too do Public Enemy's soundscapes. Their force demonstrates what
Krims (2000) calls the "Hip-Hop sublime" which defies "conventionally
representable relationships" and "aural representability for Western musical
listeners" (p. 73). This layering serves to "defeat conceptual boundaries and
unifying descriptions" (p. 74), which Krims proposes might be why "rap
soundscapes sound menacing and aggressive, [even] apart from the lyrical
content" (p. 74). Krims' vocabulary for describing the MC's flow in "reality
rap," within which he classes Public Enemy, also suggests excess: while "old-
school" rap tended to have a more "sing-songy" flow (with
antecedent/consequent couplets and matching end-rhymes, like a limerick),
the flow of 90s reality rap is "effusive" and more complex, involving "multiple
rhymes in the same rhyme complex...internal rhymes, offbeat rhymes, multiple
syncopations and violations (i.e. overflows) of meter" (p. 49).

Rap, in its layering of samples, sound, and rhyme, is greater than the sum
of its parts, exceeding what can be heard and understood in its discrete
elements. It also exceeds what can be traced—for the web of its sound samples
is so intricate that all of them cannot be teased apart, which sets up an
interesting tension. Sampling creates what Rose (1994) has called a "cultural
literacy" (p. 89) whereby the rap producers and DJs pay tribute to their creative
predecessors and contemporaries by reproducing and recontextualizing
fragments of their work. The liner notes to PE's *Fear of a Black Planet* (1990)
convey both the importance in rap of honoring one's inspirations and
supports and of the volume of these figures: the group acknowledges hundreds
of individuals and groups, organized into categories such as the "New School
8," the "Popular 14," the "Hardcore 17," the "Hall of Fame 17," the "Sister
Squad #22," and even "Sports Brothers," including "Charles Oakley" and the
"New York Knicks," creating an explicit, self-conscious tradition and
community of artists and influences. This also distinguishes a community of
listeners familiar with the works being sampled from those people who are
not. At the same time, the intensity of the layering and the degree of electronic
modification of many of the samples makes it difficult to recognize all of the
sources (a pattern continued and greatly accentuated in much contemporary

rap), and in this way undoes notions of origin, and in turn, of ownership, since for years these samples did not entail copyright fees. An interesting moment in the refiguring of origin is Public Enemy's 1988 album *It Takes a Nation of Millions to Hold Us Back*, which included war chants sampled from their first album and thus "confused the categorical status not only of PE but also the historical material" (Cross, 1993, p. 51).

Public Enemy's sample-rich sound also does something to language. Through processes such as the stretching and modification of a word so that it becomes one of a multitude of sounds, Public Enemy frees language from the rigid demands of communicative intelligibility in favor of the play of signification. The processes of electronic repetition, sampling, cutting, splicing, and mixing made possible by technology call attention to the multiple significances of words, and therefore to the intricacies of verbal connotation and nuance; the dramatic recontextualization provided by sampling brings to the fore the demands and consequences of context on meaning-making. By radically decontextualizing and manipulating language, these technologies denaturalize it and thus reveal how it works: they expose the scaffolding of previously taken-for-granted structures of communication. They also open the field of possibilities for language's reinvention.

The multiplicity of verbal meaning is, in theory, at odds with the logic of digital culture. As Perloff (1991) argues, digital space, with "its word-processing programs, its laser printers, modems, and FAX machines," celebrates invariance, for "the right input invariably produces the right output" (p. 188) through binaries such as On/Off, 1/0, Yes/No. In its emphasis on accuracy, digital culture suppresses what information theory calls "noise," which Perloff defines as "whatever modifies the message, whatever references becomes relevant, in the course of its transmission" (p. 188). What is potentially lost in the time of the computer, in other words, is "connotation, nuance, context" (Perloff, p. 187). A "poetics of artifice" has developed in response to this potential loss, for poetry intrinsically rejects the efficient transmission of facts, the input and output of information, and explores and exploits instead this "noisiness" of language and communication. Poetry aims to "'reveal' that which falls, so to speak, between the control-key cracks" (Perloff, p. 189) for it is "that which can violate the system, which refuses the formula, and the binary opposition between 1 and 2." Poetry is here imagined as the antidote to the communicative sterility and rigid control codes that have accompanied technocratic visions of the digital era.

The poetics of technology explored here expose the vision of quiet digital accuracy as a myth of technological process, suggesting instead that the information age is a very noisy one with its fluorescence of communicative media in which people are addressed, invited, enticed, and coerced in a historically unsurpassed diversity and volume of forms—this terrain is by nature a battlefield of competing voices and interests which combine, overlap, overpower, work in juxtaposition, and sometimes confuse, but which also offer multiple possibilities for making and exchanging meaning. In the poetics of technology, the terrain of contemporary communications is a source, rather than a foil, of creativity.

As in "Contract on a World Love Jam," in which words are used as raw audio materials, the message transmitted in rap music is often non-literal or semantic, its rhetorical force linked instead to tonal creations of a mood or feeling. The music video, in which lyrics and images are rarely in a literal relationship, might be the paradigm for this non-literal ethos. Neither word nor image helps to explain the other, unlike traditional book illustrations. The two texts exist in relation, most obviously because the recording artists are in most music videos, but the nature of that relation can be hard to determine: the video offers an additional field of signs open for interpretation rather than an explanatory one. This might be a technologized extension of the emphasis on indirection that has been said to be a characteristic of many oral cultures. Sobol (2002) writes of the strategies of circumlocution that:

> The power of the indirect statement lies in forcing the listener to do his or her own work, to actively make the connections between tangentially connected images and ideas. And it works, because the collision of ideas in one's own brain will always be more stimulating, and therefore more accessible, than information that requires little inner assembly. (p. 8)

That ideas are made more stimulating and accessible through the struggle over them recalls Fanon's (1965) description of the interpretive and political community in Algeria created around the white noise of the FLN radio broadcasts. And the particularly affective combination of stimulation and accessibility might explain the popularity of indirection among the producers and directors of music videos, which act as marketing devices for the song, album, and musical group, as well as the trend towards indirection in advertising.

The emphasis on the semantic value of sound in rap, sometimes indifferent to dictionary denotation, is a trait the Hip-Hop Nation Language (Alim, 2004) of rap shares with predominantly oral traditions, and in particular with African-American English, which Smitherman (1998) calls "tonal semantics," in which words are chosen for their sound effects. And yet rap's orality is not traditional; as critics such as Rose and Sobol have proposed, rap needs to be read in light of Ong's notion of secondary orality, "in which a new orality is sustained by telephone, radio, television, and other electronic devices that depend for their existence and functioning on writing and print" (Ong, 1982, p. 11). Secondary orality carries with it many of the traits of primary orality, such as an emphasis on immediacy, a concentration on the present, and the use of formulas. The style is often spontaneous and casual; however, this is a self-conscious, cultivated spontaneity and informality. Secondary orality can also foster a "participatory mystique" and sense of community, but this audience is now McLuhan's (1994) "global village."

Rap's secondary orality is shaped by both traditional and new modes of communication, a good example of William's (1977) theory of cultural co-existence. Public Enemy include transcriptions of their songs in their liner notes, unlike many rap artists, and what is immediately apparent is how inadequate the written versions of the songs are. Not only are their beats integral to the impact of the lyrics, but even the vocal component cannot be fully recorded in print. The layered samples and improvised conversations, which envelop the lyrics, cannot be confined to a written record. These textual records, like those of other oral storytelling traditions, are pale shadows of the originals. And yet while the intertextual sampling of rap suggests the collective creation of the oral tradition, the individual rap auteur is also very important; in this way rap "fuses literate concepts of authorship with orally based constructions of thought, expression, and performance" (Rose, 1994, p. 87). As well, raps are shaped by African-American oral traditions like verbal toasting and signifying, but use complex rhyme schemes that have been written down and memorized (p. 87). Cross (1993) helps explain the co-existence of the oral and written modes of expression in rap in his discussion of the differences between freestyle and formatted rap. The former "is created improvisationally to the beat; breath control, intonation, iambic pentameter and tuning are the definitive characteristics. The freestyler often makes conceptual (narrative) leaps" (p. 61). Freestyle rap's free associations revel in word play, and have links with the jazz vocal practice of "scatting." A formatted rap, on the other hand, "is one that is written, while listening to the beat, but the primary space of the creative process is the steno pad as opposed to the freestyle session" (Cross, p. 64). Rap albums usually include both the formatted raps in the body of the album and freestyle improvisations, which can act as openings to the album or individual songs and which can stand as their own separate tracks labelled as freestyle interludes. The ability to freestyle remains a crucial measure of an MC's prowess.

Central to Rose's (1994) use of Ong's concept of secondary orality is the role technology plays in rap, for rap "simultaneously makes technology oral and technologises orality" (p. 86). Examples of the technologising of orality are samples from "Contract on a World Love Jam" that sound both human and electronic to the extent that the division between the human and non-human is blurred. Also queried are the distinctions between the oral tradition and the technologised present, for although the role of performance in rap signals the oral tradition, rap's reliance on electronically produced sounds by drum machines and sampling technologies does away with the need for live musicians in the recording studio or on stage. These same digital sampling technologies keep African-American oral traditions alive and current as young rap artists cut and mix fragments from the past. As noted, this sampling itself blurs the divide between the past and the present. And despite the emphasis on longstanding oral histories, rap both relies on and transforms what Lipsitz (1994) has called some of the "newest creations of electronic, digital, fiber-optic and computer-chip mass-media technology" (p. 20).

Elsewhere Bronwen (2001) has proposed that rap's growing and ever-evolving vocabulary, shaping the idiom of contemporary youth culture and, by extension, culture more generally, speeds up processes of linguistic renewal. The accelerated pace of change of rap idiom mirrors the fast-forward evolution of Hip-Hop culture more generally, in part the result of the music industry's promotion of the new, the hot, the latest to its mostly young consumers. But the pace also reflects the multimedia accessibility of this culture, whose high-speed circuits of production, distribution, and influence include Hip-Hop magazines, music videos, numerous films featuring rap artists and Hip-Hop culture, Internet Web sites, and chat rooms. The volume of media attention, even when negative, brings the latest rap language into homes across the world. Rap's use of sophisticated digital technology also means that its producers and receivers can participate in a growing international discourse community in which innovations and material are traded and shared: for example, a rapper from South Africa might download over the Internet the latest rhythm tracks from Jamaica or sample some of the lyrics from a rap out of Atlanta, Georgia, or Toronto, Canada, resulting in the creation of a growing international discourse community of Hip-Hop.

Within the secondary orality of this technologically driven reinvention of language, the written and spoken word exist in a mutually informing relationship. For instance, the Internet has opened up new possibilities for the oral freestyle competition; there are Web sites devoted to freestyling where beginning and experienced rappers can "battle" one another, either in a series of postings without time restrictions or "live," improvising rhyming lyrics as fast as their fingers can type them. (See, for example, http://brickcity.net/default.asp) While some sites offer audio files, others rely on text only. In these, and particularly in the real-time battles, competitors invent new spellings, new words, and new abbreviations for words in a medium somewhere in between instant messaging and street-corner battling, both of which value improvised word-work "on the fly."

The transcriptions of lyrics in rap liner notes often envision a dynamic relationship between oral and written language forms which is not hampered by the demands of standardization. The liner notes for Toronto rapper Kardinall Offishall's 2001 album *Quest for Fire: Firestarter volume 1* are an example of this. The album, and in particular its signature track "Bakardi

Slang," carves out a distinct linguistic space and thus identity for the Toronto (or T-dot) Hip-Hop scene. Some of the raps are transcribed in the notes, which means that Kardi and producers not only describe the oral lexical forms of T-dot talk but also begin their unofficial orthography. Spelling choices seem to depend less on a notion of linguistic correctness than of rhetorical value. For example, in "Quest for Fire IV," the word dismissing is written "diss-missing," which evokes the put-down of the "diss," which is itself a "misspelling" of the prefix in disrespect. Here and in another track, "MIC T.H.U.G.S.," the rapper plays on the expression "to diss," a short form of the word "disrespect," which gets a lot of airtime in rap and youth talk more widely. Kardi explores the multiple significances of the prefix "dis" in a lyrical wordplay that includes the following lines (the lyrics to this track are not written down in the CD's liner notes, and so they were transcribed, using line breaks to designate pauses):

> a dissing for a dis for dis half /a dissing discrepancies/ I dismiss your dissidence and doubt your intelligence/ In disgust I disjoint/ your disk from the dispatcher/ disenthrall all of y'all from shit that's whack....

This passage acts at one level as a lesson on the uses of prefixes, which when placed at the beginning of a word qualify or adjust its meaning, as in disrespect, disjoint, or disenthrall, in which "dis" denotes the negation or reversal of an action or state. However, "dis" is not always a prefix, as in "disk" in which it is merely a three-letter syllable. And this word play at least partly evokes the use of "di" and "dis" as demonstrative pronoun in Caribbean creoles. In this passage, multilayered linguistic inquiry meets aesthetic force: the repetition of "dis" gives this string of phrases the rhythmic power that is so central to rap's lyrics. As in poetry and music, and rap is both, the phonetic element is crucial to how and what words mean: the "dis" is a hard sound, and underlines the rapper's rejection or "dissing" of the other microphone thugs. Such experiments ask us to reconsider what orality looks like on paper and what written words sound like. They suggest that both modes of expression are in a period of radical transformation, outcome unknown. And as noted above, rap's oral and written texts also co-exist with the image of the music video in a dynamic, often elliptical, relationship that tests the bounds of all three modes of expression. Their combination reflects the increasing complexity of reading and writing practices in the era of the Web, other hypertext environments, and the emergence of multimedia "characterized by the integration of different media and by its interactive potential" (Castells, 1996, p. 364) and which foreshadow the end of "the separation, and even the distinction, between audiovisual media and printed media, popular culture and learned culture..." (p. 372).

Michie Mee and the Poetics of Identity

Michie Mee is well known in Canadian Hip-Hop circles as the first Canadian rapper to get signed by a U.S. record company, First Priority/Atlantic, to produce her first album, Jamaican Funk, Canadian Style (1991). Her second album, *The First Cut is the Deepest* (2001), announces her determination to succeed despite the setbacks to her career in recent years—it took her 9 years to record a second album, a process fraught with problems including a studio which lost her DAT. Mee raps about the challenges she faces: as a performer in the racialised national context of a still nascent Canadian Hip-Hop scene ("400,000 blacks across the nation and still no radio station"—a situation changed in February 2001, with the licensing in Toronto of 93.5 FM "The Flow"); as a woman in a male-dominated industry; as a single mother; as a black woman; and as young Jamaican-Canadian faced with family expectations. In lines such "If a woman writes a love song it's about a man's mistakes/If a man writes one it's about the woman he mind rapes," Mee speaks up about double standards and injustice. At the same time, she rejects the position of passive injured party: of her role in the music industry, she proclaims, "I'm defending my ends/business never personal/what's a game if nobody wins?" In the best-known track on the album, the remake of her 12" single "Don't Wanna be Your Slave," Michie Mee states her position clearly: "I'm not gonna cry victim, I'm not gonna blame the system,/but I'm not gonna be your slave." She distances herself from a discourse of victimization, which Farred (2000) has described as one of the complications of identity politics and of "making public the oppressed self [which] rests as much upon the rejection of the pejorative identity as it does upon embracing some version of it" (p. 641). Instead, she emphasizes her power to resist confining discourses and identities, and in the process reveals an implicit theory of language and subjectivity.

A series of skits act as comic interludes between tracks on Michie Mee's album. Three are from Mee's answering machine, messages left by two male Jamaican supposed relatives, but all performed by Chris Rouse (according to the liner notes). In the first of these the "relative" leaves a message, in a strong Jamaican accent, saying that he has heard "Michelle" is putting out an "alblum" and hopes that as a family member, his picture will be in it. Teeth-sucking "Uncle Nigel" wants Mee to send him a copy of her CD on vinyl; he later calls back and reprimands her for ignoring him ("I don' like dis a-tall!"). These impersonations signal that the interludes are a place of role play and performance, despite the authenticity conveyed by the premise of the answering machine. However, there are two other messages from another Caribbean-sounding elder on the album, inviting Mee to dinner and then reprimanding her for forgetting. These messages frame the track "your daughter," and so the listener might suspect these are from a real family member, but the speaker of these clips is not identified. There are no true or false messages on the album but instead a cacophony of voices that position the rapper inside a web of (sometimes unwanted) family commitments and ties. The idea of role play also emerges in an interlude featuring Mee in which her voice has been modified to sound like a robot's; she announces in space-heroine fashion: "I must go now, my mission here is complete."

Impersonation returns as a theme in an interlude entitled "fakin jamaican" which features someone in the recording studio yelling for the "sound bwoy" and Mee screaming in laughter in response: "turn the mikes off that imitation Jamaican" and "why's he doing that?" However, if this skit is taken in relation to the Chris Rouse pieces, the distinction between real and fake Jamaican does not seem to be a given. And like Kardinall Offishall, Mee moves between languages, sometimes singing in Jamaican Creole, as in "Cut off" and the track "fun surround Dem" in which she is accompanied by a Creole-speaking male chorus. Such tracks, and the interludes featuring pretend and true Jamaican, suggest that a fluid theory of language and identity is at work, for Mee is Canadian and Jamaican, and speaks Hip-Hop English, English, and Jamaican Creole; her work reflects these multiple identities and communicative competencies.

Michie Mee firmly situates her politics and theory of the self within the telecommunications age. The title phrase of one of the most forceful tracks on *The First Cut is the Deepest*, "Time is Now," invokes rapper Flavor Flav, from Public Enemy, and his insistence in the video for the track "Fight the Power" that "we know what time it is," signaled by the stopped alarm clock he wears pinned to his shirt. Lipsitz (1994) reads this symbol as a statement of PE's belief that "time has stopped, that progress is not being made, that the need for social change is so urgent that it obscures everything else about our time" (p. 17). In Michie Mee's invocation of this charge for change, the need for it and perhaps some of its tactics are located firmly within the communicative possibilities of the digitized "now." The lyrics on this track are layered over a "wreck" of beats and sounds. Mee yells out the title phrase over an aggressive, loud bass beat, accented by the higher tones of a snare drum. The beats sound explicitly electronic, as do other elements of the track, including the high-pitched synthesizer riff, which accompanies the rap and the drum beats, the vocal reverberations, which follow Mee's proclamation, and a changing soundscape of incidental noise, which includes a digitalised sound of something "bubbling over." The piece explicitly foregrounds its technology through sounds such as the distinct grating squeal, which signals that an Internet connection has been made through the phone line. This computerized shriek peals softly several times in the piece, thematically reinforcing the comments Mee makes about owning a domain name, her Web site address, and her desire for online "hits." It then resounds full force as the endnote of the track.

Contemporary communication technologies offer a means of resisting unwanted demands and oppressive roles. The track "I'll call you" is about phone calls no one ever answers. The speaker repeatedly ignores her ringing phone, or the loud knocks on the door, rejecting the hollow offer accompanying them of "housewife/nice life you're going to make it right." This track is filled with dizzying techno/disco dance sounds, including those of lasers, and is punctuated by the electronic beeps of a touch-tone phone dial. It ends with the repeated computerized phone announcement that "the party you wish to speak to does not want to take calls right now" and the loud dial tone signaling a one-way (and therefore unsuccessful) communication over the phone. The phone and its relationship to unwelcome, interrupted, and missed communications is a structuring device on the album as a whole, as in the clips of the answering machine messages from family members. That we never hear any responses to the messages suggests that though answering machines and new information technologies make people more accessible, they are also paradoxically less available for communicative exchange—I am less likely to answer the phone knowing that I have voice mail, and only try calling someone else once, knowing that I have already left a message. Mee here seems to both query technology's usefulness and mobilize its sounds and capabilities as resources for resistance and creative expression.

The poetics of technology, like those of language, suggest that the very imperfections or inadequacies of various media open up creative possibilities for those who have been marginalized by them as a result of the exclusions of "race," gender, culture, patterns of migration and economic development, and history. Noise, static, the distortion zone, and the missed message offer spaces in which symbolic forms and speaking subjects can be made and unmade in the quest for more comfortable places within which to speak and live. Not only has experimentation—with technology and language, but also video, art, movement, fashion, and forms of production and distribution—been central to the development and continuing vitality of Hip-Hop, but it might also be one of the skills demanded by new economies and cultural systems. Ulmer (1989) suggests that the synthesizer and its capacity for digitally encoding and then manipulating sound samples, which "leads to the invention of a new world of sounds and the musicalization of new areas of experience through abstract/imaginative synthesis," (p. 14) might be an apt metaphor for the processes of academic work, of thinking and research and writing, within the age of television and video. Ulmer places a priority on the "euretic" or inventive mode as a "productive human thrust into the unknown" required in an age in which "fixed forms—whether in metaphysics, art, poetics, cultural patterns, and so forth—are under attack" (LeFevre, cited in Ulmer, 1989, p.

16). These poetics also have implications for participation in the attention economy mentioned in chapter 1. Lankshear and Knobel (2002), drawing upon Goldhaber and Lanham, underline the salience of this concept of an economy, in which attention, rather than information, is the scarce commodity. One aspect of gaining attention is sheer inventiveness: "the attention economy is based on 'endless originality, or at least attempts at originality'" (Goldhaber, cited in Lankshear and Knobel, p. 23) rather than on things one or others have already done. The rule-breaking, rule-bending, innovation ethos of Hip-Hop therefore might have value outside of the subculture.

If schools are to prepare students with such premium knowledges, they will need to think of young people as creative producers rather than as passive recipients of information and skills. In a conversation on the Black Radical Congress listserv about Hip-Hop, one contributor has a proposal with implications for a very different sort of education in technological literacy, in which we "[r]eturn Hip-Hop to a culture of production, not consumption, by creating creative spaces where kids can dance, point, rhyme, and distribute their shit. This is where the computer comes in" (Black Radical Congress listserv, 2001, from www.blackradicalcongress.org/fight.html). An important implication of rap music's high-tech production for a revitalized notion of technological literacy is that this must take into account popular uses of technology, including the drum machines, digital samplers, and turntables used in the production of music. The importance of electronic music internationally, not only in the dance club scenes but also to genres such as multimedia art and film, means that such tech skills are central to contemporary cultural production. This new technological literacy should also draw upon other popular, largely out-of-school uses of technology such as the way young people mobilize MP3 players and cell phones in the making of identities, social relations, and connections to the world. We are also arguing in this discussion of the poetics of technology that while rap producers and creators are involved in technologically literate practices, so are rap audiences through their engagements. And these practices serve to humanize technology: they insist that technology is not just a tool we work but a medium which shapes and extends us, and that we need to claim ownership of this medium, taking possession so that we can work on it from the inside.

A commitment to exploring the poetics of technology is a commitment to better understanding the ways youth are reading and writing their worlds, making their mark on language and other communicative devices and relations inherited from previous generations. These poetics represent literate engagements, which foreground the importance of language as a place for the invention of identities and communities. But this commitment also assumes that the distinction between the popular and mainstream is fluid and transitional, and that popular and youth cultures are vital sites of understanding about cultural change. A notion of literacy able to encompass rap must take seriously the possibility that distinctions between orality and writing, minority/majority languages, as well as the local and the global, are being reconfigured by technologies of communication, distribution, and production that are building new and ever expanding discourse communities. This is a theory of literacy aware of the limits of its own knowledge about evolving communicative practices, and that is accompanied by a sense of wonder and curiosity about where these might take us.

CHAPTER 8

Educating Bono:
Cultural Studies in Media Education

Michael Hoechsmann

Right in the middle of a contradiction, isn't always a bad place to be.

—Bono (Lee, 2007)

As well as appealing to educators and others to take seriously the prospect of reading youth writing in and across new and traditional literacies, this book has identified the need for modes of pedagogical address that speak to the conditions of contemporary youth. Music and fashion play a central role in the lives of youth, and the manner in which associations and affinities are mobilized by young people is a form of cultural communication worthy of consideration. If youth are writing themselves through clothing and music choices, and reading one another in relation to these elements of their cultural lives, then we must consider popular culture practices as a type of cultural production, albeit not a schooled one. The term "popular culture" is a slippery one, too often used to refer to the artifacts and emissions of the media industries, the products rather than the practices. But popular means "of the people." We are constantly making and remaking our cultural selves, one popular step at a time. As John Fiske (1990/91) points out, a CD sitting on a shop shelf is just a media artifact; a group of people dancing to it are articulating their cultural selves. We use the term articulation in the manner suggested by Stuart Hall (1986): articulation refers both to utterance and making linkage, and in the latter sense articulating self- and group-identity in relation to a broader sense of culture. The metaphorical root of linkage comes from a British usage: the cab and the trailer of a lorry (truck) are articulated together. If we want our learners to articulate themselves in our classrooms, we need to learn more about what fuels their fires, what drives them and what troubles them. What counts and what is excluded as knowledge in school and other educational settings mirrors to some extent the patterns of legitimation and exclusion that take place in the culture at large (Bourdieu & Passeron, 1964). It is beyond the scope of this book to address the broad and multiple set of practices and processes that help to determine how school knowledge is selected, legitimated, and institutionalized. The point rather is to underscore the potential for media education and popular culture to modestly destabilize existing power relationships in the classroom, and to be a point of entry into discussions that engage matters relating to everyday life in the cultures youth inhabit.

A newly refreshed engagement in youth cultural production needs to consider some of the hows and whys of intervention, the ways in which educators can engage in a cultural politics of reading youth writing, or interpreting youth production, in these new times. In our chapters on slam and youth journalism, we have provided extended examples of educational projects that have worked to make a difference in the lives of young people. In the chapters on Web 2.0 and technologies in Hip-Hop, we analyzed informal learning contexts, where peer teaching and learning is subsumed into the activity at hand. In this chapter, we raise the question of media education as it is practiced in schools and argue that this teaching context provides a useful site for reading youth popular culture as a vehicle of youth communication. Recognizing youth taste cultures as a form of expression of self and group identity is vital to this stance. As evanescent as the tastes of youth cultures and subcultures are, a set of choices and distinctions is mobilized by young people in the act of media consumption. We have considered some of the innovative ways young people make distinctions in the new mediascapes in chapter 4, but we need to advance a praxis of media education that acknowledges youth identity performance in some of the most subtle manifestations of taste and engagement in the media. To follow Johnson's model of cultural studies full circle, from production through text and reception and back to everyday culture, what is enabled and released in cultural life is recuperated back into the next moment of cultural production and hence integrated into the evolving set of messages circulating to, from, and between youth. An analysis of a contemporary media phenomenon, and some of the media events surrounding it, helps to exemplify this feedback loop. We have drawn on the figure of Bono, the rock star with political ambition, to ask and answer some questions around youth authorship behind the scenes of popular culture, and the place and role of media education in developing a curriculum of engagement in youth issues and realities.

Reading Bono

> Philanthropy is like hippy music, holding hands. Red is more like punk rock, hip hop; this should feel like hard commerce.

—Bono (Weber, 2006)

So, what does a fabulously wealthy rock star, one who moonlights as a human rights activist in the global struggles to eradicate poverty and confront the HIV/AIDS pandemic, have to teach us about youth voice in an era of globalization? If we accept the premise that the media is a distorting mirror, one that reflects back to us attitudes and worldviews already circulating in our milieu, then the answer is a lot. One of the objectives of media literacy is to cultivate the critical abilities of students—or media consumers more generally—to analyze media texts and the cultural practices associated with them such as fandom, fashion, dance crazes, remixing (or bricolage), consumerism, culture jamming, etc. Picking apart Bono as a media phenomenon seems straightforward at first blush: he is either an opportunist sell-out, using his fans' social concerns to line his pockets, or he is the second coming, a rock star who really cares, a person who will sacrifice some of the trappings of his privilege to help others. Analyzing Bono as a media text might show a folksy, populist image (the broken-down hat, the blue jeans), mixed with a dash of Monaco chic (the ubiquitous coloured shades), a cross between hyperactive hippy and down-home star. The problem with essentializing Bono, however, of treating him as a fixed object of analysis, is that we lose sight of the forest for the trees. Bono, for the sake of argument here, is a fiction created by his fans. Bono represents us—our hopes, dreams, and fears. He is but a distorting mirror which reflects back to us many of the values and norms we take for granted. Reading Bono also means reading the social and cultural conditions of our times. Reading Bono—or Britney, Kanye West, Shakira—in the classroom allows us to read and open up a discussion about that other form of youth writing, the bricolage of identity texts mobilized by young people as fans of popular culture.

Presumably Bono looked into the mirror when he went shopping at the GAP with his good friend Oprah on October 13th, 2006. Painting the town red was given a new meaning when this famous pair went on a little spending spree to celebrate the launch of the Product Red campaign, a donations-from-profit campaign that siphons on average 40% of the profits from the sale of selected products (Weber, 2006) to the Global Fund, an organization that funds direct intervention projects that target the spread and treatment of HIV/AIDS, primarily in Africa. The Red campaign, co-chaired by junior-Kennedy Bobby Shriver, aims to channel the hyperconsumerism of the global North—where 'to buy is to be' in the circuits of identity formation and performative selves—into an economic force for front line health care in Africa. Says Bono:

> AIDS in Africa is an emergency, that's why we chose the color Red. When you buy a (PRODUCT) RED product, the company gives money to buy pills that will keep someone in Africa alive. The idea is simple, the products are sexy and people live instead of die. It's consumer power at work for those who have no power at all. (Cosmoworlds, 2006)

The concept is great, once one capitulates to the 'only game in town' theory of advanced capitalism, and the ideological baggage is breathtaking. Products are sexy, consumers are powerful, and corporations are magnanimous. In one beautiful flourish, Bono held up an Amex Red Card with the words "This card is designed to eliminate HIV in Africa" written on the back. "This is really sexy to me," Bono said. "It is sexy to want to change the world" ("Bono's Red Card to Aids," 2006). Sexy is the currency of the culture of consumerism, so there is presumably nothing out of place in equating a credit card with sexiness and it might be a welcome development to make social change on a global stage appear sexy. 'Bring it on,' we might want to say. And Bono is complying, even at some risk to his reputation if one of his corporate partners turns out to be next week's child labour scandal. He remarked that "with 6,500 people dying every day, it's worth a rock star ending up with a little bit of egg on his face" (Weber, 2006).

Bono is a walking contradiction, at once a merchant of cool, a self-interested capitalist, and simultaneously one of the world's most famous social justice activists. Bono has been in the news a lot in the last few years, not just for releasing platinum-selling, Grammy-winning *How to Dismantle an Atomic Bomb* (2004) and for leading U2 on the Vertigo tour, the second highest grossing tour in rock and roll history at $377 million, but also for his lobbying of world leaders before and after the G8, his involvement in the global network of rock concerts called Live 8, his co-award with Bill and Melinda Gates as *TIME* magazine's Person of the Year in 2005, and, incredibly, his nomination with Bob Geldof two years running for a Nobel Peace Prize. There is no precedent for Bono. A fair number of celebrities step off the stage or out from the silver screen to play small parts on the global stage such as taking on the role of UNICEF goodwill ambassadors, and occasionally a celebrity or group of celebrities plays a role in an unfolding drama, such as the British ska group The Specials did in releasing the anthemic "Free Nelson Mandela." But Bono, the freelancing, moonlighting rock star politico, who is equally at home hobnobbing world leaders at Davos and performing in front of audiences of thousands, has no peer.

There is no easy answer for the Bono effect, but it is of signal importance to recognize that there is a glimmer of hope presented in his massive popularity. At a time when it appears that young people in the global north are under the thrall of mass-mediated identity texts, we would like to make the claim that many youth are "buying in but not selling out." Wandering in the streets of Granada, Spain, in 2005, Michael was struck by the slogan "Bono for Pope" on a T-shirt. Googling it at home in Montreal, he found Bono for Pope on-line petitions and blogs. This playful intervention on another media event of 2005, the naming of a new Pope, has us thinking of the role of the media in shaping our cultural worlds, in articulating values and norms that circulate among us, even while distorting them along the way. What might appear on the surface as obvious—here is a rock star trading on his celebrity to make a more lasting, positive mark on the world—is not so when we scratch below to see what he tells us about the tenor of our times. We have to understand that Bono—the person, the rock star, the lobbyist and activist who exists in a material sense—is also a "stand-in," a body double for a set of values and norms that are circulating in our world.

Cultural Studies and Media Education

Media education provides teachers and learners the opportunity to engage in the study of contemporary social and cultural values and to situate the curriculum in a meaningful manner in the lived realities of the students. It is a realm of inquiry that treats contemporary forms and practices as historically situated and thus enables the study of resonant social and cultural matters faced by young people. It is at once consumption and production oriented. Central to the project of media education is the teaching of two sets of skills and knowledge: 1) critical interpretation techniques for decoding media texts and phenomena; and 2) technical skills for producing, or encoding, media products. In this chapter, however, we would like to argue for a third aspect to media education grounded in cultural studies. Media education offers teachers the opportunity to gain some understanding of their students' lifeworlds. It is a collaborative crash course on culture and cultural change as lived by the students who inhabit the classroom or community centre. Before describing the cultural studies approach further, some terms need to be addressed. First is the distinction between media literacy and media education.

Media literacy:

1. A schooled capacity and competency, an ability to interpret and produce media texts. The result of formal media education. An essential element of citizenship engagement in a media-saturated culture.

2. Like speech, a capacity and competency also learned outside of schools, one children begin to develop years before they come to school.

Media education:

1. Teaching/learning about the media industry and how to interpret multiple forms of media. Teaching/learning codes and conventions of media genres and how to undertake semiotic and content analyses.
2. Teaching/learning to produce multiple forms of media, print, visual and oral/aural.
3. An engagement, both by educators and students, with the evolving culture(s) youth inhabit.

Two key points should be raised in relation to this distinction between media literacy as a competency or capacity and media education as a process of school learning. First, media literacy is not something only learned from teachers. Inhabiting a media-saturated world by necessity involves an immersion in the codes and conventions of media and a learning process equivalent to that of learning a first language, though later in childhood. Examples of this are the critical capacities of eight-year-olds to see through the false promises of advertising and the gradual accumulation by children of procedural knowledge of media cues (this is a flashback sequence; there was a cut in the dramatic sequence from one location to another; a close-up of an object—a knife, for example—suggests a future development in the plot). To see how television teaches its viewers these cues over time, starting simply and gradually becoming more complex, one only has to look at a typical demographic progression, say from *Barney* through *Scooby Doo* to *The O.C.* The learning curve that the typical young person embarks on is also one that the culture as a whole has undertaken over the last 60 years as television in particular, and the media in general, has become more complex and sophisticated (Johnson, 2005). Given that media literacy is not something learned only in structured learning environments, there are two wild cards embedded in media education from the start. On the one hand, there is the hand of the powerful in the mix—media corporations and those corporations whose products are pitched in the media. On the other, there is an insider knowledge already possessed by the learner, one which in many instances outstrips that of the teacher (Jenkins, 2006).

The second point to be made in relation to this unschooled media literacy is that it contains elements of the changing cultural context(s) young people experience as their immediate environment, a set of contexts that are more familiar and less alien to youth than is the school. Media education offers an opportunity par excellence to get 'in the paint' with our students, to borrow an expression from the wildly popular NBA. The vast majority of our students are consumers and fans of at least some media texts, and these texts are sites not only of pleasure and entertainment, but also of learning (Giroux & Simon, 1989; Schwoch, White, & Reilly, 1992; Steinberg & Kincheloe, 1997). These texts are produced for the most part by a media industry that relentlessly researches its audiences and that produces a great bulk of material for those demographics, including young people, who are seen to mobilize spending power in the marketplace. Discussing the cycle of symbolic exchange that leads to youth media consumption, Paul Willis states that "commerce keeps returning to the streets and common culture to find its next commodities" (1990, p. 19). The point is that commerce does not manufacture youth consciousness, but attempts to harness it. This is how and why Michael Jordan and Nike shoes became so madly popular a decade ago:

> Why do kids like Nike "Air Jordans?" Because Michael Jordan is the embodiment of cool, a vehicle for youth dreams and desires. What is cool? Well, that emerges from popular culture...not as the result of the advertisers' creative genius but through social practice, be it on the basketball court, in the school halls, or on the street corner. (Hoechsmann, 2001, p. 274)

Educators like to style themselves as 'in the know,' sensitive to and aware of the spheres of influence young people have to contend with, but they lack the resources mobilized by the media industry for extensive grounded research into the lives of young people. (See the PBS documentary *Merchants of Cool* (2001) for a description of the lengths taken by industry to identify and assess youth trends: http://www.pbs.org/wgbh/pages/frontline/shows/cool/). But this is why taking media texts seriously as windows into the lifeworlds our students inhabit is one of the great potentials of media literacy and media education. These windows open up vistas into multiple worldviews, some that are vapid and superficial, others that are harmful and problematic, still others that are inspiring sites of possibility, and the vast majority that are contradictory and complex knots of meanings in search of a referent.

Media "moments" such as that represented by Bono provide a powerful synchronic snapshot point of view of history as it is lived and felt by young people. Arguably, the Bono moment in youth culture is less pervasive than was the Michael Jordan moment. In "What We Have to Learn from Michael Jordan," Michael (2001) argued that the Jordan moment articulated youth culture, race and consumer culture in a specific and historically contingent manner. He said:

> That moment in history—when globalization, media culture, the fetishization of Afro-American culture, the marketing and popularity of the sneaker, the growth of a new global corporation (Nike), and the need in the United States for a squeaky clean black role model coalesced—will be forever Michael's. (p. 269)

In other words, Michael Jordan was, or is, an imaginary version of real social and cultural selves at a particular historical moment, a distorting mirror but one which tells a story about the state of our culture(s) at the time. The story of Michael Jordan was a powerful one in the circuits of youth culture and arguably one that drew together youth of diverse cultural heritage in a way that Bono never will. But Jordan was not nominated for a Nobel Peace prize; in fact, his reputation is somewhat tarnished, not only for his brief foray into gambling but for his association with the Nike brand and hence the problems of the underbelly of economic globalization: outsourcing North American jobs and unfair labour practices in Asia and Central America.

The point is clearly not to glorify popular culture artifacts and practices, to suggest that they could somehow stand in for the inherited curriculum, but just to recognize that they can mobilize the hopes, dreams, and fears of the young people in our classrooms. The Michael Jordan and Bono moments represent what Raymond Williams (1961) called a "structure of feeling." They circulate within a cultural moment as resonant metaphors. Williams intended with this term to express something "firm and definite as 'structure' suggests, yet [that] operates in the most delicate and least tangible parts of our activity" (1961, p. 48). The structure of feeling is "a particular sense of life, a particular community of experience hardly needing expression through which characteristics of our way of life...are in some way passed" (p. 48). It is not "possessed in the same way by the many individuals in the community," nor is it "in any formal sense, learned" (pp. 48-49). Rather it is passed down through generations, each of which innovates from the last. Says Williams:

> One generation may train its successor, with reasonable success, in the social character or the general cultural pattern, but the new generation will have its own structure of feeling, which will not have come 'from' anywhere...the new generation responds in its own ways to the unique world it is inheriting, taking up many of the continuities, that can be traced, and reproducing many aspects of the organization, which can be separately described, yet feeling its whole life in certain ways differently, and shaping its creative response into the new structure of feeling. (p. 49)

Williams argued strongly against fetishized, reified stand-ins for cultural experience, especially through the commodification of the marketplace: "the strongest barrier to the recognition of human cultural activity is [the] immediate and regular conversion of experience into finished products" (1977, p. 128). The packaging of Michael and Bono as products to be consumed gets in the way of seeing them as vehicles for understanding the convergence of certain worldviews, attitudes, feelings, and ideologies at a particular historical juncture. But this is exactly why we argue against reading these figures as commodified objects whether as stars, celebrities, or corporate pitchmen. Rather, we are making the case that they are simply reflections of our cultural selves and hence symbolic of structures of feeling to be read against specific historic backdrops.

To undertake a cultural studies analysis on Bono in a grounded manner we have to get beyond Bono's multicoloured shades, his beaten-up cowboy hat, and his public performances, both in U2 concerts and on the world stage. We have to consider what he represents, the structure of feeling to which he corresponds. In this light, we argue that Bono is a profoundly contradictory character, that he represents a historical period with no easy answers, an epoch of cultural and economic flux when contradictory worldviews are a reasonable response to social, cultural, and economic conditions in which youth find themselves. Whereas young people may appear to be buying in to a culture of consumerism, there is more at play. Paul Willis (1990) speaks of the "necessary symbolic work" (p. 26) at play of young people grappling to make meaning in a period of profound change. Reflected in, and refracted through, Bono, this "necessary symbolic work" of youth identity formation coalesces with the expression of critical youth voice on some of the more pressing social and cultural issues of the day.

In *Common Culture* (1990), Willis argues for a conception of media and consumer production that has less to do with DJs and VJs than it does with fans on the street and in their homes. Willis argues for a principle of "symbolic creativity" that involves a bricolage, or mixing, of products and practices, of posters, clothing styles and musical tastes. It is a creativity in the reception of television and music that eschews a one-size-fits-all interpretation. It is, to all extents, a broad act of reading the popular and the vernacular, a symbolic form of encoding the body, the place one lives, and the streets one haunts. Willis is ruthless in his critique of cultural theorists who do not share his vision of a new symbolic creativity alive in all of its contradiction:

> Mistaking their own metaphors for reality, they are hoist by their own semiotic petards. They are caught by— defined in professionally charting—the symbolic life on the surface of things without seeing, because they are not implicated in, the *necessary* everyday role of symbolic work, of how sense is made of structure and contradiction. (1990, p. 27)

Willis calls in effect for a theory of youth expression that is not a literacy as much as a social and cultural semiotic. He seeks an approach to youth communication that recognizes all symbolic creativity as meaningful. This approach to youth voice, and the reading of youth communication, offers up for analysis an explosion of youth expression that helps to fill in the gaps missing from more traditional readings and forms of reading. While we do not wish to substitute a theory of symbolic creativity for the teaching of writing in schools, we nevertheless wish to argue for an engagement in media education that recognizes the semiotic richness of youth lives.

This often means reading the contradictions in the lives of youth, and recognizing youth lives as profoundly contradictory, hence opening up a way of seeing young people that is less condemnatory and more forgiving. Ultimately, it is important to mark the uneven development that distinguishes people's mediations with their social realities. An impure criticism must grapple with the contradictions and signal the differences which exist between young people. Perhaps, for example, some youth who are particularly compelled by the circuits of consumer culture have succeeded in foreseeing a future of underemployment in the growing service sector, and are getting the headstart that they will need to sustain the consumer desires that older generations or richer kids have been able to take for granted. Some young people enact performative selves through clothing choices—this might be a Hip-Hop styling, a queer celebratory identification, a grunge statement, or just a working-class kid trying to fit in by wearing expensive jeans—and these are entirely expressive choices of style, neither more nor less than body design and performance of identity selves. Whatever the case, it is too simplistic, too deterministic to give up on a generation just because it is buying in, to some extent, to the dreamworld of consumption.

The question arises when reading youth lives whether there is an incipient ethos or politics which coexists with participation in consumer and mainstream media culture. Given the permeation of corporate values into every sphere of everyday life, it is necessary to ask if youth even have access to the language in which they could articulate their social concerns. Of course, the term 'youth'—its masculinist bias notwithstanding—yokes together an enormous array of young people who have diverse experiences and histories. Arguably, young people are highly conscious of the many social, economic, and environmental problems they will inherit. The shifting sands of economic fortune in North America create the conditions of possibility for new emancipatory agendas by linking diminishing economic prospects for young people with the collapsing of the social safety net and environmental degradation. As much as we wish to contest economic determinism, the incipient ethos we are describing is emerging right from under our noses in the mothballed factories, in the specter (or, for some young people, the reality) of homelessness, the rise of terrorism and the resurgence of warfare, and finally in the deceptively beautiful but rapidly despoiling environment.

The problem for educators and cultural workers becomes one of teasing out the incipient critique which is only waiting to be articulated. To ignite the imaginations of young people, or to scaffold their emergent consciousness in imaginative ways, it is important to concede that the rhetoric of social change of an earlier generation does not resonate in the same way today. Without buying in to the dominant narratives of the Left, or the mythologizing of the end a social consciousness somehow tied to the 1960s, it seems nonetheless that we educators cannot simply impose our slogans onto young people. The fire must burn from within emergent consciousnesses and fresh songs and symbols. If educators are to understand the nature of today's contradictory popular politics, in order to engage young people in dialogue, we must be willing to learn. Talking about Bono in the classroom will not solve all of these problems. In fact, for some students, it will appear meaningless and out of touch. Given the fine distinctions made by young people over popular culture choices, and the highly resonant nature of music as a descriptor and symbol of self and group identity, Bono's popularity will be limited to only some students. But his performance away from the mic, the stewardship of economic and health issues through some of the world's most important political forums, is certainly worth taking up. And his status as rock star—even among non-fans—would be likely to invigorate debate and study of some of the compelling social and economic problems of the day.

Digital Futures

Young people are learning all the time, inside and outside of schools. Given that they spend many hours immersed in media consumption across varying platforms, it is of increasing importance that this learning be addressed by educators. We worry that they are becoming "vidiots" and audio slaves, hooked on the high of computer gaming and oblivious to the grand silences that informed our learning in university libraries and late nights hovering over our typewriters. David Buckingham (2003) argues against a media education approach which positions youth as innocent victims who need to be protected from media influences, and suggests that we empower young people to read and produce media instead. Some of the young people we work with are taking this approach without our tutelage in the new Web 2.0 platforms such as MySpace, YouTube, and Facebook. As discussed in chapter 4, *TIME* magazine named the interactive "you" of the millions who have contributed to the new electronic public spheres as the 2006 Person of the Year. There is an element of play at play in the new media technologies and popular culture of today that can enable a wholesale revolution in the manner in which we view teaching and learning. This is a 'learn to play—play to learn' era, and the young folks who still have a foot in the sand box have an advantage. They don't have to think 'out of the box' because they haven't yet begun to shut the lid. Those young people with the technological advantage are those with the means (time + money x motivation) to play. The gizmo world we live in is a tinkerer's paradise. Most of the new tools/toys have multiple capacities that can only be discovered by the most dedicated among us.

Outside of the institutions of formal education, many non-profit organizations are providing a context for youth to use technologies as innovative tools for learning and self and group expression. One of the key features of how the use of new media technologies in the non-profit sector differs is in an outcome-oriented sense of project. Non-profits in Canada and elsewhere, run in many cases by and for youth, are producing innovative new media work on issues that concern them such as social justice, the environment, anti-bullying campaigns, anti-racism, or getting the youth vote out to the polls. These types of organizations are realizing the potential of the Internet as the printing press and broadcast hub of the new era, taking advantage of the new two-way flow of information to make youth voices heard. Another common feature of new media work in the non-profit world is a non-hierarchical approach to the sharing of expertise, breaking down the old distinction between teacher and learner characterized by Freire's banking model. Of course, the idea that Generation Net is technology savvy is a truism postulated in the popular and academic press, and lived on a day-to-day basis by many educators in and outside of schools. But, in general, outside of schools this unsettling of historical teacher-student relationships is not seen as threatening, whereas in schools the jury is still out. In the non-profit world, there is no one-size fits all approach to learning, and no real reason for everyone to know everything. In many of these contexts, young people are working in teams, combining talents in design, music and writing to produce multimodal material. In these contexts, purpose and play intersect.

Capacity building. Empowerment. Citizenship engagement. These are the buzzwords the non-profit sector regularly uses when applying for grants to fund innovative new media projects for youth. Compare this to educational discourse: media literacy, new literacies, multiliteracies, and scaffolding learning. We are still, of necessity, caught in paradigms of times past, teaching new-fangled versions of the traditional 3 R's. Is that a wrong-headed approach? No. As much as times have changed, print literacy continues to be hegemonic in the distribution of social privilege in a text-based society. Like "Juana, la Cubana," we move "dos pasos p'adelante, dos p'atras, pero con ganas" [two steps forward and two steps back, but willingly] (Fito Olivares, 1988). Once bitten, twice shy, we are still nursing our wounds from grand battles such as those between phonics and whole language, ebonics and standard English. Policymakers want results, business lobbies clamour for back-to-the-basics approaches to the curriculum and the apocalyptic words of pundits such as the late Allan Bloom still ring in our ears. "Our students have lost the practice of and taste for reading," he intoned (1987, p. 62). "As long as they have the Walkman on, they cannot hear what the great tradition has to say. And, after its prolonged use, when they take it off, they find they are deaf" (p. 81). And given that Bloom peddles in half-truths, he can't be all wrong. Despite the grave pronouncements of Bloom and others who missed the postmodern turn on the path to the present, many of us have striven to include popular culture in the curriculum, usually within the context of media literacy lessons. This has been, in part, a fulfillment of the Freirian challenge: to teach we must be willing to learn and to take seriously the culture of our students. But even at its apogee, circa 1990, media literacy has remained a curricular add-on, inconsistently applied from one jurisdiction to the next and not undergirded with sufficient professional development to ensure quality teaching. Ironically, this apogee predates the greatest impacts of new technologies on everyday life and learning. Like a thief in the night, the new technologies in education snuck in under the radar to become education's new Janus-faced prize. School districts are under intense pressure to purchase ever more sophisticated equipment and pre- and in-service teacher education programs are responding by shifting their course offerings into this domain. For example, in a 2003 survey of course offerings in educational technology and media education by Canadian faculties of education, Michael found that of 309 courses, 250 focused on educational technology, 59 on media education.

Bono is but one of many media moments worthy of study in media education contexts, now complicated—but potentially much enhanced—by new technologies. The best media education is dialogic and foregrounds the background and experience of the learner (Buckingham, 2003). It is a humbling fact of media education contexts that educators cannot know everything and require the active involvement of learners to pursue the multitude of topics that arise in the study of the media and the cultures in which it is situated. In the rush to introduce new technologies into education—whether inside or outside of Canadian schools—objectives and outcomes can be lost sight of, overwhelmed by the "gee-whizzery" of techno-fetishism, often on the part of educators unfamiliar with, and intimidated by, the new technologies themselves. Of course, for every sceptic, there is a dedicated teacher out there making a difference with the new tools now at our disposal. If anything, the results are uneven. Good teaching in the new technologies is often the luck of the draw: an inspired teacher, a privileged school, or an innovative program for at-risk students. Media educators do need to have the conceptual tools, and at least some of the technical know-how, to undertake analysis and interpretation of media texts and to enable media production. Though media educators increasingly need to have the capacity to produce media of all types, the interesting wrinkle that has emerged as new technologies became cheaper and more accessible is that learners across multiple spectrums have begun to come into media education settings with adequate or better knowledge bases in production than teachers. This too has revolutionized media education settings and unsettled the relationship between teacher and learner. Ultimately, what media educators need more than almost anything else is an open mind and the capacity and desire to read youth writing their lives. As educators with visions of critical literacy dancing in our heads, we try to enable new forms of expression in schools, while balancing our roles as the gatekeepers of the social pyramid of symbolically mediated power relationships and, in the service of social justice, as advocates of fair play. It is in enabling and reading youth writing across literacies new and old that the pedagogy of possibility grows wings and prepares to take flight in new social futures and new creative lives.

CHAPTER NINE

Conclusion: Writing the Future

Hollywood knows how to spin a feel-good yarn, and the film *Freedom Writers* (LaGravenese, 2007), based on a true story and book about a new teacher who makes a difference in the lives of a group of alienated, angry high school students in south L.A., is no different. Like the teachers, filmmakers, activists, and youth media organizations discussed in this book, this teacher goes against the grain of educational indifference and takes seriously her class of incorrigibles by giving them journals and encouraging them to write meaningful personal narratives. Despite the warnings and protestations she faces from colleagues and superiors, Erin Gruwell, played by Hilary Swank, decides that she can break through student resistance and indifference by taking the students seriously as authors of their own stories. By the time the students collect their writing in a book, they develop critical thinking skills, discover the value of education and literacy, and find friendships across race lines unimaginable before this teacher taught them to respect themselves and others. They call themselves the freedom writers in honor of the civil rights activists known as the "freedom riders." That the miracle worker is cast as an attractive white woman, the Florence Nightingale of urban education, speaks more to the myth machine of Hollywood than to the diversity of hard-working teachers across North America and the world. For every Swank/Gruwell, there are many less glamorous, hard-working teachers out there trying to make a difference. That said, *Freedom Writers* is a significantly different film than *Dangerous Minds* (1995), that other Hollywood teacher-as-miracle-worker fantasy, also based on a true story, discussed in chapter 6. Unlike LouAnne Johnson, Erin Gruwell recognizes that her students have stories of their own to tell that matter which warrant the attention and interest of their peers, teachers, and communities.

Freedom Writers represents to us the potential that youth writing can have in the lives of young people, whether undertaken in schools, community settings, or alone in front of computer terminals or on pads of paper. We too have met freedom writers, many of the students in Bronwen's classrooms and writers in Michael's youth media organization. Freedom writers are also among the millions of young people in community settings or at home who have picked up a pen or a camera, or sat down to a keyboard to tell their stories. And potential freedom writers are among the countless young people who have not had the opportunity to articulate their points of view to an audience who cares, those who are waiting to be taken seriously and to register their voices in the public domain.

Conflating freedom and writing might, however, be raising the bar too high. The aspirational context of education as a process of enlightenment is good for goal setting, but does not represent well the long learning curves—and detours—many young people go through. We observe in chapter 4 that a good deal of youth writing and cultural production is very lighthearted and superficial, and also demonstrate there, and in the case studies which follow, that a sense of audience has much to do with how and what young people write or produce. In chapter 3 we cautioned against idealistic readings of youth voice, arguing instead for close critical engagement with youth cultural production and our own investments in what youth say or do not say. Furthermore, we want to register a caveat about pedagogy. Teachers and community educators are not miracle workers. What appears to change the lives of youth in a given context might not in the next setting. Pedagogies never come with guarantees, and so we advocate for an orientation to teaching and learning that strives to make a difference and to open meaningful dialogue, but is not a haughty, prescriptive tutelage. Despite our best efforts, there is no guarantee that youth voice will be representative and insightful. But measures can be taken to improve the rate of success. Reading youth writing, it appears to us, is a critical, intergenerational dialogue, one that is biased towards adults reading the discourse, and discourses, of young people. The challenge is for us educators to constantly interrogate our own teaching, to refine the debate while young people define it, always with an ear bent towards the utterances of young people.

Gruwell helped her students turn a corner in *Freedom Writers* when she challenged them to step outside the immediacy of their contexts and build links with broader historical narratives, in this case the Jewish Holocaust. Telescoping from the local story to other powerful stories, including stories of survival and resistance, helped free the young participants from the fatalism associated with the present day reality they live in. It helped them to think of themselves as historians, but also as historical subjects, caught, but not trapped in, systems and histories of oppression. This returns us to the discussion in chapter 3 about the limits of "the real," and Fleetwood's (2005) argument that discourses of street authenticity could "other" the urban youth she worked with in media programs and limit the stories they told about their lives. It also reminds us that Goodman's (2003) point that the project of having youth document "the way things are" needs to be accompanied by research on why they are that way and how they might become otherwise.

This book is about adolescent literacies, writ large, multi and new. But at the same time it is a reflection on the possibilities that these multiple literacies offer for strengthening education, intergenerational communication, and the processes of citizenship engagement, both in relation to life pathways and work futures. Hence, we need to consider a framework that transcends literacy as an end per se and instead situates literacy practices in productive and fulfilling lives.

No More Monday Mourning

> We need altogether a new approach in education. Let us give the devil of work what is due, let us pay necessary homage to the goddess of technology, but then why not use the rest of humanity's currency for the widest possible imaginative exchanges and sensuous purposes. Education/training should re-enter the broader plains of culture and the possibilities there for the full development of human capacities and abilities, this time not led by the elite culture, but by common culture. (Paul Willis, 1990, pp. 147–148)

Paul Willis' treatise on "common culture" helps us close this book by offering a number of important suggestions for educators facing up to the challenges of a changing culture, a globalizing economy, and rapid technological evolution. Though written before many of the ruptural transformations that have massively sped up processes of change, Willis' arguments are salient and incisive. First, he argues that we should "give the devil of work what is due." Despite our contention that schools serve a greater good than only to orient students to a world of work, most students will eventually need jobs, and youth cultural production holds some significant potential for employment. For one, given the increasing importance of the culture industries to the economy, the student producing videos on her home computer might be carving out the beginnings of a career for herself, whether as a documentary maker or as a communications assistant in a large corporation. We are not the first to make that point. Angela McRobbie (1999) argues that cultural studies needs to pay more attention to the policy implications of the cultural phenomena under investigation, including the possibilities of "cultural entrepreneurialism" and how popular cultural practices might transfer into the market economy. She reminds us that "culture has to be considered not only as a practice of consumption but as a substantial sector of the economy, a sizable mode of production, and also a field of employment, increasingly of self-employment" (p. 26). Many young people are creating job opportunities for themselves in the culture industries, choosing to forge ahead on their own rather than resign themselves to the less rewarding jobs offered by the service sector or some of the less fulfilling lifestyles in the corporate world. Work pathways which might stem out of the hobbies and interests of young people could include professional blogging and magazine writing or production; fashion design; Web site design/information architecture; concert and cultural event organizing; and, in relation to Hip-Hop, jobs such as DJing, rapping, teaching break dancing, Hip-Hop-inspired graphic design and clothing design, and music production (especially with the multiple uses of electronic music across media, as mentioned in chapter 7). If schools better understand the employment possibilities of the culture industries, they can help young people develop skills and aptitudes to match career aspirations in these fields.

Furthermore, educational systems should strive harder to recognize the value of cultural and creative skills in a range of occupations including, but also beyond, the traditional associations of arts and culture industries (Oakley, 2006). New literacies are central to new ways of thinking, being and working. As we have argued throughout the book, drawing and focusing attention is an important capacity in an information-saturated environment. Where attention is an increasingly rare commodity, creativity is vital for capturing and keeping people's interest. This means that the encouragement and support of creativity should no longer be a curricular add-on but should instead be central to curriculum. The education in storytelling offered by both Young People's Press and the slam performance poetry curriculum is an education in drawing people's attention, but is predicated on the conditions of willingness on the part of newspapers and a school. The conditions we chronicle in chapters 5 & 6 are less dependent on institutional involvement and more the free will of young people making culture in groups or on their own.

These capacities and competencies are central to young peoples' survival in the workforce of the future. "New work order" (Gee, Hull, & Lankshear, 1996) economies which are increasingly competitive, interconnected, and international are shaped by discourses about workers and workplaces which emphasize "networking, flexibility, cooperation, collaboration" (p. 39). The community of poets fostered in Tim's classroom (chapter 6) has other implications for the "devil of work." In this community, people were willing to take risks, trying out new identities and modes of engagement. Students were also committed to each other's success, both through their participation in classroom workshops where the collective acted to make each individual's poem and performance stronger, and in the slams in which students came together to form an audience actively (and loudly!) invested in the poems and poets. The community of poets is also a model community of learners—and of workers in the new workplaces envisioned and changed by new-capitalist rhetoric.

Schools have always taken the tasks of educating workers seriously, for better or worse, and an introduction and apprenticeship in prevailing "literacies" has been central to this mission. This brings us to Willis' second suggestion that we "pay necessary homage to the goddess of technology." We are witnessing an explosion of what literacies are and could be in the era of new information technologies, and we need to acknowledge that some youth are closer to the frontline of change than are their parents and teachers. In this context, literacy educators and theorists need to observe young people and youth-driven popular culture as important sites to learn from about evolving communicative practices. For instance, many students come to classrooms with skills and abilities learned from IM communication and video gaming. As Gee (2003) and Johnson (2005) point out, the latter in particular can involve the development of complex, highly nuanced competencies and capacities. And as we have discussed in this book, while paradigm cases of new mindsets and literacies can be found among the many middle-class kids with modems and high-speed Internet access who populate Web 2.0 domains, they also exist among less privileged youth forging the dynamic, interactive, performative, and innovative spaces of Hip Hop culture as well as in the low-tech peripheral spaces of spoken word. At the same time, the embrace of new technology-driven environments, and perhaps even new mindsets, is uneven regardless of class or other identity markers, as Michael has found in the creative media arts course he teaches to teacher education students at the undergrad level; while some of the students in their late teens and early twenties come in with knowledge of programming language, others need instruction on using simple software and Web applications. Thus, we cannot assume that all young people know how to navigate, contribute to, and critically engage with new media spaces; that said, many are further ahead than their teachers.

Another argument we have worked to make here, drawing upon Raymond Williams and others, is that cultural change is uneven and unpredictable, that much of the new is still deeply imbricated in older ways of doing things. As Bronwen found in her work with Tim and his students, while the teacher felt he had much to learn from his students about contemporary spoken word poetics, his students also benefited greatly from his years of experience as a teacher of creative writing and as a poet himself. Tim was able to have them pay close and careful attention to their own and each other's words, which strengthened their written poems as well as their ability to listen to and to respond to each other's work. This was training in the arts of critical reading and listening as well as writing, all of which have been and remain vital literacy skills in an employment era of hyper-communication in which people are increasingly being addressed and asked to speak or write in a variety of modes, including e-mail, instant messaging, lists serves, report writing, teleconferencing, and PowerPoint presentations. The "new work order" is increasingly shaped by "information-processing" activities rather than "material production" (Gee, Hull, & Lankshear, 1996, p. 37), as an increasing percentage of workers in developed countries spend the majority of the work day trading in "'data, words, oral and visual representations'" (Reich in Gee, Hull, &Lankshear, 1996, p. 37).

From work futures to life pathways, we cannot lose sight of the primary objective of educating and raising an enlightened citizenry. Willis' third injunction is that education should enable the "full development of human capacities and abilities, this time led not by elite culture, but by common culture." This challenges us to consider how to adapt our literacy pedagogies to enable forms of engagement by young people that are meaningful and relevant to their lives. Willis suggests that the lived culture of everyday life be valorized in schools alongside the inherited curriculum of elite culture, and he also posits that we should "become fully developed cultural producers" (1990, p. 150). By this, he does not mean we all must become television producers, performance artists or novelists. Rather, he asserts that we must recognize our roles as appropriaters and reworkers of an inherited symbolic universe, which includes today the practices and artifacts of new and old literacies. States Willis:

> The democratic mastery of symbolic materials is being made a common thing, especially in the work of play—no matter what the imperatives, the materials, the media, the forms. Education becomes less relevant to this every day, whereas it should be in the vanguard of how we can proceed fully to take control, to live and master al of our present and past cultural experience. Incidentally, this would also be the best route, the future-oriented route, to the creation of the 'high quality' workforce...and to an entrepreneurial opening up of new industries, though the direct purpose would be to produce fully developed cultural citizens. (1990, p. 148)

A recognition of the significance of a capacity to manipulate and interpret symbolic and semiotic domains means acknowledging that youth are already reading and writing themselves and their worlds in complex and sophisticated ways. Schools need to better understand the worlds of cultural play inhabited and often driven by young people. And, as discussed in chapter 8, there is a crucial role for media education in this process. Ultimately, however, we are not arguing for a post-literate education dedicated only to the new literacies and television. And it makes us nervous to see that Willis does not make much of a distinction between critical and uncritical relations to the symbolic material of everyday life, so that just watching television is framed as an active reworking of it. We wish to add critique to this formulation of appropriation and reworking, aware of the support young people (and others) need in developing critical relations to mass-mediated culture, as in, for instance, the limited narratives Hollywood offers about what it means to be young, urban, and black. We feel that the "fully developed cultural citizen" needs to be a critical citizen.

Given a chance to express themselves in a context where they feel their views will be taken seriously, many young people will set an agenda for themselves, and for society at large, that is ambitious and transformative. When Michael undertook the content analysis of YPP youth-written articles published in the *Toronto Star*, he coded the data for optimistic versus fatalistic worldviews. In particular, he looked for kernels of hope and demands for change. Less than 20% of the articles registered a fatalistic outlook, the vast majority either suggesting that change is possible or that it should be struggled for. Whether access to a meaningful soapbox prompts idealistic prose or not, the reality is that many young people are trying to imagine a just world for themselves and others. Critical consciousness and intergenerational communication is the first crucial step towards developing a model for youth participation and citizenship engagement that is inclusive and meaningful. If we set out to enable youth expression and develop contexts for it, we will have succeeded in beginning the process of self and group actualization.

Key to encouraging and fostering critical literacy in youth, however, must be helping them to move from talk to action. This is not meant to minimize the importance of free expression on the part of young people, the central argument of this book. We feel that social engagement requires first of all seeing yourself as an author of your own opinions, as someone willing to stand up and speak out, to try out ideas and politicized identities. However, a further step follows on the heels of fueling the discourse and enabling expression of youth identity. Carlos, one of the keenest students in Tim's performance poetry course, shared his frustrations with Bronwen after one of the slams. He said that while his classmates were talking the politicized talk in their slam poems, most were not walking the walk. This is a salient criticism if the objective of the spoken word curriculum is to not only give students a platform and a language for self-expression but to enable them to become agents of social change. A slam course might be a powerful experience for all or most of the participants, but it also needs to be seen as a jumping off point for other kinds of experiences of participation, advocacy, and decision making in both the school and the larger community and its organizations.

Ultimately, we argue for a hybrid approach to literacy that encompasses the residual and the emergent elements of communication, one that is critical and productive. Crucial to encouraging and fostering a critical and productive literacy in youth is to enable meaningful forms of participation in the sites where literacy work is being undertaken and in society at large. Reading youth writing is an active approach to taking young people seriously and hence opening up horizons for them and vistas for us; it is a form of intergenerational dialogue and respect that invokes a willingness to learn on the part of educators and other adults, and issues an open challenge for young people to step up and make themselves be heard.

Bibliography

Ahmed, M. (2007). Young people lose out in media coverage, survey finds. Retrieved July 31, 2007, from http://www.communitycare.co.uk/Articles/2007/06/25/104914/young-people-lose-out-in-media-coverage-survey-finds.html?key=TNS%20OR%20ILLITEGENCE

Alexa: The web information company. Retrieved September 7, 2007, from http://www.alexa.com.

Algarín, M. (1994). Introduction: The sidewalk of high art. In M. Algar_n & B. Holman (Eds.), *ALOUD: Voices from the Nuyorican Poets Café* (pp. 3–28). New York: Henry Holt.

Algarín, M., & Holman, B. (Eds.). (1994). *ALOUD: Voices from the Nuyorican Poets Café*. New York: Henry Holt.

Alim, S. (2004). Hip hop nation language. In Finegan & Rickford (Eds.), *Language in the USA: Themes for the 21st century*. Cambridge: Cambridge University Press.

Althusser, L. (1971). Ideology and ideological state apparatuses (B. Brewster, Trans.). In *Lenin and philosophy, and other essays*. London: New Left Books.

Alvermann, D. (2002). *Adolescents and literacies in a digital world*. New York: Peter Lang.

Alvermann, D., Moon, J., & Hagood, M. (1999). *Popular culture in the classroom: Teaching and researching critical media literacy*. Newark: International Reading Association and National Reading Conference.

Anthony, L. (2006). Goth culture feeds off teen angst and takes it into adulthood. *CBC News*. Retrieved September 14, 2006, from http://www.cbc.ca/cp/Home+Family/060914/U091414U.html.

Atwell, N. (1987). *In the middle: Writing, reading, and learning with adolescents*. Upper Montclair, NJ: Boynton/Cook.

Bailey, C. (1999). A cinema of duty: The films of Jennifer Hodge de Silva. In K. Armatage et al. (Eds.), *Gendering the nation: Canadian women's cinema* (pp. 94–108). Toronto: University of Toronto Press.

Barthes, R. (1972). *Mythologies* (A. Lavers, Trans.). New York: Hill and Wang.

Barton, D. (1994). *Literacy: An introduction to the ecology of the written language*. Oxford: Blackwell Publishers.

Barton, D., & Hamilton, M. (1998). *Local literacies: Reading and writing in one community*. New York: Routledge.

Barton, D., Hamilton, M., & Ivanic, R. (Eds.). (2000). *Situated learnings: Reading and writing in context*. London: Routledge.

Bloom, A. (1987). *The closing of the American mind*. New York: Simon & Schuster Inc.

Bono's red card to Aids. (2006, January 26). *Evening Standard*. Retrieved December 9, 2006, from http://www.thisismoney.co.uk/taxadvice/giving/article.html?in_article_id=406594 &in_page_id=153.

Bourdieu, P. (1984). *Distinction: A social critique of the judgement of taste* (R. Nice, Trans.). Cambridge, MA: Harvard University Press.

Bourdieu, P., & Passeron, J. C. (1964). *Les heritiers: Les etudiants et la culture.* Paris: Les Editions de Minuit.

Buckingham, D. (2003). *Media education : Literacy, learning and contemporary culture.* Cambridge: Polity.

Calkins, L. (1994). *The art of teaching writing.* Portsmouth, NH: Heinemann.

Callahan, M., & Low, B. (2004). At the crossroads of expertise: The risky business of teaching popular culture. *English Journal, 93*(3), 52–57.

Castells, M. (1996). *The rise of the network society.* Cambridge, MA: Blackwell Publishers, Inc.

Clanchy, M. (1979). *From memory to written record: England, 1066–1307.* London: Arnold.

Clark, L. (Director/Writer). (2005). *Kids* [Motion Picture]. USA: Excalibur Films.

Clarke, G. (1990). Defending ski-jumpers: A critique of theories of youth subcultures. In S. Frith & A. Goodwin (Eds.), *On record: Rock, pop, and the written word.* New York: Pantheon Books.

Cohen, S. (1980). *Folk devils and moral panics.* London: MacGibbon and Kee.

Connor, J. (1997). Radio free Joyce: *Wake* language and experience of radio. In A. Morris (Ed.), *Sound states: Innovative poetics and acoustical technologies* (pp. 17–32). Chapel Hill: University of North Carolina Press.

Cope, B., & Kalantzis, M. (Eds.). (2000). *Multiliteracies: Literacy learning and the design of social futures.* London: Routledge.

Cosmoworlds. (2006). Bono and Bobby Shriver launch (RED)TM in the U.S.   Retrieved December 9, 2006, from http://www.cosmoworlds.com/product_red.htm.

Crichter, C. (1976). Structures, cultures, and biographies. In S. Hall & T. Jefferson (Eds.), *Resitance though rituals: Youth subcultures in post-war Britain.* London: Hutchinson.

Cross, B. (1993). *It's not about a salary...Rap, race and resistance in Los Angeles.* New York: Verso.

Cross, D. (Director). (1997). *The street: A film with the homeless* [Documentary]. Montreal: NFB/Necessary Illusions.

Cross, D. & Denis, Eric. (Directors). (2001). *S.P.I.T.: Squeegee Punks in Traffic* [Documentary]. Canada: Atopia.

Cuban, L. (2001). *Oversold and underused: Computers in the classroom.* Cambridge, MA: Harvard University Press.

Dery, M. (1994). Black to the future: Interviews with Samuel R. Delany, Greg Tate, and Tricia Rose. In *Flame wars: The discourse of cyber-culture.* (pp. 179–222). Durham, NC: Duke University Press.

Diversity Watch. (2004). Who is telling the news? Race and gender in Canada's daily newsrooms. Retrieved on Sept. 14, 2007, from http://www.diversitywatch.ryerson.ca/home_miller_2004report.htm.

Dorsey, J. (Director). (2006). *The Point* [Motion Picture]. Canada: NFB/Silo Productions.

11 hours before murder. (2006, September 15). *National Post,* p. A1.

Ewen, S. (1976). *Captains of consciousness: Advertising and the social roots of the consumer culture.* New York: McGraw-Hill.

Fanon, F. (1965). *A dying colonialism.* New York: Grove Press.

Farred, G. (2000). Endgame identity? Mapping the new left roots of identity politics. *New Literary History, 31*(4), 627–648.

First-person shooters. (2006, September). *Harper's Magazine*, 19–21.

Fisher, M. (2005). From the coffee house to the school house: The promise and potential of spoken word poetry in school contexts. *English Education, 37*(2), 115–131.

Fiske, J. (1990/1991). An interview with John Fiske. *Border/Lines*, 4–7.

Fleetwood, N. (2005). Authenticating practices: Producing realness, performing youth. In S. Maira & E. Soep (Eds.), *Youthscapes: The popular, the national, the global* (pp. 155–172). Philadelphia: University of Pennsylvania Press.

Folksonomy. (2007). *Wikipedia.* Retrieved May 19, 2007, from http://en.wikipedia. org/wiki/Folksonomy.

Frith, S. (1983). *Sound effects: Youth, leisure, and the politics of rock*. London: Constable.

Frow, J., & Morris, M. (2000). Cultural studies. In N. Denzin & Y. Lincoln (Eds.), *The handbook of qualitative research* (pp. 315–346). London: Sage.

Gallagher, K. (2002). *Teaching adolescent writers*. Portland, ME: Stenhouse.

Gee, J. (1996). *Social linguistics and literacies*. London: Taylor and Francis.

——. (2003). *What video games have to teach us about learning and literacy*. New York: Palgrave Macmillan.

——. (2004). *Situated language and learning*. New York: Routledge.

Gee, J., Hull, G., & Lankshear, C. (1996). *The new work order: Behind the language of the new capitalism*. Boulder, CO: Westview.

Gelder, K. (Ed.). (2005). *The subcultures reader* (2nd ed.). London: Routledge.

Gerard-Cosh, D. (2006, September 15). Gill attracted to gun violence. *National Post*, p. A5.

Gilbert, J. (2007). Risking a relation: Sex education and adolescent development. *Sex education: Sexuality, society and learning, 7*(1), 47–62.

Gilroy, P. (1996). British cultural studies and the pitfalls of identity. In J. H.A. Baker, M. Diawara & R. H. Lindeborg (Eds.), *Black British cultural studies: A reader*. Chicago: The University of Chicago Press.

Giroux, H. (1994). *Disturbing pleasures: Learning popular culture*. New York: Routledge.

——. (1996a). *Fugitive cultures: Race, violence, and youth*. New York: Routledge.

——. (1996b). Hollywood, race, and the demonization of youth: The "kids" are not "alright." *Educational Researcher, 25*(2), 31–35.

Giroux, H., & Simon, R. (Eds.). (1989). *Popular culture, schooling and everyday life*. Granby: Bergin and Garvey.

Goldfarb, B. (2002). *Visual pedagogy: Media cultures of education in and beyond the classroom*. Durham, NC: Duke University Press.

Goodman, B. (Director). (2001). *The merchants of cool* [Documentary]. Alexandria, VA: PBS Educational Video Series.

Goodman, S. (2003). *Teaching youth media: A critical guide to literacy, video production, and social change*. New York: Teachers College Press.

Graff, G. (1987). *The legacies of literature: Continuities and contradictions in Western culture and society*. Bloomington: Indiana University Press.

Gramsci, A. (1971). *Selections from prison notebooks* (Q. Hoare & G. N. Smith, Trans.). New York: International Publishers.

Grossberg, L. (1992). *We gotta get out of this place: Popular conservatism and postmodern culture*. New

York: Routledge.

Grossberg, L., Nelson, C., & Treichler, P. (Eds.). (1992). *Cultural studies*. New York: Routledge.

Grossman, L. (2006, December 13). Time's person of the year: You. *TIME*, 14–15.

Hall, S. (1980). Cultural studies: Two paradigms. *Media, Culture and Society, 2*, 52–72.

——. (1986). On postmodernism and articulation: An interview with Stuart Hall. *Journal of Curriculum Inquiry 10*(2), 45–60.

——. (1992). Cultural studies and its theoretical legacies. In L. Grossberg, C. Nelson & P. Threichler (Eds.), *Cultural studies*. New York: Routledge.

Hall, S., & Jefferson, T. (Eds.). (1976). *Resistance through rituals: Youth subcultures in post-war Britain*. London: Unwin Hyman.

Harrison, B., & Rappaport, A. (2006). *Flocabulary: The Hip-Hop approach to SAT-level vocabulary building*. Kennebunkport, ME: Cider Mill Press.

Harrold, M. (2006, September 21). Hard lesson for school. *Montreal Gazette*, p. F1 & F4.

Harvey, D. (1989). *The condition of postmodernity*. Oxford: Basil Blackwell.

Heath, S. B. (1983). *Ways with words: Language, life, and work in communities and classrooms*. Cambridge: Cambridge University Press.

——. (2004, February). *The rush to romanticize: Cautions and some reminders about language and learning*. Paper presented at the National Council for the Teaching of English Assembly for Research, Berkeley, CA.

Hebdige, D. (1979). *Subculture: The meaning of style*. London: Menthuen.

——. (1988). *Hiding in the light*. London: Routledge.

Heinrich, J., Cherry, P., Larouche-Smart, M., & Bruemmer, R. (2006, September 14). Bloody Wednesday. *Montreal Gazette*, p. A1.

Hewitt, D. (Producer). (1999, November 28). Slam [Television series episode]. *Sixty Minutes*. New York: CBS.

Hoechsmann, M. (1996). I am white, male, and middle class in a global era: Marketing (to) Generation X. In M. Pomerance & J. Sakeris (Eds.), *Picture of a generation on hold* (pp. 85–96). Toronto: Media Studies Working Group.

——. (2001). Just do it: What Michael Jordan has to teach us. In D. L. Andews (Ed.), *Michael Jordan, Inc.: Corporate sport, media culture, and late modern America* (pp. 269–276). Albany, NY: SUNY Press.

Hoggart, R. (1957). *The uses of literacy: Aspects of working-class life, with special reference to publications and entertainments*. London: Chatto & Windus.

Holman, B. (1994). Congratulations: You have found the hidden book. In M. Algar_n & B. Holman (Eds.), *ALOUD: Voices from the Nuyorican Poets Café* (pp. 1). New York: Henry Holt.

Hull, G. (2003). Youth culture and digital media: New literacies for new times. *Research in the Teaching of English 38*(2), 229–233.

Hull, G., & Schultz, K. (2001). Literacy and learning out of school: A review of theory and research. *Review of Educational Research, 7*(4), 575–611.

——. (Eds.). (2002). *School's out: Bridging out-of-school literacies with classroom practices*. New York: Teachers College Press.

Huq, R. (2006). *Beyond subculture: Pop, youth, and identity in a postcolonial world*. London: Routledge.

Jarecki, E. (Director/Writer). (2005). *Why we fight* [Documentary]. USA: BBC Storyville.

Jenkins, H. (2006). *Convergence culture*. New York: New York University Press.

Jocson, K. (2005). "Taking it to the mic": Pedagogy of June Jordan's Poetry for the People and partnership with an urban high school. *English Education* 37(2), 132–149.

——. (2006). Bob Dylan and Hip Hop: Intersecting literacy practices in youth poetry communities. *Written Communication, 23*(3), 231–259.

Johnson, R. (1996). What is cultural studies anyway? In J. Storey (Ed.), *What is cultural studies? A reader* (pp. 75–114). London: Arnold.

Johnson, S. (2005). *Everything bad is good for you: How today's popular culture is actually making us smarter*. New York: Penguin.

Kaiser Family Foundation. (2005). Generation M: Media in the Lives of 8–18 year-olds. Retrieved March 7, 2007, from http://www.kff.org/entmedia/entmedia030905pkg.cfm.

Kardinall Offishall. (2001). *Quest for fire: Firestarter volume 1* [CD]. Canada: MCA Records.

Kitwana, B. (2002). *The Hip-Hop generation: Young blacks and the crisis in African-American culture*. New York: Perseus Books Group.

Koza, J. (1999). Rap music: The cultural politics of official representation. In C. McCarthy et al. (Eds.), *Sound identities: Popular music and the cultural politics of education*. New York: Peter Lang.

Krims, A. (2000). *Rap music and the poetics of identity*. Cambridge: Cambridge University Press.

KRS-One. (2000). *KRS-One: A retrospective*: USA: Zombia Group (RCA).

LaGravenese, R. (Director/Writer). (2007). *Freedom writers* [Motion Picture]. United States: Paramount Pictures.

Lanham, R. (2006). *The economics of attention*. Chicago: University of Chicago Press.

Lankshear, C., & Knobel, M. (2002). Do we have your attention?: New literacies, digital technologies, and the education of adolescents. In D. Alvermann (Ed.), *Adolescents and literacies in a digital world* (pp. 19–39). New York: Peter Lang.

——. (2003). *New literacies: Changing knowledge and classroom learning*. Buckingham: Open University Press.

——. (2006). *New literacies: Everyday practices and classroom learning*. New York: Open University Press.

Lee, C. (2007). The U2 frontman expresses his support for a new Joe Strummer documentary. Retrieved March 30, 2007, from http://www.u2station.com/news/archives/miscellaneous_news/index.php.

Levin, M. (Writer/Director). (1998). *Slam* [Motion Picture]. USA: Trimark Pictures and Offline Entertainment Group.

Levinson, P. (1997). *The soft edge: A natural history and future of the information revolution*. London: Routledge.

Lewin, Tamar. (2003, April 30). Writing in schools is found both dismal and neglected. *New York Times*. Retrieved on May 2, 2007 from http://www.nytimes.com/2003/04/26/education/26WRIT.html.

Lipsitz, G. (1994). We know what time it is: Race, class, and youth culture in the 90's. In A. Ross & T. Rose (Eds.), *Microphone fiends: Youth music and popular culture* (pp. 17–28). New York: Routledge.

Lopez, L. (1994). Generation Mex. In E. Liu (Ed.), *Next: Young American writers on the next generation*. New York: W. W Norton & Co.

Low, B. (2001). "Bakardi slang" and the poetics of T-dot hip hop. *Taboo: The journal of culture and education. Special issue: Hip hop pedagogies and youth cultures, 5*(2), 15–31.

——. (in press). Poetry on MTV? Slam and the poetics of popular culture. *Journal of Curriculum Theorizing.*

Luke, A., & Freebody, P. (1997). The social practices of reading. In S. Muspratt, A. Luke & P. Freebody (Eds.), *Constructing critical literacies: Teaching and learning textual practice.* St. Leonards, N.S.W.: Allen & Unwin.

Luke, A., & Luke, C. (2001). Adolescence lost/childhood regained: On early intervention and the emergence of the techno-subject. *Journal of Early Childhood Literacy, 1*(1), 94–111.

Marchessault, J. (1995). Reflections of the dispossessed: Video and the "Challenge for Change" experiment. *Screen, 36*(2), 131–146.

McKenna, C. (Director). (2006). *The Year Before* [Documentary]. Montreal: National Film Board.

McLuhan, M., & McLuhan, E. (1988). *Laws of media: The new science.* Toronto: University of Toronto Press.

McLuhan, M. (1994). *Understanding media: The extensions of man* (1st MIT Press ed.). Cambridge: MIT Press.

McRobbie, A. (1999). *In the culture society: Art, fashion, and popular music.* London: Routledge.

Media Awareness Network. (2005). Young Canadians in a wired world. Retrieved March 7, 2007, from http://www.media-awareness.ca/english/research/ycww/index.cfm.

Michee Mee. (1991). *Jamaican funk, Canadian style* [CD]. New York: First Priority / Atlantic.

——. (2000). *The first cut is the deepest* [CD]. New York: Koch Records.

Mitchell, T. (Ed.). (2001). *Global noise.* Middletown, CT: Wesleyan University Press.

Montgomery, S., & Heinrich, J. (September 15, 2006). Killer fantasized about the day he'd wreak carnage. *Montreal Gazette,* pp. Al, A8.

Morrell, E., & Duncan-Andrade, J. (2004). What they do learn in school: Hip-hop as a bridge to canonical poetry. In J. Mahiri (Ed.), *What they don't learn in school: Literacy in the lives of urban youth* (pp. 247–268). New York: Peter Lang.

Morrison, T. (1995). Nobel lecture. *The Georgia Review, 49*(1), 318–323.

Mudede, C. (2000). Hip Hop rupture. *ctheory, 92* from http:// www.ctheory.com .

Muggleton, D., & Weinzierl, R. (Eds.). (2003). *The post-subcultures reader.* Oxford: Berg.

Oakley, K. (2006). Include us out: Economic development and social policy in the creative industries. *Cultural Trends, 15*(4), 255–273.

O'Hear, S. (March 15, 2007). Social network traffic up 11.5 percent; MySpace still dominates. *ZDNet Blogs.* Retrieved April 10, 2007, from http://blogs.zdnet.com/social/?p=114.

Olivares, F. (1988). *Juana, la Cubana* [CD]. Houston, TX: Gil Records.

Ong, W. (1982). *Orality and literacy: The technologizing of the word.* New York: Menthuen.

Perloff, M. (1991). *Radical artifice: Writing poetry in the age of the media.* Chicago: University of Chicago Press.

Perry, I. (2004). *Prophets of the hood: Politics and poetics in Hip Hop.* Durham, NC: Duke University Press.

Pettitt, T. (2007). *Opening the Gutenberg paranthesis: Media in transition in Shakespeare's England.* Paper presented at the Media in Transition 5 conference, Massachussetts Institute of Technology.

Public Enemy. (1987). *Yo! Bum rush the show* [CD]. USA: Def Jam/Columbia Records.

——. (1988). *It takes a nation of millions to hold us back* [CD]. USA: Def Jam/Columbia Records.

——. (1990). *Fear of a black planet* [CD]. USA: Def Jam/Columbia Records.

Rioux, C. (December 3, 2005). La faute aux rappeurs? *Le Devoir,* pp. A1, A10.

Rogoff, B. (2003). *The cultural nature of human development*. Oxford: Oxford University Press.

Rose, T. (1994). *Black noise: Rap music and black culture in contemporary America*. Hanover, NH: University Press of New England.

Ross, A. (1989). *No respect: Intellectuals and popular culture*. New York: Routledge.

——. (1990). Ballots, bullets, or batmen: Can cultural studies do the right thing? *Screen, 31*(3), 26–44.

——. (1994). Introduction. In A. Ross & T. Rose (Eds.), *Microphone fiends: Youth music and popular culture* (pp. 1–13). New York: Routledge.

Rothenberg, J. (1981). *Pre-faces & other writings*. New York: New Directions.

Sample of song lyrics. (2006, September 15). *National Post*, p. A5.

Sandoval, G. (2006). Video of teacher rant gets students in trouble. *CNET News*. Retrieved January 27, 2007, from http://news.com.com/2100-1025_3-6138172.html.

Sarkar, M., Low, B., & Winer, L. (2007). "Pour connecter avec le peeps": Québéquicité and the Quebec Hip-Hop community. In M. Mantero (Ed.), *Identity and second language learning: Culture, inquiry and dialogic activity in educational contexts* (pp. 351–372). Charlotte, NC: Information Age Publishing.

Scherpf, S. (2001). Rap pedagogy: The potential for democratization. *Review of Education/ Pedagogy/Cultural Studies, 23*(1), 73–110.

Schwoch, J., White, M., & Reilly, S. (1992). *Media knowledge: Readings in popular culture, pedagogy and critical citizenship*. Albany: State University of New York Press.

Sellers, P. (2006). MySpace cowboys. Retrieved August 24, 2006, from http://money.cnn.com/magazines/fortune/fortune_archive/2006/09/04/8384727/index.htm.

Shandler, S. (2000). *Ophelia speaks: Adolescent girls write about their search for self*. New York: HaperCollins.

Sharpley-Whitling, T. D. (2007). *Pimps up, ho's down: Hip Hop's hold on young black women*. New York: New York University Press.

Shelley, P. B. (1989). A defense of poetry. In D. Richter (Ed.), *The critical tradition: Classic texts and contemporary trends* (pp. 323–340). New York: St. Martin's Press.

Shklovsky, V. (1989). Art as technique. In D. Richter (Ed.), *The critical tradition: Classic texts and contemporary trends* (pp. 737–748). New York: St. Martin's Press.

Sitomer, A. L., & Cirelli, M. (2004). *Hip-Hop poetry and the classics for the classroom*. Beverly Hills, CA: Milk Mug Publishing.

Smith, J. (Director/Writer) (1995). *Dangerous minds* [Motion Picture]. In D. Simpson & J. Bruckheimer (Producer). USA: Hollywood Pictures.

Smith, P. (1992). Skinhead. In *Big towns, big talk*. Cambridge, MA: Zoland Books.

——. (2007). Building Nicole's mamma. *Rattle e.2, Spring*, 49.

Smitherman, G. (1998). Word from the hood: The lexicon of African American Vernacular English. In Mufwene et al. (Eds.), *The structure of African American Vernacular English*. New York: Routledge.

Sobol, J. (2002). *Digitopia blues: Race, technology, and the American voice*. Banff: The Banff Centre Press.

Soep, E. (2006). Beyond literacy and voice in youth media production. *McGill Journal of Education, 41*(3), 197–213.

Spivak, G. C. (1988). Can the subaltern speak? In Nelson & Grossberg (Eds.), *Marxism and the interpretation of culture*. London: Macmillan.

Steinberg, S., & Kincheloe, J. (Eds.). (1997). *Kinderculture: The corporate construction of childhood.* Boulder, CO: Westview Press.

Storey, J. (Ed.). (1996). *What is cultural studies? A reader.* London: Arnold.

Stratton, R., & Wozencraft, K. (Eds.). (1998). *Slam.* New York: Grove Press.

Street, B. (1995). *Social literacies: Critical approaches to literacy in development, ethnography, and education.* New York: Longman.

——. (Ed.). (2005). *Literacies across educational contexts.* Philadelphia: Caslon.

Talarico, R. (1995). *Spreading the word: Poetry and the survival of community in America.* Durham, NC: Duke University Press.

Tapscott, D., & Williams, A. (2006). *Wikinomics: How mass collaboration changes everything.* New York: Portfolio.

The Utube Blog. (2007). From http://theutubeblog.com/

Thompson, E. P. (1963). *The making of the English working class.* London: Gollancz.

Toop, D. (1991). *Rap attack 2: African rap to global Hip Hop.* London: Serpent's Tail.

Ulmer, G. (1989). *Teletheory: Grammatology in the age of video.* New York: Routledge.

Virilio, P. (1986). *Speed and politics: An essay on dromology.* New York: Semiotext(e).

Wah, F. (2000). *Faking it: Poetics of hybridity: Critical writing 1985–1999.* Edmonton: NeWest Publishers.

Watson, P. (1970). Challenge for change. *ArtsCanada, April,* 20.

Weber, T. (2006). Bono bets on Red to battle Aids. *BBC News.* Retrieved December 9, 2006, from http://news.bbc.co.uk/2/hi/business/4650024.stm.

Williams, R. (1958). *Culture and society, 1780–1950.* London: Chatto & Windus.

——. (1961). *The long revolution.* New York: Columbia University Press.

——. (1976). *Keywords.* London: Fontana Press.

——. (1977). *Marxism and literature.* Oxford: Oxford University Press.

——. (1989). *What I came to say.* London: Hutchison Radius.

Williams, T. (Director). (2005). *Harlem diaries: Nine voices of resilience* [Documentary]. USA: Discovery Channel Pictures.

Willis, P. (1990). *Common culture: Symbolic work at play in the everyday cultures of the young.* Boulder: Westview Press.

Yon, D. (2000). *Elusive culture.* Albany, NY: SUNY.

Index

Colin Lankshear, Michele Knobel,
& Michael Peters
*General Editor*s

New literacies and new knowledges are being invented "in the streets" as people from all walks of life wrestle with new technologies, shifting values, changing institutions, and new structures of personality and temperament emerging in a global informational age. These new literacies and ways of knowing remain absent from classrooms. Many education administrators, teachers, teacher educators, and academics seem largely unaware of them. Others actively oppose them. Yet, they increasingly shape the engagements and worlds of young people in societies like our own. The *New Literacies and Digital Epistemologies* series will explore this terrain with a view to informing educational theory and practice in constructively critical ways.

For further information about the series and submitting manuscripts, please contact:

Michele Knobel & Colin Lankshear
Montclair State University
Dept. of Education and Human Services
3173 University Hall
Montclair, NJ 07043
michele@coatepec.net

To order other books in this series, please contact our Customer Service Department at:

(800) 770-LANG (within the U.S.)
(212) 647-7706 (outside the U.S.)
(212) 647-7707 FAX

Or browse online by series at:

www.peterlang.com